Politics and the
American Economy

Politics and the
American Economy

James J. Gosling
University of Utah

 LONGMAN

An imprint of Addison Wesley Longman, Inc.

New York • Reading, Massachusetts • Menlo Park, California • Harlow, England
Don Mills, Ontario • Sydney • Mexico City • Madrid • Amsterdam

Editor-in-Chief: Priscilla McGeehon
Acquisitions Editor: Eric Stano
Marketing Manager: Megan Galvin-Fak
Full Service Production Manager: Mark Naccarelli
Project Coordination, Text Design, and Electronic Page Makeup: Nesbitt Graphics, Inc.
Cover Designer/Manager: Nancy Danahy
Cover Illustration/Photo: © John Sposato/SIS
Senior Print Buyer: Hugh Crawford
Printer and Binder: The Maple-Vail Book Manufacturing Group
Cover Printer: The Lehigh Press, Inc.

Library of Congress Cataloging-in-Publication Data

Gosling, James J.
    Politics and the American economy / James J. Gosling.
        p. cm.
    Includes bibliographical references and index.
    ISBN 0-321-07044-5
        1. United States—Economic policy—Decision making. 2. United States—Economic conditions—1981-
    3. Democracy—United States. 4. Capitalism—United States. 5. Finance, Public—United States. I. Title.

HC106.8.G67—2000
338.973—dc21   99-046530

Copyright © 2000 by Addison Wesley Longman, Inc.

Please visit our website at http://www.awlonline.com

ISBN 0-321-07044-5

1 2 3 4 5 6 7 8 9 10—MA—02010099

To Charles W. Anderson,
mentor and friend

Contents

List of Figures and Tables

Preface

E conomic policymaking involves political choice—choice that is value based. Should economic policies be followed that sacrifice employment and personal income to control inflation? Economists can describe and explain the consequences of that tradeoff, but policymakers decide whether or not it should be pursued. Policymakers make choices within institutional frameworks and processes that advantage some interests and disadvantage others in their efforts to shape economic policy in line with their interests and preferences. The study of economic policymaking requires that the politics of decision making not be divorced from the economics of decision making—choice should be based on what we know about how national economies work. The two are highly interrelated, as the student will soon learn.

Politics and economics are inextricably linked in the fabric of American democracy. The condition of the economy affects political decision making, and the political choices of economic policymakers can affect the economy. *Politics and the American Economy* not only equips students to appreciate that interrelationship but also gives them the tools they need to evaluate economic performance and assess both its political implications and the extent to which politically influenced economic policy choices affect the course of the economy. This book also equips students to understand and weigh the significance of economic problems, appreciate the interrelationships among them, and evaluate competing prescriptions for solving them. Yet for these tools to be useful, they must be applied. The chapters that follow do just that, focusing primarily on the performance of America's political economy and its implications in the 1980s and 1990s, but looked at in the context of its ideological and historical inheritance.

In exploring these relationships, the organization of this book parallels a course of the same title that I teach at the University of Utah. Like so many other authors, I decided to write this book because I could not find a core text that approaches the subject matter the way I wanted to treat it in the course. Although the subject matter is intellectually challenging and possibly intimidating to those who shy away from economic theory and its specialized language, this examination of the interrelationship of politics and economics makes a special effort to explain basic concepts carefully and to apply them using well-chosen illustrations, many of which students will see covered regularly in the media.

Instructors may wish to use this book as their primary text in the several variously entitled courses on America's political economy. I wrote *Politics and the American Economy* to be accessible to both undergraduates, including students majoring in something other than political science or economics, and graduate students enrolled in master's programs in public administration and public policy, who come into these programs with a wide variety of undergraduate degrees and who may not have been exposed to the material in their undergraduate studies. This book could also serve as a supplementary text in introductory courses on American government or American public policy.

Several colleagues in political science and economics commented on the individual chapters, for which I am indebted. Special thanks go to Andrew Cortell and Ted Hebert, who followed this project from the very beginning and offered many helpful suggestions. The external reviewers commissioned by Addison Wesley Longman, including James Anderson of Texas A&M University; Alan Buckley of Santa Monica College; Bill Hudson of Providence College; David Nice of Washington State University; and Graham Wilson of University of Wisconsin–Madison, deserve thanks for their many insightful comments. I also want to express my appreciation to Paul Smith and Eric Stano, who guided this endeavor to publication.

James J. Gosling
Salt Lake City, Utah

CHAPTER 1

An Introduction to America's Political Economy

olitics and economics are inextricably linked in the fabric of American democracy. The condition of the economy can affect political choice, and political decision making can influence the course of the economy. An economy in recession—a condition in which the real (inflation-adjusted) gross domestic product (GDP) declines for two consecutive quarters—affects both government revenues and spending. Personal income declines as a result of the increased unemployment that accompanies a sustained drop in the economy's output of goods and services. As aggregate personal income falls, so does aggregate consumption, and this lowered demand translates into reduced corporate profits. Thus both personal and corporate income tax revenues decline as a result of their shrinking tax bases, hitting the federal government the hardest, given its heavy reliance on income taxes. Although states also see their income tax revenues fall, they suffer an even bigger loss of sales tax revenues, since the sales tax remains their primary revenue source. Local governments that make sizable use of these tax instruments feel similar effects. Those that depend primarily on property taxes are less immediately affected, although a prolonged recession and slow recovery will typically drive down property values and correspondingly reduce the property tax base.

A recessionary economy packs a one-two punch. Not only does it depress revenues; it also drives up public expenditures. As unemployment rises and personal income declines, more and more people become eligible for government programs that provide need-based public assistance. Welfare roles and unemployment compensation claims rise, as do applications for publicly supported medical assistance. The latter, with medical care costs rising well in excess of general inflation, puts the greatest pressure on government budgets. The federal government and the states feel the fiscal pinch the most. All persons who meet eligibility standards for the joint federal- and state-supported Medicaid program have a legal (statutory) entitlement to receive the services it supports.

These fiscal pressures can wreak havoc on government budgets. Expenditures rise faster than revenues. The federal government can make do by incurring a budget deficit and using debt to finance costs over current revenues. In contrast, all states, except for Vermont, must balance their budgets; and a deficit leaves governors and legislatures little choice but to cut expenditures or raise additional revenues, both painful prospects politically.

Economic woes not only affect taxing and spending decisions; they can also influence partisan political relations. The minority party is usually not shy about attributing a declining or flat economy to the leadership and policies of the majority party. Economic problems invite fanfare. The media, loving demonstrative controversy, zeros in on the escalating partisan attacks. That attention, in turn, crystallizes the popular association of economic troubles with the administration in power. As might be expected, the political consequences can be dramatic. Witness the experience of presidents Carter and Bush. President Carter had the misfortune of serving during a period of "stagflation," in which high inflation accompanied slow economic growth and higher-than-expected unemployment. President Bush, basking in the afterglow of America's military successes in the Persian Gulf, soon found his popularity undermined by the politically ill-timed (at least from his perspective and that of his supporters) national recession of 1990. The recession's fiscal effects pushed up the fiscal year (FY) 1992 deficit above $290 billion, a level that Democratic candidate Bill Clinton exploited in the 1992 presidential campaign. The recession also all but wiped out the fiscal gains expected from the Budget Enforcement Act of 1990, a major deficit-reduction package that included a highly controversial tax increase. It was President Bush, not Congress, however, who soaked up most of the attention and blame for raising taxes, since he agreed to the tax increase not long after proclaiming on national television, "Read my lips, no new taxes."

The euphemism that "a rising tide lifts all boats" aptly applies to political economy. Political leaders of a national economy that experiences strong, sustained growth, with full employment but without excessive inflation, enjoy a veritable win-win situation. Favorable economic numbers are commonly associated with the high political popularity of elected public officials. Full employment with widely shared rising personal income provides the means for people to get ahead and improve their standard of living. It also swells public treasuries, giving governments the financial ability to meet the claims of groups and interests that would not be met in tight economic times. Even faced with a budget deficit, strong economic growth can allow policymakers to meet some claims for added spending while contributing to deficit reduction.

President Clinton, in his campaign for reelection, benefited from a sound economy. Taking full advantage of favorable economic reports preceding the 1996 election, he used almost every public forum to tie his administration's fiscal policies to the economy's strength. The litany commonly included the following evidence of success: a 12-month, 3.4 percent increase in real (inflation-adjusted) GDP from the fourth quarter of FY 1995 to the fourth quarter of FY 1996, capped by a 4.7 percent increase from July through September 1996; the lowest combined rate of unemployment and inflation—the so-called misery index—since the administration of Lyndon Johnson; the creation of over 11 million jobs since he took office; a reduction of over two million recipients on the welfare rolls over the same period; and a national budget deficit at the end of FY 1996 that reached its lowest point since 1981 in current dollars, and its lowest point since 1974 as a percentage of the GDP. With this economic record as a backdrop, President Clinton went on to defeat Republican challenger Bob Dole handily. Not surprisingly, national polls showed that the condition of the economy significantly influenced voter support for the president.[1]

Public policymakers, professional economists, business interests, the media, and the general public look to these and other aggregate measures to assess how well the economy is doing. In a sense, they also use them to judge how well America and its political leaders are doing. Individuals, however, look to their own personal situation to judge how they are faring, and they compare their own lot with the composite picture of national well-being. Again, national polls preceding and following the 1996 presidential election showed that most Americans felt that their individual situation had improved, even though a number worried about their long-term economic prospects.[2]

Beyond individuals' comparisons of how they are doing in light of how they believe the nation is doing, few measures of how national economic growth is distributed among the population are regularly available for popular consumption. This is not to suggest that scholars and economic analysts fail to examine questions of distribution and equity, for they certainly do. Their findings can indeed have an impact on the national debate over how well America is faring. Assessments of who benefited from the strong economic recovery following the deep 1981–1982 recession provide a case in point. The consensus among analysts is that the wealthiest and highest income individuals benefited the most, which is discussed in greater detail later in this chapter.

That conclusion shaped the nature of President Clinton's deficit-reduction initiatives of 1993, introduced shortly after his election to a first term. Over half of the $433 billion in deficit reduction over five years approved by Congress, at the president's behest, was to come from tax increases, drawn primarily from the personal income tax. Yet what is most salient for this discussion is the way in which that additional revenue was to be raised—with the bulk coming from an increase in the top income tax rate from 31 percent to 36 percent, along with a 10 percent surcharge on taxable income over $250,000. The well-off, in a sense, were asked to give back some of the gain they disproportionately enjoyed in previous years.

Just as the economy can affect policy choice and its associated politics, political decisions can influence the performance of the economy. As discussed earlier, national political leaders see a healthy economy as advancing their political fortunes. Policymakers worldwide do what they can to support economic prosperity. The tools they use may differ, but their goals are pointedly similar: economic growth, full employment, stable prices (or at least acceptably low levels of inflation), and a favorable balance of payments from international trade. The trick for policymakers pursuing economic growth is to expand the economy fully to its potential for production, but being careful not to exceed that potential and run the risk of promoting accelerated inflation and the rising unemployment that follows.

Beyond this common list of goals, governments also may want to pursue policies that extend economic development to underdeveloped regions of their nation. Directed regional growth, tapping resources and labor that had not previously been exploited to their potential, holds the promise of both enlarging the national economic pie and minimizing problems that result from a heavy concentration of industrial activity and population. In the United States, the federal government has largely been inactive in using policy tools to direct economic development geographically, in comparison to other national governments. Its closest venture has come in creating the Tennessee Valley Authority and the Appalachian Commission as investments in infrastructural support for regional economic development.

In addition to directing economic development geographically, governments can use their regulatory authority, taxing powers, and financial resources to prevent, discourage, or encourage certain *kinds* of economic development within their borders. Or they can take action into their own hands and develop and own the means of production themselves. Here, again, the U.S. federal government plays little direct role in shaping the composition of industrial production. It has, however, engaged in limited assistance to selected industries, employing a diverse and somewhat incoherent assortment of devices such as tax expenditures (special provisions in the tax code reducing liability), loans and loan guarantees, financial support of basic and applied research, and job training assistance, a topic receiving further discussion in Chapter 2.

State and local governments have gone the furthest in supporting economic development.[3] States have established agencies whose job it is to promote economic development, making special efforts to entice large manufacturing and service industries to open new plants and offices within their borders. States often compete against each other over economic development, using tax incentives, loans, subsidized labor training, relaxed regulations, and highway improvements and freeway access as their primary enticements.

Local governments also strive to attract new and expanded development within their jurisdictions, which puts communities in competition with one another. In that competition, they tend to employ some of the same tools used by the states, turning most often to tax abatements, which can consist of reduced tax rates; deferrals of tax liability; or outright exemption from taxation. Beyond tax considerations, local governments also can forgive corporations from their share of the costs of physical infrastructure needed to support an industrial plant or large service enterprise, including the costs of curbs and gutters, street lighting, power sources, and extension of sewer lines. In addition, where permitted by their state, they can offer relaxed regulations to attract development, most commonly in the form of variances from planning requirements or land-use restrictions.

Corporations put these incentives in the larger context of a state's or a community's business climate and the quality of life it offers. Business climate includes the types of taxes a government employs and the tax effort it makes, prevailing wage rates and the extent of unionization in the area, the preparedness and cost of labor, and the overall regulatory climate. Quality of life refers to such considerations as quality of schools and higher educational institutions, crime rate, climate, neighborhoods and available housing, and recreational opportunities. Industries also consider other factors that bear on the soundness of business decisions, such as the ready availability of raw materials and energy resources, proximity to suppliers and transportation facilities, and access to key markets. In fact, research over the past three decades suggests that it is these elements of a sound business decision that influence locational choice the most.[4] State and local government incentives appear to exercise only a marginal influence, primarily when the traditional elements of a sound business decision are essentially equal. Yet this knowledge has not dulled state and local officials' enthusiasm for development incentives. They have not been willing in a highly competitive environment to take the chance of losing ground because they fail to match or exceed the concessions offered by their competitors. It has, however, prompted state officials to redirect a good part of their efforts toward keeping industries within their state's borders and encouraging them to expand there. It also has increasingly prompted them to offer development incentives only after a corporation has narrowed its geographic search based on sound business considerations.

While these limited efforts to direct economic development geographically and the selective efforts to support industrial development of a certain kind have some effect on the economy, the real influence of government on the U.S. economy comes from the national government's efforts to influence the performance of the economy overall. Two macroeconomic policy instruments loom largest toward that end: fiscal policy and monetary policy.

Fiscal policy, which is covered in detail in Chapter 2, deals with national governments' use of taxing and spending to affect aggregate demand and thereby influence the course of the economy in desired directions. Legislative bodies make taxing and spending decisions in most democratic industrial nations, and the United States is no exception. Yet those choices are typically shaped by presidents or prime ministers, who use the budgetary process to set their nation's fiscal agenda. Their budget recommendations suggest how much a nation should spend in a given fiscal period, how it should raise revenues to finance that spending, and how much debt should be incurred to support spending not covered by current revenues. In the United States, it is the president who initiates fiscal policy and prioritizes spending among the many federal government programs. The Congress then decides the extent to which it will follow the president's lead, although its decentralized decision-making structures and process mitigate Congress's ability to produce a coherent alternative to the president's agenda, despite its attempts to reform the budgetary process toward that end.

Although states and local governments engage in taxing and spending, the fiscal effects of those choices are overwhelmed by national economic forces. Moreover, since nearly all states and local governments must balance their budgets, state and local decisions about taxing and spending usually run counter to national fiscal policy directions. When a national recession broadly depresses state economies, reducing revenues and increasing the costs of public assistance programs, state policymakers have little choice but to increase taxes or fees, or cut spending in certain programs and reallocate that budget authority to others. Both tacks reinforce the recession's dampening effects. In contrast, federal policymakers use fiscal policy in an economic downturn to stimulate the economy through increased national government spending or decreased taxes. Local governments' taxing and spending decisions have even less effect on the national economy than do those of states. Their heavy reliance on the property tax and the high percentage of their budget devoted to personnel costs give local government policymakers little flexibility to affect aggregate demand.

Monetary policy, also discussed in Chapter 2, attempts to alter the supply of money in circulation to influence the direction of the economy. Like fiscal policy, monetary policy is a national economic policymaking tool that aims to affect aggregate demand, but uses changes in the money supply—not taxing and spending decisions—to achieve that objective. Monetary policy works on the expectation that additions to the money supply get spent, fueling aggregate demand, while contractions of the money supply constrict aggregate demand. Changes in the money supply take place through the medium of a nation's credit system. Governments usually do not just print more currency to increase the money supply, a proven recipe for inflation; they influence the availability and cost of loanable funds. Restricted availability and the increasing cost of credit lowers aggregate demand, and liberal availability and the declining cost of credit raises it.

Unlike fiscal policy, monetary policy is not the direct responsibility of presidents or prime ministers. The responsibility for monetary policy lies with a nation's central bank; however, it would be naive to suggest that presidents and prime ministers do not influence monetary policy. Yet the degree of that influence varies with the relative political insulation of the central bank. In the United States, the Federal Reserve System functions as our central bank, and it is structurally insulated from presidential or congressional control.

The Federal Reserve has employed monetary policy differently over time. Most often it has used monetary policy to combat inflation, but the Fed has also used it to stimulate a stagnant economy or strengthen a slow recovery. The Fed's inflationary fighting has taken either a reactive, crisis-interventionist approach or an incremental, preventive one. A dramatic example of the former is the Federal Reserve's strike against double-digit inflation in the early 1980s. At that time, Americans faced a slow-growth economy but with runaway inflation fueled by skyrocketing oil prices and declining productivity. In response to seemingly uncontrollable inflation, an increasingly unpopular President Carter, who would face a reelection campaign the next year, appointed a conservative monetarist, Paul Volcker, to chair the Federal Reserve Board. Dogged by a rising federal budget deficit, President Carter and the Congress faced a tough policy predicament. Should they follow a course of raising taxes to reduce the deficit and slow the growth of inflation but face the risk of throwing an already weak economy into recession, or try to stimulate the economy's growth and fuel further inflation? Congress did neither, opting instead for marginally higher budget cuts, a direction initially supported by Carter in his January budget address to Congress. But with the election just four months away, the president proposed higher spending and some last-minute tax cuts. Congress demurred, as it looked to the electoral outcome for direction.[5]

Chairman Volcker ultimately had another course in mind, one intent on squeezing inflation out of the economy through the use of a highly restrictive monetary policy. Since that course would have had sure recessionary consequences in an election year, he and the Fed chose not to pursue it. However, with the election of Ronald Reagan to the presidency and with the Republicans in control of the Senate, the stage was set for the kind of restrictive monetary policy necessary to deal a blow to inflation. In relatively short order, the Fed's abrupt efforts to increase the cost of credit and shrink its availability had their desired effects. Interest rates charged by banks rose markedly, both aggregate consumption and spending declined, and rising unemployment followed. The United States soon found itself in the worst recession since the Great Depression of the 1930s. High inflation had been broken, dropping to under 4 percent for the 1982 fiscal year. Unemployment, however, rose to double-digit levels. The Volcker-led Federal Reserve had made an inherently political choice, to trade off high inflation for high unemployment.

As the economy recovered from the recession, the Federal Reserve pursued a strategy of using monetary policy to manage the economy in the direction of sustained growth with price stability. That prescription led the Fed to provide additional bank reserves and drive down interest rates when aggregate demand showed signs of slackening significantly, but it also led it to reverse course when aggregate demand grew sufficiently to threaten a new wave of increased inflation. On balance, the Fed has followed a strategy of striking proactively to promote economic growth while keeping inflation in check. That clearly has been the operative policy of Volcker's successor, Alan Greenspan.

Critics argue that the Federal Reserve under Greenspan's leadership has worried excessively about inflation and been too eager to raise interest rates before a good case could be made for dampening demand. They see the Fed's inflation-fighting initiatives as costing would-be jobs and higher personal income. Supporters of preemption, in contrast, view the Fed's action as using short-term intervention to lay the foundation for acceptable levels of sustained long-term economic growth with low inflation. Once accomplished, they see the Fed's job as providing a monetary policy supportive of growth in line with the increased capacity of the economic system to provide goods and services over the long run. That job also entails acting to lower interest rates when demand slackens, as the Fed did on three separate occasions in the fall of 1998 to counter the dampening economic effects produced by East Asia's financial crisis.

Beyond national governments' use of fiscal and monetary policy as instruments of general economic management, both national and subnational governments, motivated by other economic and social goals, use their regulatory powers in ways that affect sectors of the economy differently. For example, both the U.S. federal government and the states regulate the industrial discharge of air and water pollutants. They do so to protect the broader public interest over the narrow interests of industrial firms. For example, industries bear the costs of making the capital improvements necessary to clean up the pollutants they emit. Those resource commitments reduce their financial bottom line. Thus, from a financial perspective, it is in the interest of industries in a market economy to keep their costs of pollution mitigation as low as good relations with their customers will allow. Government, on the other hand, must concern itself with how industrial leaders' choices will affect the general public welfare, protecting the rights of its citizens, in this example, to breathe healthy air and use clean water. In protecting those rights, the challenge facing government is to decide *how* clean air and water should be, recognizing the different costs of attaining the various possible levels of air and water quality. The more restrictive the regulations, the more it costs industry to comply with them. Other government regulations that entail private-sector costs of compliance target a panoply of practices, including workplace safety, consumer information and product safety, labor relations, and affirmative action, to cite just a few. Regulation is covered comprehensively in Chapter 5.

THE NORMATIVE INHERITANCE OF AMERICA'S POLITICAL ECONOMY

Economic policymakers in the United States do not make decisions in a vacuum. Their options are limited by the structure and processes of America's political institutions, by competing political interests with different power bases and resources at their disposal, and by ideologies. Ideologies influence whether conditions should be treated as problems, how problems are to be defined, and the standards of judgment to be used in evaluating competing alternatives.[6] Classical liberalism, with its roots largely in the writings of seventeenth- and eighteenth-century British economic and political theorists, provides an ideology that still conditions the way American policymakers and even the general public look at government, think about their relationship to it, and hold expectations of it. In both economic and political affairs, liberalism draws a sharp line between the private and public spheres of citizens' lives. The central organizing tenet of liberalism is that individuals are the best judge of what is in their self-interest. They, therefore, should be free to pursue their own interests as they see them, as long as that pursuit does not abridge the rights of others to exercise freedom.

Government exists to protect the rights of people. For John Locke, a contract exists between government and the people, under which government protects individuals from having their rights to personal freedom and property infringed upon by others, in exchange for citizens' support of limited government. As part of that contract, government action is legitimate only when it protects individual rights better than individuals can protect them alone.[7] Government's protection of civil liberty, and the market's facilitation of economic choice, serve as vehicles toward self-actualization. For John Stuart Mill[8] and other utilitarians, that pursuit of self-interest by individuals leads in the aggregate to the greatest collective good for the greatest number.

The market allows buyers and sellers to come together of their own volition to benefit themselves: buyers obtaining what they want, and sellers receiving payment for their goods or services that are wanted. In a competitive marketplace, both buyers and sellers look to prices as a gauge of whether it is in their self-interest to enter into a transaction. Buyers compare the price charged with their sense of the expected quality of the product or service, and sellers price their wares with a sense of how the quality of their product or service compares with others available. A transaction occurs when the buyer believes he or she has found something of acceptable quality at an acceptable price. Competition keeps prices down, since the buyer can usually find the same or a similar product or service in the marketplace; and, when that is the case, price tends to become the determining factor, although customers also may consider the quality of service that sellers provide. The market makes goods and services available that people want because someone believes that he or she can earn a profit by making or selling them. But the market turns on someone wanting something in the first place. Sellers use advertising to create wants, and to entice consumers to identify with their products and services.

For Adam Smith[9] and other economic liberals, the striking thing about the market is that economic order can emerge as the unintended consequence of the actions of many people, each seeking his or her own self-interest. The market itself sets priorities for private resource investment and expenditure, and the market exchange of supply and demand determines value. The important point here is that the market becomes a device for coordinating the economy, but without top-down, centralized command. It is the market, not government, that defines the substance of the economic product, the specific array of goods and services available, their quality, and their distribution.

Classical liberal theory, however, does acknowledge a role for government in the economy, and that is to ensure the integrity of the market while not distorting the natural operation of market forces. For the market to work efficiently, government must protect personal property, protect the respective rights of buyers and sellers, and thwart monopolies. Yet in those relatively few instances when the nature of the enterprise leads to monopoly, such as traditionally with public utility services, government has elected to regulate them in the public interest, approving rate structures and profit margins (although power generating and telecommunications industries in the United States have recently undergone significant deregulation).

John Maynard Keynes, a British economic theorist, writing in the early twentieth century, accepted the tenets of classical economic theory but also espoused a broader, more activist role for government in the market economy.[10] Accepting the proposition that government must justify its intervention in the economy, Keynes added to the short list of legitimate justification. For Keynes, government has an obligation to secure the reliable performance of the economy as a whole. Although he recognized the power of the market to function as an invisible hand to coordinate the economy, he also realized that the economy is subject to periods of expansion and contraction. In a slumping economy, consumers are more wary of satisfying their material wants, and more inclined to save rather than to spend. The resulting downturn in aggregate demand induces businesses to reduce inventories and postpone orders for new products, thus prompting manufacturers to cut back on production and lay off unneeded workers. This snowballing effect further propels the economy into decline and increases unemployment.

The Great Depression thrust unemployment to record heights in both Great Britain and the United States. Contrary to classical economic theory, the economy showed no signs of self-correcting. The high unemployment of the Great Depression appeared not to be transitional, as the classical theory of self-adjusting labor markets suggested. Keynes feared that the economy would remain in the doldrums as long as low demand persisted.

Increased saving was not the answer for Keynes. In fact, he viewed saving as the enemy of recovery. Spending was the answer—spending that would increase aggregate demand. The problem for him was how to achieve increased demand in an environment of sustained underemployment of resources. That is where government comes in. National governments can use debt to finance spending beyond their ability to cover the costs out of current revenues. Keynes saw major deficit-financed government spending as the spark that could ignite the economy, propelling aggregate demand that would revitalize markets and bring the unemployed back to work. For Keynes, a large pool of trained workers existed during the depression who were ready and willing to go back to work if only there were sufficient demand in the economy for the products they produce. Massive government spending could create that demand, and Keynes viewed government as having an obligation to step in and get the economic ball rolling in a depressed economy.

Keynes, however, also saw that obligation as not just limited to recessionary conditions. An activist government should work to manage aggregate demand whenever market forces prove insufficient to create enough demand to keep unemployment at acceptable levels. Although Keynes preferred increased government spending as government's foremost instrument to expand demand, he recognized that demand could be fostered through tax cuts as well. But for tax cuts to generate increased demand, those benefiting from them would have to spend their increased after-tax income rather than save it. In worrisome economic conditions, people might be more inclined to save rather than to spend. Significantly increased government spending, on the other hand, obviates that uncertainty; it translates directly into higher aggregate demand.

Keynesian theory also gives national economic policymakers the expectations and tools to cool down an overheated, inflationary-prone economy. The recipe again lies with government action to influence demand, reducing it by decreasing spending or increasing taxes. Keynes' primary concern, however, was not how to slow down an overheating economy but how to stimulate an economy operating below capacity, bringing it to full employment and sustaining it there.

The major political contribution of Keynesian theory is its justification for government intervention in the economy. Remember that classical liberal theory prescribes a limited role for government, and requires that government justify its intervention in society and the economy. Keynes not only legitimized government intervention to secure national economic prosperity; he honored it. In doing so, his activist orientation has had lasting political implications. Those supporting activist government, believing that government has a highly constructive role to play in improving the quality of life and conditions of its citizens, broadened the agenda to include other forms of government intervention, including justification for a growing welfare state. Such adherents have been labeled political liberals—modern liberals, not in the sense of classical liberals, as discussed earlier. (Ironically, as an aside, those who espouse the values of classical liberalism have been popularly tagged as modern-day political conservatives.)

In focusing on government intervention in managing aggregate demand to achieve full employment, Keynes did not worry much about the inflationary effects of overstimulating the economy beyond its productive capacity, because his primary concern was how to mobilize underutilized resources. That concern fell to his intellectual successors. One prominent disciple, A. W. Phillips, identified an inverse relationship between unemployment and inflation.[11] He found that as unemployment falls, inflation rises, since the growing scarcity of labor drives up wage rates; and higher wage rates typically inflate the cost of the products or services provided, that is, unless they are accompanied by proportionally increased productivity. He found the converse also to be true: inflation drives up the cost of labor, inducing employers to attempt to get by with less of it. Thus governments face a dilemma. Their efforts to increase aggregate demand can lead to inflation that rises to unacceptable levels. Conversely, their efforts to control inflation can lead to growing unemployment.

The tradeoff apparent in the so-called Phillips' curve reinforced the interventionist inclinations of Keynesians. It became incumbent on economic policymakers to anticipate the effects of this tradeoff, and to use fiscal and monetary policy tools (with Keynesians preferring the fiscal policy variety) to mitigate its negative effects, striving for an acceptable balance between unemployment and inflation. In employing policy tools to achieve that objective, policymakers tend to err on one side or the other. They may be willing to accept a little more unemployment for a little less inflation, or the converse. That choice represents an inherently political judgment.

FISCAL POLICY CHOICE AND THE ASCENDANCY OF MONETARY POLICY FOR ECONOMIC MANAGEMENT

The widespread acceptance of the perceived realities of the Phillips' curve was first shaken by the experience of the mid- to late 1970s. High inflation coexisted with high unemployment, at least higher unemployment than occurred during the first part of the 1970s and particularly during the 1950s and 1960s. For 1978, inflation rose to almost 8 percent while unemployment stood at a little over 6 percent, an unemployment level well in excess of the Carter administration's policy of 4 percent unemployment. By 1979, unemployment remained essentially flat, but prices rose by 11 percent. And although inflation became America's most pressing economic problem, unemployment remained much higher than economic theory suggested it should be, or that policymakers were willing to tolerate.

The perceived inadequacy of Keynesian theory to explain stagflation and deal with it effectively through demand-side fiscal policy prompted a few economists and journalists, influential in conservative Republican circles, to offer a competing model, although it failed to win many adherents among economists. *Supply-side economics*—espoused by Jude Waninski, Arthur Laffer, Robert Mundell, and others—targeted inflation as its principal economic problem, not unemployment, as did Keynesian theory. Yet it embraced Keynesianism's primary objective of achieving and sustaining economic growth without inflation. Therein lay its appeal to a Reagan administration that shared the supply-siders' antipathy toward the inflation it had inherited, but that also found itself thrust into a deep recession induced by the monetary shock therapy of the Federal Reserve. The trick for supply-siders was to rescue the nation from recession and establish the conditions for a sustainable economic recovery without excessive inflation. Instead of spending its way out of recession, as Keynesian theory dictates, supply-siders called for the federal government to support public policies that would encourage saving, leading to increased investment.

Remember that Keynes feared saving, because it dampened demand. The supply-siders, in contrast, viewed increased savings as providing the investment capital necessary to sustain a long-run recovery in the business cycle. They theorized that the growth in savings would finance the investment that would create jobs and increase aggregate income over the long run while providing the productive capacity to keep aggregate demand in line with the growth of productive capacity, thus keeping inflation under control.

Yet how can government foster increased saving? A major part of the supply-siders' answer in the early 1980s was to cut taxes, providing the largest tax cuts to those who have the greatest marginal propensity to save, that is, those with the highest incomes. As the theory goes, individuals with relatively low incomes are more likely to spend additional after-tax income, not save it, although they would still benefit from the greater employment opportunities and higher incomes made possible by the increased investment created by the savings of others.

Contrary to the theory's expectations, personal savings declined as a percentage of disposable income during the 1980s.[12] Recipients appear to have spent their higher after-tax income instead of saving it. In fact, it appears that people behaved just as Keynesian theory would have predicted. They used the tax cut to spend the nation toward economic recovery, providing an economic stimulus beyond what normally could be expected as a result of the upward swing of the business cycle.

Economic recovery from the 1981–1982 recession brought with it a panoply of favorable economic indicators. Real GDP grew by 3.6 percent annually between 1982 and 1989, the unemployment rate declined from slightly less than 10 percent in 1982 to about 5 percent by 1989, and the inflation rate declined from its 1980 peak of over 13 percent to about 6 percent in 1982, falling even further to under 5 percent by 1989.

With these economic indicators moving in the desired direction, and with an economic expansion lasting longer than any previous post–World War II expansion, save that of the 1960s, the president and Congress gave little attention to national economic management. What preoccupied them in the 1980s was a rising national budget deficit, created as a product of their taxing and spending decisions. The combination of the large revenue-removing tax cut of 1981, substantial real-dollar increases in defense spending, and unbridled entitlement spending pushed the federal budget deficit to $221 billion at the end of the 1986 fiscal year. Subsequent payroll tax increases and a significant reduction in the growth rate of defense spending dropped the deficit to $153 billion at the end of the 1989 fiscal year. The 1990 recession, however, ended the seven-year period of economic expansion and pushed the deficit up to $290 billion by the end of the 1992 fiscal year. It increased entitlement spending and also cut into the revenue growth promised by the tax increase enacted by Congress in October 1990, with President Bush's support—a tax increase employed not as a tool of fiscal management but as a symbolically laden message sent in the waning days before the midterm election that those in power could finally get the job of deficit reduction done.

The federal budget deficit, not economic management of the economy, continued to preoccupy both branches during the Clinton presidency. It is true that President Clinton offered Congress a modest economic stimulus package shortly after his election to a first term, but Congress rejected the greater part of it, as Congressional Budget Office economists and most others warned against its passage as potentially inflationary—timed with the lag time between passage and implementation to coincide with the normal recovery to which the leading economic indicators were beginning to point. Despite the prospects for recovery, President Clinton and the Democratic majority in Congress still faced a projected near-$300 billion federal budget deficit by the end of Clinton's first year in office. With the Democrats in control of both the presidency and Congress for the first time since the Carter administration, they felt a collective responsibility and political need to deliver on President Clinton's campaign pledge to make a sizable dent in a seemingly insurmountable deficit.

That came through the enactment of a deficit-reduction package of tax increases and budget cuts, the second of the young decade. The Omnibus Budget Reconciliation Act of 1993 passed without a single Republican vote in either chamber of Congress. Of greatest political significance, it included $240 billion projected to come from tax increases, a response to candidate Clinton's admonition that deficit reduction would likely have to include tax hikes. Some observers, including Republican leaders, criticized the tax increases as wrongly conceived and ill-timed, threatening the sustainability of economic recovery. Democrats worried that they could later face a political backlash in the 1994 elections, which they did. Exit polls, however, indicated that the tax increase, which primarily affected the top two percent of income earners, was only one ingredient in a growing diffuse alienation of American voters, who were in a "throw the bums out" frame of mind. Their distrust of government seemed to grow, as did their distaste of government solutions to problems: witness the public's lack of enthusiasm for the sweeping Clinton health care reform proposals that preceded the 1994 election. Moreover, both popular media commentary and public opinion polls pointed to a mounting concern among workers about the security of their own jobs in an economy of slow growth and corporate downsizing and consolidation.[13] Voters responded by electing conservative Republicans to office and giving the Republicans control of both chambers of Congress for the first time since the early years of the Eisenhower administration. They also replaced Democrats with Republicans in statehouses across America, increasing the ranks of Republican governors from 19 to 30.

The Republicans in Congress, particularly those in the House, under the leadership of their new Speaker, Newt Gingrich, saw the 1994 election as a mandate to reduce the size of government and its programmatic and regulatory reach. They pursued that mission with apostolic zeal. Buoyed by the national attention given to their "Contract with America," the House Republicans pushed their Senate counterparts to support a budgetary agenda that sought to make deep cuts in the deficit, in significant part by eliminating entitlement status for the Medicaid and Aid to Families With Dependent Children (AFDC) programs, and by cutting their rates of growth. The Republican agenda also included reducing the growth in Medicare spending and requiring more out-of-pocket payments from higher income recipients. In response, President Clinton vetoed the budget reconciliation bill, and promised an alternative deficit-reduction plan. The Republicans—unable to garner enough support to override the president's veto, yet feeling ideologically secure as a result of their solid electoral victory—persisted in their cause at the same time the president remained unmoved. The resulting stalemate led to Congress's refusal to enact additional continuing resolutions necessary to keep all government departments operating. During the protracted budget battle, breaks in coverage forced the shutdown of several federal agencies and the furloughing of employees for two stretches, the longest lasting for 22 days.

Polls suggest that the general public tended to blame the Republicans for the stalemate and government shutdown.[14] President Clinton skillfully reinforced that perception and used the presidential podium to paint the Republican leadership as extreme, pointing to their efforts to cut Medicare (even though the legislation called for reducing growth, not cutting the program), reduce student loans, and weaken environmental protection. Political moderates, in response, called on Congress and the president to turn aside confrontation and work closer together in addressing pressing national problems. Getting the political message, the President and Congress agreed essentially to continue spending at the current level, except for a few politically sensitive spending additions sought by the Clinton administration, and to await the outcome of the 1996 presidential and congressional elections as a sign of voter sentiment.

As the election neared, President Clinton lent his support to Republican-initiated welfare reform legislation that eliminated the AFDC entitlement program and replaced it with discretionary block grants to the states, giving voters further evidence of their ability to work together and enact legislation favored by the public. National opinion polls registered widespread voter approval,[15] and both the president and Congress took credit for "ending welfare dependence." Not everyone shared that enthusiasm, however. Liberals (in the modern-day, not classical, sense) viewed the end of entitlement as an unwelcomed departure from the traditional values of the Democratic Party. The welfare reform package not only divided Democrats in Congress, but in the Clinton administration as well. Recent accounts portray the internal lack of consensus among Democratic Party leaders, and one former cabinet secretary attributes his departure to the president's choice of political pragmatism over principle in welfare reform.[16]

Along with their growing hopefulness that the president and Congress had finally recognized the need to cooperate and accommodate their respective interests if progress was to be made on matters the public cares about, Americans also were increasingly optimistic about the national economy and their own fortunes. Economic indicators continued to point in the right direction, and income disparities began to show signs of narrowing. Both President Clinton and congressional incumbents benefited from this state of affairs. The president won reelection easily, and the Republicans maintained majorities in both chambers, although they suffered some losses in the House. Voters did not use the electoral opportunity to take sides, to answer unambiguously whether they supported the "Republican Revolution" or President Clinton's more moderate stance, as many observers had expected. Instead, voters seemed to sanction the status quo of divided government—a relationship that appeared to be working better as of late. In that environment, both the president and Congress appeared less willing than before to rock the political boat.

Democrats seemed content to ride the waves of prosperity for a time, and Republicans looked to make further gains in polishing their quickly tarnished image. Both parties' agendas became less ambitious and controversial, centering primarily on further reducing the federal budget deficit. The Democrats' attention to the details of deficit reduction, however, soon became diverted by growing allegations of influence peddling and campaign finance irregularities, directed at both Clinton and Vice President Albert Gore personally. Yet the issue never became the scandal that the Republicans had hoped it would become. Political accommodation and the strength of the economy helped to keep President Clinton's approval rating at historically high levels.[17] This confluence of fledgling but unrealized scandal and public support for the outcomes of political accommodation set the stage for further cooperation on deficit reduction. For President Clinton, a major further deficit-reduction package would deflect the public's and the media's attention away from allegations of campaign finance abuse and reinforce the public's perception of him as a leader who could work with the other party in Congress to get things done. For the Republicans, it would help to repair further their popular image as hardliners who preferred ideological purity to getting things done.

On May 2, following the election, President Clinton and Republican congressional leaders reached agreement on further deficit reduction aimed at balancing the federal budget by 2002, an agreement subsequently enacted into law in late July 1997. The margin of congressional approval was especially noteworthy, given the record of partisan divisiveness and rancor marking congressional debate and action on previous deficit-reduction packages. The House passed the tax portion of the plan by a lopsided vote of 389–43, punctuating its vote with a hearty round of applause, and the Senate followed with a nearly unanimous vote of 92–8. In a similar fashion, the House voted 346–85 in favor of the spending package, and the Senate followed suit, by an 85–15 vote. A year later, in the fall of 1998, Congress continued its bipartisan support of the budget, with the House passing the Omnibus Budget Act by a 333–95 margin, and the Senate supporting it by a vote of 65–29. Although Chapter 3 covers in detail the substance and implementation of the budget deals, it is sufficient for our purposes here to note that both White House and Republican congressional leaders saw them as win-win propositions.

In 1997, the White House could claim that the deal would lead to a balanced budget that reflected the values and priorities of the president, including increased spending for education, environmental protection, expanded medical assistance coverage for uninsured children in low-income families, restored public assistance benefits for legal immigrants, and tax incentives for businesses to hire welfare recipients, among other provisions. Overall, the budget agreement would allow domestic discretionary spending to increase by $70 billion over the five-year period, capping its growth at projected inflation—a looser cap than the spending freeze that preceded it. President Clinton and his advisors were careful to label the higher domestic spending as "vital domestic investment."

Republican leaders, in turn, could point to $95 billion in net tax cuts, prominently including a reduction in the tax rate on capital gains, a $500 per-child tax credit, a doubling of the estate-tax exemption, and a liberalization of the deductibility of individual retirement accounts (IRAs), making them available to higher income taxpayers. Republicans could also take credit for putting Medicare on a sounder financial footing, through controls on reimbursements to hospitals and health care providers, along with increases in the premiums paid by middle- and upper-income beneficiaries, jointly producing a projected reduction in entitlement spending of $115 billion—savings that would offset the cost of increased domestic spending and tax cuts. In addition, both parties could highlight new tax credits for lower- and middle-income taxpayers to offset the costs of higher education, even though many of the more ideological Republicans voiced their preference for other forms of tax relief that would contribute more directly to economic growth.

In the following year, the 1998 deal gave President Clinton and the Democrats more in discretionary spending than Clinton had requested in his February budget submission,[18] and it included the president's hard-fought $1.2 billion initiative to aid local school districts in reducing class size in the early grades.[19] For Republicans, the Omnibus Budget Act contained an increase in defense spending and funding for new antidrug programs.

It is unclear whether this decidedly bipartisan support for the budget represents a new consensus on policy direction for the nation, following decades of clashing priorities, or rather a serendipitous opportunity to use favorable revenue flows to advance the political fortunes of incumbents, whatever their political stripe. Yet it probably has elements of both. It is clear that the near $70 billion budget surplus reported for the end of the 1998 fiscal year, together with forecasts of further surplus growth, has given Congress the fiscal room to ease up on the restrictions that kept spending in line during most of the 1990s. Whether they will do so remains to be seen.

As the President and Congress devoted their attention to deficit reduction and its attendant politics in the 1990s, the Federal Reserve exercised responsibility for continued management of the economy. Under its chairman, Alan Greenspan—originally appointed by President Reagan at the end of his presidency, and reappointed by President Clinton—the Fed followed an active and often proactive strategy of employing monetary policy to control economic fluctuations. It steeply increased the federal funds rate (the rate of interest that lending institutions charge one another for overnight loans—a benchmark that affects commercial interest rates, as is discussed more fully in Chapter 2) in 1988 and early 1989 to slow down what it viewed as an overheated economy. Then, it lowered the federal funds rate in response to signs of the looming recession, following the initial decrease by a series of successive downward adjustments that lowered interest rates by about a third from where they were in 1989, aimed at softening the effects of the recession and shortening its duration. Yet it did not stop there. As the economy strengthened and expanded, the Federal Reserve followed a policy of graduated preemptive strikes against the inflation that could result from growth beyond economic capacity.

Inflation remained the principal problem for Greenspan and his fellow policymakers, as it had been for the Volcker-led board, even though inflation had stabilized at about 3 percent in the mid-1990s and dropped below 2 percent in 1997 and 1998—a level reminiscent of the 1950s and 1960s. The Fed stood ready to squelch the threat of inflation in the name of sustaining economic growth with price stability. In just the short period between early 1994 and early 1995, the Greenspan-led board hiked interest rates seven times. It continued to follow that policy strategy after the 1996 election, raising the federal funds rate by 25 basis points (a quarter of 1 percent) in March 1997, in response to signs of faster economic growth than expected. Yet as the economy showed that it could grow strongly with stable or even declining inflation and historically low unemployment, Greenspan and the Fed demonstrated a new willingness to allow that growth to continue unimpeded by monetary policy, believing that strong economic fundamentals could sustain growth within the economy's capacity to accommodate it.

That posture remained unchanged until late September 1998, when the Federal Reserve changed direction and *lowered* the federal funds rate by a quarter percent, in response to signs that the serious financial crisis in several East Asian nations was beginning to tighten credit markets in the United States. In a surprise move, it lowered the rate by another quarter percent in mid-October, just about one month later, and followed in November with an additional quarter percent reduction. The U.S. stock markets responded enthusiastically, and the Dow Jones Industrial Average recovered from a significant correction to reach a new all-time high in late November. Other world markets rose as well, encouraged by the U.S. markets' performance and by signs of improved financial conditions in East Asia. Chapter 4 discusses how economic conditions in the rest of the world can affect the U.S. economy, and it examines the East Asian situation in greater detail.

PUTTING RECENT ECONOMIC AND POLITICAL PERFORMANCE IN PERSPECTIVE

Capitalism and Democracy

Our classical liberal inheritance holds that individuals know best what is in their self-interest. America's capitalistic market economy and its democratic political system provide avenues for individuals to act in their own interest, whether they act individually or participate as members of enterprises or associations. In the market, individuals or collective enterprises participate as self-interested buyers or sellers. In democratic politics, individual participation takes a number of forms: expressing political opinions and policy preferences publicly, supporting candidates for office, voting, and contacting elected representatives and other public officials. Individuals also seek to further their personal interests by joining their forces in organized groups. As members of interest groups, individuals contribute to their organization's financial support and stand ready to add their voice to its collective voice when called upon. In both markets and democratic politics, people participate to advance their interests, although some participants—a distinct minority—see their individual interests in light of what they view to be in the broader public interest, particularly if that support or action does not cost or inconvenience them much personally. A person who buys an American-brand automobile because it is good for the country, even though he or she would really prefer a more highly rated or socially prestigious import, is an example of the former, and a citizen who supports increased taxes to finance expanded tax credits or public assistance programs for the needy is an example of the latter.

Both markets and democratic politics distribute things that people value. Participants judge the extent to which these systems produce outcomes that are indeed in their interest and commensurate with what they believe they deserve. This sense of just deserts lies at the center of Robert Lane's important comparison of market justice and political justice.[20] He argues that Americans regard the market as more just than democratic politics. The public readily recognizes the value they derive from market transactions. They feel that they deserve what they get, for they are putting either money or product on the line, and the competitive interaction of supply and demand is yielding a fair price for what they are getting in return. The relationship between cost and return is direct and evident. Such is not the case for politics. National taxpayers typically question the value they get from government in relation to what they pay in taxes. They typically recognize few tangible benefits that directly affect their lives, while they see their tax dollars supporting benefits received by others. They also may question the amount of government spending in support of nondivisible goods, such as national defense and environmental protection, viewing it in excess of what they believe is needed to accomplish national objectives. On the other hand, they may exclude collective goods altogether from any calculus of personal benefit, as Robert Lane suggests. In general, too, Americans share a sense that there is "fat" in government programs, that government agencies can operate more efficiently with fewer resources devoted to administrative overhead. This belief stems in part from how Americans view the public sector in relation to the private sector.

In the private sector, individuals and enterprises assume risks in their pursuit of rewards. The quest for an acceptable profit margin motivates risk taking. Sole owners or partners invest their own resources in entrepreneurial ventures, commonly incurring debt to finance new businesses. Large corporations may turn to the broader public for financing, offering shares of stock for sale in the financial marketplace. Here corporate officers take risks with theirs' and other people's money, and the return received depends on how well the corporation does financially, although corporate officers often are insulated personally from the consequences of underperformance, as their base level of compensation frequently remains intact nonetheless. Moreover, corporate contracts commonly provide executives with severance pay should they be terminated. With small businesses, it is the owners who directly suffer the consequences of underperformance or failure: their profits decline or their losses mount, potentially forcing them into bankruptcy. But risk is a recognized part of entrepreneurial activity. Investors, however, put their money behind what they believe are good economic ventures—benefiting when right, and losing when wrong. A certain direct responsiveness and accountability exists.

In citizens' relationship with government, they may vote for elected officials to represent their interests, and may use a number of avenues to influence their representatives' decisions, but it is the elected officials and their appointees who make the choices that shape public policies and allocate resources. Responsibility and accountability are far from direct. Individuals do not control their own destiny through their political participation. Their interests compete with the interests of others and get mediated through the politics of mutual partisan adjustment. It is not surprising, then, that people tend to see the private sector as more responsive and fairer than the public sector.

A growing economy with both low inflation and low unemployment, however, predisposes citizens to look more favorably at their elected officials. Strong growth gives citizens greater market power by increasing the personal resources they have at their disposal, that is, as long as the benefits of growth are reasonably widely distributed and governments do not increase taxes, significantly reducing that gain. If individuals do indeed value the market more highly than politics, it is not surprising that a combination of strong economic growth and government restraint tends to elicit a favorable popular response. That seems particularly to have been the case in the second half of the 1990s, and incumbents in 1996 and 1998 benefited accordingly, although the Republicans experienced a net loss of five House seats in 1998, the latter likely a product of voter backlash over how the GOP used Clinton's sexual escapades with White House intern Monica Lewinsky to gain partisan advantage. The recent political stances and relatively limited agendas of the president and Congress appear to be shaped by this realization of the economy's influence on electoral outcomes, as is discussed in Chapter 7.

The Problem of the Noncompetitive

Americans, on the whole, reject the idea of an essentially equal distribution of material rewards. They prize equality of opportunity and display a healthy distaste for forms of discrimination that would keep anyone from his or her place at the starting line. Yet, at the same time, they distrust government advantaging anyone in that competition, particularly when government action benefits someone else. The problem remains how to deal with those who fail to succeed. What about those who "fall through the cracks" of capitalism? What obligation does government have to them? Further, if the public regards redistributive programs suspiciously, how can they be expected to support or tolerate them politically?

If people generally believe that they get about what they deserve in the marketplace, as Lane argues and public opinion research continues to support, how can they be expected to treat those who get very little? In dealing with this issue, most Americans tend to differentiate conceptually between the "deserving needy" and the "not-so-deserving needy." Since the working presumption is that people want to get ahead, and will act in their self-interest toward that end, those who find themselves in need through no fault of their own, such as those who have become disabled on the job, merit public assistance of some sort. Conversely, those who do not make substantial effort to compete, even if it may mean competing at the lowest rungs on the social ladder, are seen as less deserving of public assistance. Yet within this rigid characterization, people struggle most with questions about government's obligation to those who are gainfully employed but earn barely enough to keep them out of poverty, or about those whose economic fortunes have fallen, who have lost well-paying jobs, for example, as a result of corporate downsizing, and who have exhausted their personal savings while waiting for comparable employment.

In putting these issues in perspective, Americans tend to fall back on the principles of market justice. If a person falls on hard times, he or she needs at least to get by as best as possible—if necessary taking a job well below one's previous station in life. Even better, this American ethic calls upon that individual to regroup; seek retraining, if available; and start anew. Yet reality attests to the many practical obstacles that thwart such a turnaround.

Conventional wisdom suggests that government does have an obligation to assist people caught in certain circumstances to help themselves. For instance, few question the value of unemployment compensation. Most see government as having a legitimate obligation to provide the means of support to those who find themselves temporarily out of work. Their approval no doubt rests in part on the fact that they, as taxpayers, are not paying for unemployment compensation; employers are. Similar support exists for Social Security, in which the criterion of just deserts influences how people perceive the largely compulsory retirement program administered by the federal government. With Social Security, people who meet minimum employment requirements during their working years contribute, along with their employers, to their own retirement. Retirees are just getting back what they deserve, or at least that is how most Americans see it. But what about the longer-term needy, those who have been unemployed for a protracted period, or those who work part- or full-time but who fail to earn enough to keep them out of poverty? That is the subject of discussion in Chapter 6.

The debate preceding recent welfare reform in America addressed these questions and reinforced the notion of temporary assistance directed at getting the downtrodden back on their feet. Reformers decried welfare as an institution on which millions of recipients have become dependent. The challenge for reformers was how to get recipients off welfare and back into the economy as competitors. Work experience and job training became part of the formula for success. Yet it was widely recognized that a combination of insufficient jobs and budgetary constraints that limit training opportunities left a large number of chronically unemployed still dependent and without any improved means to compete. For them, government's admonition became: just do your best. Federal funds would no longer be available to support welfare benefits for those who exceed government-imposed time limits on aid. The question, however, persists: What will happen to those who remain unemployed and needy? Whose obligation—if anyone's—is it to provide assistance? In reality, does that obligation pass from the federal government and the states to local communities and private charities? Or, is that obligation reduced, in practice, to a minimum, as government policy squeezes dependency out of its system of public assistance? The verdict is still out, but we can expect that millions will continue to fall through capitalism's cracks.

The Test of Inequality

Americans like to see themselves as part of the broad middle class, who have reached that stature through their own efforts. Survey research shows that a wide span of income earners place themselves within the middle class, even though they might assign themselves within the lower- or upper-middle-class brackets. Relatively few identify themselves as members of the upper or lower class.[21] Americans tend to minimize the economic and social distance that divides them from others. At the lower end, they want to see themselves as central sharers in the fruits of prosperity. Yet they recognize whether their lot is improving or worsening, and whether others seem to be faring better or worse than they. As long as their own situation appears to be improving, individuals tend to pay less attention to their relative position to others. When they perceive their fortunes to be in decline, they become more attentive to how others are doing. That is why political theorists argue that widely shared economic growth fosters support for political regimes and enhances governmental legitimacy. As Charles W. Anderson observes, "Growth fulfills the mandates of the liberal state to improve the human condition yet endorses no specific conception of human ends."[22]

The benefits of growth, however, may not be widely shared. The experience of the 1980s and the early 1990s provides a clear case in point. Despite seven years of sustained economic growth during the 1980s, economic analysts broadly agree that income inequality increased and the size of the middle class declined during the 1980s, and continued that decline into the 1990s. They disagree, however, about what underlies that growing inequality.

Between 1983 and 1989, the top 1 percent of income recipients received 37 percent of the growth in personal income over that period, the rest of the top 20 percent received 39 percent, and the remaining 80 percent of income earners received 24 percent. The benefit gap is even wider when we examine wealth instead of income. Over the same period, the top 20 percent of wealth holders received all but about 1 percent of the total gain in marketable wealth, with the top 1 percent realizing a 37 percent gain.[23]

Using a somewhat longer time period for analysis, another oft-cited study found that the top 1 percent of family income earners realized an average 115 percent income gain in inflation-adjusted dollars between 1977 and 1992. The average real income of the next 4 percent grew by a much smaller, but still significant, 23 percent, while that of the next 5 and 10 percent brackets grew by only 11 and 9 percent, respectively. The picture is far less sanguine for those on the middle and lower ends of the income spectrum. Those in the fourth-highest quintile saw their real incomes remain essentially flat, while those in the bottom 60 percent experienced a decline in real income.[24] To be fair, this analysis omits the value of noncash government benefits, such as food stamps and publicly supported medical care, received by those in the bottom income quintile.

The above analyses use before-tax income. When the focus shifts to after-tax income, the average inflation-adjusted gain of the top 1 percent grows to 136 percent over the same period, with the other 99 percent doing about the same or slightly worse.[25] In other words, the supply-side income tax cuts enacted in 1981, the rate and tax expenditure changes included in the 1986 tax reforms, and increases in payroll taxes enacted during that period combined to benefit those with highest incomes the most.

Most analysts and observers drawing on the findings of these temporal point-to-point studies have used them to illustrate what they believe to be a serious problem facing American policymakers, and they pose that problem in variations on the themes of growing inequality and a stagnating or shrinking middle class. Books and articles entitled *The Endangered American Dream; Boiling Point: Republicans, Democrats, and the Decline of Middle-Class Prosperity; The Downsizing of America; Silent Depression;* "If the GDP Is Up, Why Is America Down?"; and "America's Anxiety Attack" explore the consequences of the growing concentration of wealth and increased income inequality.[26] It is striking that the vast majority of analysts and commentators agree that economic inequality grew in the 1980s and early 1990s. They disagree, however, over the causes and the implications.

The conventional explanation points to a number of factors: supply-side tax policy; the loss of well-paying manufacturing jobs and their replacement with comparatively lower-paying service-sector jobs; the growth of high-paying employment in the information technology field; industrial restructuring; the shift of employ-ment in several industries from the United States to foreign soils in search of cheaper labor; unfair competition and restrictive foreign trade policies; and the weakening of American labor unions. Each variation on problem definition carries its own set of policy prescriptions aimed at solving the problem as defined, but they come together in characterizing the middle class, variously defined, as the loser. They portray the rich's success as having come at the expense of the middle class, and they see unaddressed rising class tensions as promoting political distrust and ap-athy, and thereby weakening the foundation of American democracy.

Another, less conventional and more positive finding holds that the shrinking of the U.S. middle class during the 1980s was due to improvement, not decline, in economic well-being. Employing a statistical technique that allows analysis of the movement of households across income groups over time, rather than based on freeze-frame comparisons of income distributions at two single points in time, a re-cent Federal Reserve research paper concludes that the middle class shrank not by adding to the ranks of the poorer off, but by adding to the ranks of the richer. In-equality surely increased, but it came not because the middle class found their eco-nomic fortunes in decline. On the contrary, their economic situation improved, but just not as much as that of upper-income families; and where there was middle-class movement, the vast majority was into the ranks of the upper-income earners. In other words, as the report concludes, "The vast majority of the middle class that vanished did so not by being left behind, but by moving forward."[27]

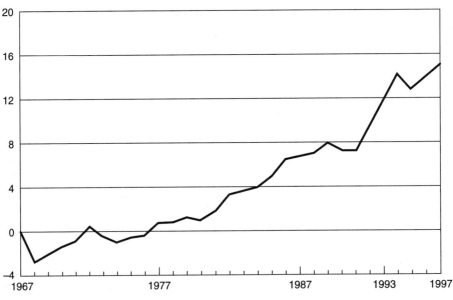

FIGURE 1.1   Percent Change in Household Gini Coefficients, 1967–1997

SOURCE: *Money Income in the United States: 1997* (Washington, DC: U.S. Bureau of the Census, September 1998), xiii.

The U.S. Bureau of the Census measures income inequality using an index of income concentration referred to as the Gini index, which incorporates detailed income shares data into a single statistic that summarizes the dispersion of income across the entire income distribution. The index ranges from 0, indicating equality, to 1, indicating the greatest inequality. The Census Bureau's analysis indicates that not only did income inequality grow sharply in the 1980s, with the Gini index rising by approximately 7 percent over the decade, but it experienced an even sharper increase during the brief period from 1991–1994, rising by about 7 percent (the greatest three-year growth since the Great Depression) as the American economy recovered from recession (see Figure 1.1). In the latter case, income inequality grew markedly at the same time that inflation-adjusted median household income declined.[28] In contrast, the growth of income inequality for most of the 1980s accompanied the growth of real median household income (see Figure 1.2).

Median household income, when valued in 1997 dollars, declined from its all-time high of $37,303 in 1989 to $34,700 in 1993—its lowest point since 1984. Then, after fledgling marginal growth in 1994, real median household income grew by a solid annual average of 1.9 percent between 1995 and 1997.[29] Standing at $37,005 in 1997, the median household income indicator regained almost all of its loss since 1989. The good news is that households with midpoint income improved their standard of living over that eight-year period. The bad news is that they were no better off in 1997 than they were in 1989. The poverty rate dropped and income inequality flattened out after 1994, as strong economic growth and declining

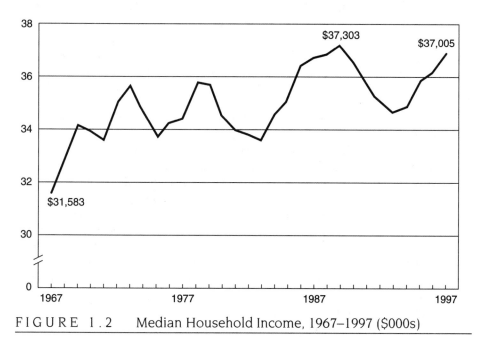

FIGURE 1.2   Median Household Income, 1967–1997 ($000s)

Source: *Money Income in the United States: 1997* (Washington, DC: U.S. Bureau of the Census, September 1998), vi.

unemployment bid up the cost of low-paying jobs.[30] Yet America's income distribution remained far more unequal than it had been at the beginning of the 1980s, the departure point of rising income inequality.

ASSESSING THE NEAR-TERM FUTURE FOR AMERICA'S POLITICAL ECONOMY

The U.S. economy's post-recessionary growth in the 1990s surpassed that of the 1980s. At the close of 1998, after nearly eight years of economic growth, America's measures of economic well-being looked good. Consumer confidence remained strong, after having reached its highest level in 29 years earlier in the year; unemployment averaged about 4.5 percent, a 25-year low; inflation held level at less than 2 percent; and real GDP continued its record of solid growth—averaging a strong 3.9 percent average rate of growth for 1998, following a respectable 3.4 percent average rate of growth for the preceding two years.[31]

Fueling optimism about the prospects for continued economic improvement, labor productivity in the nonfarm business sector rose by an average of 2 percent for the first three quarters of 1998, up slightly from its 1.8 percent average increase for 1996 and 1997, after having grown under 1 percent annually between 1993 and 1995.[32] Increased output per worker holds the promise of rising household incomes and improved living standards. To appreciate that relationship, one needs only to compare the relationship between productivity and median household income over two periods: 1947–1973, and 1973–1992. Productivity doubled during the former period, averaging 2.8 percent a year and leading to a doubling of real median household income. In contrast, both productivity and real income essentially stagnated during the latter period, growing by only about 5 percent over the entire 20 years.[33]

The distinguished economist Paul Krugman calls productivity growth "the single most important factor affecting America's economic well-being"[34] but admits that economists have difficulty explaining why productivity declined, and why it has increased recently. The most prominent explanations of productivity decline include the stifling effects of expanded government regulation and reduced investment in physical and human infrastructure. Yet Krugman finds each lacking. He notes that productivity growth in Japan and most Western European nations exceeded that of the United States from the 1960s through the 1980s, even though its economies are more highly regulated than the U.S. economy. He also points out that the American economy placed about as high a share of its resources into investment, and a larger share into education, in the 1970s and 1980s as it did in the 1950s and 1960s. It just did not work as well, and the reasons seem to escape us.[35]

Although explanations of why productivity declines and rises appear to fall short on empirical validity, that fact does not curtail advice about how to increase productivity. The orthodox prescription of deferring current consumption in order to increase savings, and thereby expand capital, still has the most adherents. Others, such as Robert Reich and Lester Thurow, advocate greater government intervention in the economy through industrial policy, by which government uses its financial and regulatory resources to bias the incentives of the private sector to direct capital into those uses that would increase worker productivity and result in the greatest growth.[36] However, industrial policy, outside of wartime, has failed to gain a foothold in America's liberal political culture.

The bottom line is that America's economy is enjoying a period of sustained growth, and worker productivity appears to be improving. People seem to be more content with their lot and more hopeful about the future. They also appear to be less antagonistic to politicians, following a mid-decade period of rising discontent and alienation, and more optimistic about the ability of the president and Congress to work together cooperatively.[37]

Government policymaking and resource allocation reflect values; the question is whose values are being reflected? Recent accommodations between President Clinton and Republican congressional leaders appear to be moving national policy-making away from lack of consensus and confrontation, and toward mutual adjustment. President Clinton said it best himself, when commenting on the May 2 budget deal: "I wanted a balanced budget with balanced values."[38] In signing the actual legislation that implemented the budget deal, the president continued on this theme of bipartisan cooperation, commenting:

> Today, it should be clear to all of us, without regard to our party or our differences, that, in common, we were able to transform this era of challenge into an era of unparalleled possibility for the American people. I hope we can tap this spirit of cooperation and use it to meet and master the many challenges that remain before us.[39]

In balancing values, the budget deal and the welfare reform package that preceded it appear to have reflected the preferences of a growing political center, which has shifted somewhat to the right. Yet that shift has its detractors. Liberal Democrats see it as abandoning the traditional New Deal values of their party, and the right wing of the Republican Party view it as compromise-driven politics that moves too far away from the Reaganite ideological inheritance and the tenets of the GOP Contract with America. The latter's true believers regard increased nondefense domestic spending as an ideological anathema, and they prefer much deeper tax cuts, particularly those that contribute to investment. Overall, however, Americans appear to be regaining some lost faith in their elected officials' ability to govern—in a way that balances the principle of limited government with a popularly acceptable justification for government action. Similarly, strong economic growth through most of the 1990s has reinforced Americans' faith in the responsiveness of its market economy. One ponderable is whether the growing popular sense of political responsiveness can be sustained in a protracted period of economic downturn, one in which, as history suggests, incumbents will be the losers. As the turn of the century approaches, worries increase that the global fallout from the Asian financial crisis will significantly slow U.S. economic growth, although the U.S. economy has weathered the storm well in the waning months of the twentieth century. Another unanswered question whether partisan differences over impeachment and trial will lead to political confrontation, rather than cooperation, on matters of policy and budget, even in good economic times.

NOTES

1. *New York Times/CBS News Poll*, September 6, 1996.

2. Ibid.; *Los Angeles Times Poll: National Survey*, February 5–6, 1997; The Pew Research Center for the People and the Press, May 23, 1997.

3. Peter K. Eisinger, *The Rise of the Entrepreneurial State* (Madison: University of Wisconsin Press, 1988); Dan Pilcher, "The Third Wave of Economic Development," *State Legislatures* 17, no. 11 (November 1991).

4. Lawrence Lund, *Factors in Corporate Locational Decision* (New York: The Conference Board, 1979); Roger Schmennee, *Making Business Locational Decisions* (Englewood Cliffs, NJ: Prentice-Hall, 1982); Michael Kieschnick, "Taxes and Growth: Business Incentives and Economic Development," in *State Taxation Policy*, ed. Michael Barker (Durham, NC: Duke University Press, 1983), 155–280; and Richard H. Mattoon, *Economic Perspectives* 17, no. 3 (May/June 1993), 11–23.

5. Herbert Stein, *The Fiscal Revolution in America*, 2d ed. (Washington, DC: AEI Press, 1996), 580–581.

6. Charles W. Anderson, *Statecraft: An Introduction to Political Choice and Judgment* (New York: John Wiley & Sons, 1977), 17–22.

7. John Locke, "The Second Treatise of Government," in *Two Treatises of Government*, 3d ed., ed. Peter Laslett (New York: Cambridge University Press, 1988), 265–429.

8. John Stuart Mill, *On Liberty* (New York: Liberal Arts Press, 1958).

9. Adam Smith, *An Inquiry into the Nature and Causes of the Wealth of Nations* (New York: Modern Library, 1937).

10. John Maynard Keynes, *The General Theory of Employment, Interest and Money* (New York: Harcourt, Brace, 1964).

11. A. W. Phillips, "The Relation Between Unemployment and the Rate of Change of Money Wage Rates in the United Kingdom, 1861–1957," *Economica* 25 (November 1957), 263–299.

12. Paul Krugman, *Peddling Prosperity* (New York: W.W. Norton & Co., 1994), 126; James Tobin, "Reaganomics in Retrospect," in *The Reagan Revolution?*, ed. B. B. Lymlicka and Jean V. Matthews (Chicago: Dorsey Press, 1988), 885–886; and Robert S. McIntyre, *Inequality and the Federal Budget Deficit* (Washington, DC: Citizens for Tax Justice, 1991), 13.

13. A good summary can be found in Alfred J. Tuchfarber, et al., "The Republican Tidal Wave of 1994: Testing Hypotheses about Realignment, Restructuring, and Rebellion," Presented at the Annual Meeting of the American Political Science Association, Chicago, August 31–September 3, 1995.

14. *New York Times/CBS News Poll*, January 23, 1996.

15. *New York Times/CBS News Poll*, November 3, 1996; The Pew Research Center for the People and the Press, November 3, 1996.

16. Robert B. Reich, "Up From Bipartisanship," *The American Prospect* 32 (May–June 1997), 26–32.

17. *Los Angeles Times Poll National Survey*, February 5–6, 1997.

18. *Congressional Quarterly Weekly Report* 56, no. 45 (November 14, 1998), 3081.

19. Andrew Taylor, "Congress Wraps Up and Heads Home on a Trail of Broken Budget Caps," *Congressional Quarterly Weekly Report* 56, no. 42 (October 24, 1998), 2887.

20. Robert E. Lane, "Market Justice, Political Justice,"*American Political Science Review* 80 (June 1986), 383–402.

21. *New York Times/CBS News Poll*, February 9–11, 1993; Sam Roberts, "Another Kind of Middle-Class Squeeze," *The New York Times*, May 5, 1997, 1, 6.

22. Charles W. Anderson, *Pragmatic Liberalism* (Chicago: University of Chicago Press, 1990), 105.

23. Edward N. Wolff, "How the Pie Is Sliced," *The American Prospect* 22 (Summer 1995), 58–64.

24. Robert S. McIntyre, *Inequality and the Federal Budget Deficit*, 5–6.

25. Ibid., 6–7.

26. Edward N. Luttwak, *The Endangered American Dream* (New York: Simon & Schuster, 1993; Kevin Phillips, *Boiling Point: Republicans, Democrats, and the Decline of Middle-Class Prosperity* (New York: Random House, 1993); New York Times Special Report, *The Downsizing of America* (New York: Times Books, 1996); Wallace C. Peterson, *Silent Depression* (New York: W.W. Norton & Co., 1994); Clifford Cobb, et al., "If the GDP Is Up, Why Is America Down?," *The Atlantic Monthly* (October 1995) 5–21; Ronald Brownstein, "America's Anxiety Attack," *Los Angeles Times Magazine*, May 8, 1994, 14–20.

27. Mary C. Daly, "The Shrinking Middle Class?," *FRBSF Economic Newsletter*, 97–07 (March 7, 1997).

28. Daniel H. Weinberg, "A Brief Look at Postwar U.S. Income Inequality," *Current Population Reports*, P60 (June 1996).

29. *Money Income in the United States: 1997* (Washington, DC: U.S. Bureau of the Census, U.S. Department of Commerce, September 1998), B-3.

30. Ibid., xiii; Daniel H. Weinberg, *Press Briefing on 1997 Income and Poverty Estimates*, U.S. Census Bureau, September 24, 1998.

31. U.S. Department of Commerce, "Selected Indicators," *The State of the Nation*, 1998 Edition, www.statusa.gov, November 27, 1998; *Statement of Alan Greenspan Before the Subcommittee on Domestic and International Monetary Policy, Committee on Banking and Financial Services, U.S. House of Representatives*, February 24, 1998; U.S. Department of Commerce, *Bureau of Economic Analysis News Release*, Table 1, April 30, 1999.

32. *Productivity and Costs: Third Quarter 1998* (Washington, DC: U.S. Department of Commerce, November 10, 1998).

33. *Economic Report of the President*, 1998, 338; Martin Neil Baily and Alok K. Chakrabarti, *Innovation and the Productivity Crisis* (Washington, DC: Brookings Institution, 1988), 3.

34. Paul Krugman, *The Age of Diminished Expectations* (Cambridge, MA: The MIT Press, 1994), 22.

35. Ibid., 18–22.

36. Robert B. Reich, *Tales of a New America: The Anxious Liberal's Guide to the Future* (New York: Random House, 1987); Robert B. Reich, *The Work of Nations: Preparing Ourselves for 21st Century Capitalism* (New York: Alfred A. Knopf, 1991); Lester C. Thurow, *The Zero-Sum Solution: Building a World-Class American Economy* (New York: Simon & Schuster, 1985); Lester C. Thurow, *Head to Head: The Coming Economic Battle Among Japan, Europe, and America* (New York: William Morrow, 1992).

37. Richard L. Berke, "Americans Foresee Harmony in Capital, *New York Times*, January 20, 1997 www.archives.nytimes.com/archives; *New York Times/CBS News Poll*, January 14–17, 1997.

38. *Statement by the President on Budget Agreement*, Office of the Press Secretary, The White House, May 2, 1997.

39. *Remarks by the President at Signing of the Balanced Budget Act of 1997 and the Taxpayers Relief Act of 1997*, Office of the Press Secretary, August 5, 1997.

CHAPTER 2

Managing America's Economy: Fiscal and Monetary Policy

T he benefits from a sound, growing economy are many and widespread, ranging from the financial to the political, as discussed in Chapter 1. A good economy increases personal income, generates resources for investment, creates favorable conditions for job growth, enhances citizen support for government, and advances the political standing of incumbents. Yet economic prosperity cannot be taken for granted. History shows alternating periods of economic growth and decline. Workers, businesses, and elected public officials reap the benefits of growth, and suffer the consequences of decline. In one sense, they are captive of the vagaries of economic cycles and fluctuations. In another sense, however, all share the conviction that government can and should act to stabilize the economy at desired levels of economic performance—our Keynesian intellectual inheritance. United States government policymakers rely primarily on fiscal and monetary policy tools to manage the economy.

Although fiscal and monetary policy share the same objective of promoting economic growth and full employment, but within acceptable levels of inflation, fiscal and monetary policymakers go about that task differently. Fiscal policy deals with the tax and spending decisions of national governments and the relationship between them. In the United States, that means the tax and spending decisions of Congress, as affected by actions of the president. Tax and spending choices influence the national economy by affecting aggregate demand. Government taxes reduce aggregate demand because they take resources away from individuals and businesses that might otherwise be spent. Tax increases transfer additional resources from the private to the public sector and reduce the purchasing power of the former. Conversely, tax cuts transfer resources from the public to the private sector and increase after-tax disposable income that can be spent. Tax policy, depending on its structure, can also affect aggregate supply, to the extent that it provides strong incentives for individuals or firms to save rather than to spend.

Government spending adds to aggregate demand through the purchases that government makes directly or through those made by the recipients of government financial assistance, whether they be individuals or other governmental units. In the latter case, states and local governments in the United States spend federal aid directly or distribute it to individuals who, in turn, spend it. In either case, this added spending increases aggregate demand. Government spending can also influence the level and potential growth of a nation's economy, depending on the nature of that spending. Government spending on physical infrastructure, such as highways and bridges, and on education, technology development, and basic research, commonly referred to as human infrastructure, can provide the basis for increased productivity and the higher personal income that follows.

Spending must be financed. Governments can use current revenues to pay for their expenditures or, where permitted by law, can borrow to cover costs in excess of revenues. In the past, the U.S. federal government has typically run an annual deficit and sold Treasury securities to obtain the financial resources needed to cover expenditures in excess of current revenues. The resulting debt, then, must be paid off to security holders over the life of the bond or note. The federal government budgets that debt-service obligation as part of its operating budget, thus increasing pressure on the expenditure side of the budget. As debt obligation grows, either additional revenues must be found to pay the bill, or offsetting reductions must be made somewhere else in the budget.

The federal government faces no constitutional or statutory requirement to balance its budget. Most states and local governments are required to balance their operating budgets, but are allowed to have separate capital budgets, within which they can incur debt to finance capital projects such as buildings and roads. Yet, as with the federal government, any resulting debt-service obligation must be met in the operating budget, which at the state and local level is subject to the balanced-budget requirement.

The federal government's license to run a deficit and finance it through debt constitutes an important tool of national fiscal policy, for if it had to close the fiscal year in balance, the president and Congress would have no way to expand spending beyond current revenue constraints. Lacking that ability, national policymakers would lose a powerful tool to increase aggregate demand in times of economic malaise. Without the federal government's ability to deficit-spend, economic policymakers would be without an important tool to fight unemployment.

What about cutting taxes to stimulate aggregate demand? Tax reductions can contribute toward increased aggregate demand, as long as the additional after-tax income is spent rather than saved. Facing a stagnant economy or sharp economic downturn, people tend to behave conservatively, putting off major purchases, largely restricting spending to meeting their basic needs, and saving for an uncertain future. In that environment, increased government spending becomes the only sure fiscal policy tool to stimulate demand.

To what extent can monetary policy, which affects the cost of loanable funds, be used to stimulate the economy? Can it be used effectively to jump-start the economy when aggregate demand is down and consumers lack confidence in the economy and in their personal futures? Monetarists believe that it can. They base that assessment on the premise that people act in their self-interest. Individuals and businesses look to exploit situations to their advantage. A stagnant or declining economy is not conducive to major new economic endeavors, all other things being equal. Flat or depressed demand tends to discourage increases in both personal and corporate spending. For corporations, why would it be in their best interest to expand productive resources or acquire new equipment when demand is insufficient to meet existing production? It would make more sense, instead, for them to draw down current inventories and either lay off workers, or at least not add any, while postponing investment. The catch, however, lies in the caveat of all other things being equal. Can policymakers act in such a way that would-be spenders or investors will judge that the time is indeed right to act? That is where monetary policy can be used to bias the incentives of economic actors.

What if the cost to individuals and corporations of making major capital purchases can be lowered significantly? Might that influence their decision to go ahead, even in a poor economy? That depends in part on the availability and cost of credit. If loanable funds become available at an attractive rate, and if would-be consumers believe that they are more likely to go up later, rather than down, that perceived lower cost of money might just be enough to get them to borrow and make the investment.

Monetary policy can also be an effective tool in an overheated economy, in which inflation exceeds acceptable levels. The objective in that condition is to lower aggregate demand, trading off reduced inflation for some increase in unemployment. Monetary policymakers act to tighten the availability of credit and increase its costs. A steep increase in the cost of loanable funds creates a disincentive for credit-financed spending. Consumers and businesses tend to wait for more favorable interest rates. If enough people behave that way, aggregate demand declines, unemployment rises, and inflation drops.

Monetary policy cannot control long-term interest rates. They are set in a highly competitive market in which borrowers bid for capital. But, as noted above, monetary policy can influence short-term rates. Not only does the short-term cost of loanable funds affect the relative willingness of borrowers to take on debt, but short-term interest rates send important signals about what the future economy might portend. Investors who believe that a modest increase in short-term interest rates presages a series of future increases are less likely to purchase long-term securities than are those who see a solitary adjustment acting to nip inflationary tendencies in the bud. Thus interest rate changes, the way they are positioned by monetary policymakers, and the perspectives of would-be investors can all influence the behavior of participants in capital markets.

POLITICAL INSTITUTIONS AND ECONOMIC POLICYMAKING

The U.S. Constitution gives Congress the authority to tax and spend on behalf of the national government. That power to tax and spend gives Congress the fiscal policy tools to influence the course of America's economy. The Constitution also gives Congress the authority to borrow and coin money, and to regulate its value. This vesting of authority in Congress for economic policymaking should not be interpreted to mean that Congress exercises sole, or even primary, influence in shaping U.S. economic policy. In fact, Congress has acted over time to delegate a great deal of operational authority over macroeconomic policymaking to other governmental institutions, most notably to the president and the Federal Reserve Board, an independent agency created by Congress in 1913. For the president to be successful in putting his distinctive stamp on America's fiscal policy, Congress must cooperate, approving the president's recommendations on taxing and spending. More often than not, Congress's choices represent an amalgam of compromises and accommodations that have presidential initiatives as their starting point. This still remains the case, despite the GOP's attempt to set the national agenda through its "Contract with America," following the wave of electoral victories in 1994 that gave it control of the House and the Senate. The Federal Reserve Board, in comparison, is statutorily positioned to enact monetary policy on its own, without any needed concurrence by either the president or Congress.

This section looks first at fiscal policymaking, examining the relative institutional roles and power of the president and Congress in shaping fiscal policy in the United States. It will then turn to a discussion of monetary policy, assessing the roles and influence of the president and Congress in a system designed to provide the Federal Reserve Board with a great deal of policymaking autonomy.

Fiscal Policy

The president plays a highly influential role in fiscal policymaking, if not the dominant role. Although Congress possesses the ultimate authority over taxing and spending, it is the president who exercises primary responsibility for shaping America's fiscal policymaking. Both acts of Congress and executive initiatives have institutionalized that responsibility. Congress has given the president responsibility for setting America's fiscal policy agenda, and presidents have expanded their own role.

The Executive Branch

Among all of the tools available to the president to influence macroeconomic policy, it is the president's responsibility to submit a national budget to Congress that gives him an edge in fiscal policymaking. Using his authority to develop an executive budget, the president recommends how much the federal government should tax, spend, and borrow in a given year. Working off the current year's budget, the president's recommendations set priorities that depart from that base. Those might include new programmatic initiatives, increases and cuts in funding for existing programs, and reallocations from some programs to others. The executive budget shapes the terms of the national budgetary debate and typically puts Congress in a reactive posture.

Even though the president's ascendant position in fiscal policymaking has evolved over time, it is rooted in Congress's passage of the Budget and Accounting Act of 1921. That act created the vehicle of the executive budget and required that agencies submit their budget requests to the president instead of directly to Congress, as was done previously. The president could then decide whether to include, exclude, or modify agency requests. The executive budget was to become the president's budget, carrying the stamp of presidential priorities.

To assist the president in carrying out his budgetary responsibilities, Congress created the Bureau of the Budget in 1921, which became the Office of Management and Budget (OMB) during the Nixon administration. Originally placed within the Department of the Treasury, the bureau was moved in 1939 to the newly created Executive Office of the President. The Great Depression, and President Franklin Roosevelt's activist New Deal initiatives in response to it, created the need for greater policy coordination and management oversight within the executive branch. The Executive Office of the President consolidated presidential staff assistants who were charged with those tasks. Although the number of presidential aides never exceeded twelve during FDR's years in office, the executive office's creation gave birth to the modern White House professional staff.[1]

In those early years, neither the Bureau of the Budget nor the Executive Office of the President played an explicit leadership role in shaping national fiscal policy. The bureau assisted the president in putting together the executive budget, but it played only a limited role in initiating policy development. Nor did it articulate an economic strategy that integrated its budgetary recommendations to the president. Before the Depression, the bureau followed the common inherited wisdom that the budget should be balanced except in times of war.

President Roosevelt remained a devotee of the balanced budget paradigm throughout his first term and early into his second term, even though he soon came to realize that governmental action was necessary to cut into the Depression's sustained high unemployment. To address the problem of high and rising unemployment, FDR followed a simple approach: use government to put unemployed people to work and give them income. Roosevelt put primary value on the benefits that gainful employment provided to people, and not so much on the aggregate economic stimulus it provided. Government intervention was to be a temporary stop-gap measure, providing relief to a hurting populace. According to Herbert Stein, Keynesian theory provided a later "sophisticated rationale" for the increased government spending of the New Deal, without the president or his economic advisors having to worry about the theorized consequences of deficit-financed spending on aggregate demand or private-sector borrowing. It was not until midway into his second term that FDR came to appreciate the stimulative power of public expenditures to expand purchasing power, to raise recovery to a level at which it would run by itself.[2] Ultimately, the massive job-creating defense spending in support of U.S. involvement in World War II broke the back of unemployment. America did indeed spend itself into prosperity.

Keynes and his later disciples legitimized the New Deal's approach and provided the theoretical justification for demand-side expansionist policies of administrations to follow.[3] By the end of World War II, Keynesianism had won broad acceptance within the academic community and within the nation's capital. Government was widely seen as having a responsibility to use its fiscal policy tools to maintain full employment; and the institution of the president, in the wake of Roosevelt's political leadership, was acknowledged as the locus of governmental initiative. The public had come to expect presidential leadership in economic management, and it was ready to hold the president accountable for the economy's performance.

With Keynesian theory firmly in place, Congress acted in 1946 to institutionalize the national government's responsibilities for economic management by passing the Employment Act of 1946. A product of Keynesian-trained New Deal economists in the White House and their allies in Congress, the legislation formally strengthened the president's role in economic management—a role that Congress hoped would lead to an economy that could provide "maximum employment" and absorb the millions returning from military service. The act created the Council of Economic Advisors (CEA) to provide assistance to the president, and it required the president to report to each new Congress on the condition of the economy. That report, now called the annual *Economic Report of the President*, sets the stage for the president's executive budget recommendations that follow, which contain the tax and spending measures that embody the administration's fiscal policy.

Today, the OMB and the Department of the Treasury join the CEA in assisting the president to carry out his economic leadership. Of the three, the CEA operates at the broadest, macro level. Its job is to apprise the president on the state of the U.S. economy and to offer advice about what measures can be taken to improve the nation's economic performance. In addition to its formal responsibility to prepare the president's economic report, the three-member council, and particularly its chair, advises the president on how the economy works, helping the president to sort out complicated economic relationships and be able to handle them in public discourse. Council members also assist in the preparation of presidential speeches on economic matters, and help prepare the president for press conferences at which questions about the economy can be expected.

Council members have been drawn primarily from academe, serving a few years in office, then returning to their university appointments. Presidents appoint members for their economic expertise; but, in doing so, they look for candidates who share their views of the proper role for government in the economy. However, the CEA is not divorced from politics or partisanship.[4] Members and top-level staff assistants realize they have a duty to provide the president with sound analysis drawn from their academic and professional expertise; yet they are not disinterested in the president's political fortunes. They share an interest in making the president look as good as possible in the public arena. That combination can translate, on the one hand, into offering frank assessments of the state of the economy and how the administration's economic policies are working, and, on the other, into putting a positive gloss on the administration's accomplishments. A careful reading of annual economic reports shows their public relations value to the president.

Compared to the CEA, the OMB is the operational arm of presidential fiscal policy. Fiscal policy must be translated into concrete tax and spending decisions. The OMB assists the president in developing and presenting the executive budget to Congress. At its inception, as the Bureau of the Budget, the office was charged with reacting to agency requests and recommending courses of action to the president on each. Over time, it has become a proactive force in policy initiation and budgetary development. Today, it not only analyzes agency requests but also articulates a policy and budgetary framework within which executive agencies are expected to work. That framework includes policy prioritization and fiscal limitations put on agency requests.

The director of the OMB is a member of the president's cabinet and a key policy architect within the president's small circle of top policy strategists. The director's role differs significantly from the other cabinet officers, however. Unlike department heads, who have administrative authority over their agencies and are charged with both initiating and implementing policy in their respective areas, the OMB director is responsible for influencing and advancing presidential initiatives across agency jurisdictions. In exercising that responsibility, the complexity and technical demands of the budget place the director in a unique position among cabinet peers. The director sees the big budget picture and how the many pieces to the budgetary puzzle fit together and interrelate. He can suggest that a cabinet secretary does not fully understand the interprogram and interagency effects of a given budgetary recommendation, or the overall fiscal constraints under which the executive budget is formulated. That comprehensive perspective not only enhances the influence of the director in budget development but also positions him to act as the administration's spokesman on the budget.[5]

The third executive branch institution that can influence national fiscal policy is the Department of the Treasury. Its influence on fiscal policy has been more a product of the broad-reaching role of the Treasury secretary and the stature of the individuals appointed to the post than of the administrative functions the department performs. Its primary functions are operational—collecting federal taxes and other revenues, managing cash flow and paying the federal government's bills, borrowing money and managing the national debt, printing and coining currency, and administering the U.S. balance of payments with other nations. The Treasury secretary also serves as U.S. governor of the International Monetary Fund, the World Bank, the Inter-American Development Bank, the Asian Development Bank, and the African Development Bank.

One of the oldest cabinet departments, the Treasury was established in 1789, and Alexander Hamilton served as its first secretary. As officially the second-ranking cabinet officer, the Treasury secretary serves as the chief financial officer of the U.S. government and as a key presidential advisor on tax policy. The secretary's domestic economic influence comes not from overseeing departmental operations, but from the ways in which presidents have chosen to use the incumbents as economic policy advisors. In most administrations, presidents have accorded their Treasury secretary a prominent role and strong voice in economic policymaking, one that has often been built on a close personal relationship between the two. Recent examples include Ronald Reagan's appointment of James Baker, and Bill Clinton's appointment of Robert Rubin.

Presidents have differed in how they have institutionalized economic counsel within their administrations. President Nixon chose to centralize macroeconomic policy advice under Treasury secretary George Schultze, who was also designated as assistant to the president for economic affairs. His predecessors, Presidents Kennedy and Johnson, preferred to chair an informal economic advisory committee composed of the Treasury secretary, the chair of the CEA, and the director of the OMB. Presidents Reagan and Bush formalized this collective approach, and broadened the membership to include a number of additional cabinet officers, including those from the Departments of Labor, Transportation, Commerce, and State, along with the president's U.S. trade representative. President Clinton enlarged the membership even further—adding the vice president, presidential assistants for economic and domestic policy, the secretaries of the Departments of Agriculture, Energy, and Housing and Urban Development, and the director of the Environmental Protection Agency (EPA)—as he established the new National Economic Council (NEC). Chaired by the president, the NEC was created "(1) to coordinate policy advice to the president, (2) to coordinate the economic policymaking process with regard to domestic and international economic issues, (3) to ensure that economic policymaking decisions and programs are consistent with the president's stated goals and to ensure that those goals are being effectively pursued, and (4) to monitor implementation of the president's economic policy agenda."[6]

Clinton's first presidential assistant for economic policy, Robert Rubin, played a significant role in guiding the council's agenda. As a result of his effective staff work and the president's growing confidence in his ability and advice, President Clinton named Rubin as Treasury secretary, replacing Lloyd Bensten. In that position, the new secretary has emerged not only as the administration's key spokesperson on economic affairs, but as a key political strategist as well.

Across presidential administrations, it is clear that even though personal relationships between presidents and key administration officers and aides have a bearing on policy influence, institutional role still is the best indicator of influence. When the focus is narrowed from economic affairs—defined broadly—to fiscal policy, presidents have turned most often to their secretary of the Treasury and OMB director for counsel, putting their advice in the context of the CEA's analysis of the nation's economic condition and likely future, and in the context of the political realities as viewed by the president's chief-of-staff. Among the three economic advisors, however, it is the OMB director, whose task it is to put together the tax and spending plan, who most directly shapes the president's budgetary choices, as is illustrated in Chapter 3.

Congress

Although the U.S. Constitution gives Congress the power to tax and spend, Congress is not well positioned to set the nation's fiscal policy agenda. That continues to be true even after congressional reform of the federal budgetary process. Before the budget reform of 1974, Congress possessed little institutionalized ability to substitute its collective vision of national fiscal policy and budgetary priorities for that of the president's. Congressional decisions on taxing and spending were decentralized and fragmented, built on a foundation of "contained specialization."[7] Congressional subcommittee and committee leaders enjoyed considerable autonomy in their decision making. Mutual adjustment and reciprocity characterized the politics of aggregating committee recommendations within each chamber. No plan of congressional action informed committee choices. Congress's imprint on taxing and spending became the aggregate product of numerous discrete and often disconnected decisions.

While Congress lacked a collectively endorsed plan for its tax and spending actions, entitlement spending grew rapidly without Congress needing to make annual decisions on appropriations. With this automatic spending feature, largely a creation of Great Society legislation, entitlement spending grew three times faster than discretionary spending between 1960 and 1974 alone.[8] Spending seemed to be out of control, and Congress appeared to have no agreed-on strategy to deal with it.

Congress turned in 1974 to budgetary reform, to be used both to bring coherence to congressional budget making and to limit the president's ability to impound funds appropriated by Congress. Facing a president weakened by the Watergate crisis, Congress passed the ambitious Congressional Budget and Impoundment Control Act of 1974 by overwhelming margins, 80 to 0 in the Senate and 401 to 6 in the House. Congressional leaders hailed the act's passage as a "historic legislative development," providing a "new process by which Congress determines national spending priorities."[9] Congress was to set these priorities within the backdrop of its own fiscal policies, not those of the president's administration. It would start out by deciding how much the federal government should spend in the coming year and the extent to which it would cover that spending through taxes, fees, and debt.

The act altered the federal budgetary process and created structures to give Congress the ability to map out its fiscal direction. It created new budget committees in both the House and the Senate, each with its own staff, along with a new congressional staff agency named the Congressional Budget Office (CBO). Congressional leaders conceived of the CBO as Congress's own alternative to the CEA and the OMB. The CBO would be responsible for developing its own, independent economic projections and estimates of revenues and spending, freeing Congress from its dependence on executive branch numbers.

The act also modified the federal budgetary process, changing the fiscal year and creating the procedural devices of concurrent budget resolutions and reconciliation. Concurrent budget resolutions, which do not require presidential approval, must be passed in identical form by both chambers of Congress. The budget act provided for two distinct resolutions. The first had to be adopted before either chamber could act on legislation that provides new spending authority, appropriates budget authority, or results in changes in revenues or in the public debt. It represented Congress's fiscal game plan for the session, establishing aggregate-level ceilings on budget authority and outlays (actual expenditures), and projecting revenues to be generated based on the CBO's economic forecasts and the resolution's assumptions about tax law, including any planned changes in current law. Comparing planned expenditures and anticipated revenues, the resolution yielded a projected level of deficit or surplus. Macro choices were to precede micro choices.

Following passage of the first resolution, the Senate and House budget committees, aided by staff assistants, parceled out budget authority and outlay targets to its chamber's committees and subcommittees to guide them in their budgetary decision making. When the resolution called for changes in entitlements, the budget committees instructed the committees having jurisdiction over those entitlement programs to report legislation out that implemented the resolution's provisions. Similarly, the tax writing committees—Ways and Means in the House, and Finance in the Senate—were charged with acting on any tax changes called for in the budget resolution. The new budgetary timetable created by the act gave committees less than four months to complete action on all spending and tax bills. If the committees reported bills out that were not in line with the resolution's limits and intent, Congress had the opportunity to pass a second concurrent resolution—adjusting the first resolution's targets to conform to committee actions, making selective modifications in the resolution while retaining other provisions, or reaffirming the first resolution's targets and including reconciliation instructions to bring committee actions in line with the recommendations of the budget committees. If committees failed to comply, the budget committee could then roll the changes into a single bill, called the reconciliation bill, which would then be reported to the floor for a vote, bypassing the recalcitrant standing committees.

Congress has since done away with the second resolution, retaining a single resolution and the process of reconciliation. Congress today still uses reconciliation to bring committee actions into accord with the concurrent resolution's provisions; yet it also uses reconciliation to make last-minute changes that commonly emerge out of budgetary negotiations with the president or key presidential aides. Thus reconciliation cannot be viewed solely as a procedural tool internal to Congress, one that Congress uses to put the final touches on its own budgetary alternative to the president's. Instead, presidents and their key aides have used reconciliation as an eleventh-hour device to bring congressional budgetary decisions closer in line with presidential priorities, in a sense co-opting a process originally designed to serve Congress's own internal decision-making needs.

David Stockman, Reagan's first OMB director, set the precedent for using Congress's reconciliation process to advance an administration's policy goals. Working with a supportive Republican majority in the Senate and a sizable coalition of Republicans and conservative Democrats in the House, Stockman and other OMB officials hurriedly crafted omnibus reconciliation legislation late in the 1981 session that contained reductions in entitlement spending. These reductions, together with separate legislation that greatly cut individual income taxes, demonstrably launched the promised "Reagan Revolution"—a policy campaign that lost much of its steam during the remainder of the Reagan administration.

Subsequent OMB directors followed Stockman's early lead in working with Congress to fashion omnibus reconciliation bills that advanced presidential policy agendas. The Omnibus Budget Reconciliation Act of 1993 provides a salient illustration of strong executive-led reconciliation, as OMB Director Leon Panetta fashioned a major deficit-reduction package of tax increases and spending cuts that Congress passed with the exclusive support of Democrats, who were then in the majority in both chambers of Congress. Four years later, during President Clinton's second term in office, even though congressional Republican leaders played the lead role in structuring deficit-reduction reconciliation bills, one for tax law changes and another for spending adjustments, presidential negotiators significantly influenced the nature of that legislation. And the administration's contribution was the product of a team effort—composed of the president's chief-of-staff, OMB director, and Treasury secretary—rather than the work of a chief-of-staff or a budget director acting as the president's principal negotiator.

Presidential Leadership in Fiscal Policymaking

Presidents have largely set America's fiscal policy agenda; nonetheless, sentiments in Congress have influenced presidential postures. Presidents know that they need Congress's cooperation to get their policies enacted into law. Congress, in turn, looks for presidential leadership in steering the U.S. economy toward growth with price stability. That is not to suggest that economic policymaking is free of partisan overtones. Yet both individual members of Congress and the president share a common interest in promoting the nation's economic health. Beyond their desire to secure what is good for the country, they realize that a strong economy enhances their reelectability. At the same time, political partisans are not adverse to casting aspersions when others can be blamed for poor economic conditions. This tension between promoting the greater good and advantaging oneself and one's partisan colleagues has been variously played out over time. This section examines that connection as it traces presidential leadership in fiscal policymaking, starting with the Great Depression.

Herbert Hoover, when faced with a rapidly declining economy in 1931, supported a tax increase to replenish shrinking revenues. He chose to honor the widely accepted principle of budget balance, even if it risked further dampening demand and exacerbating recessionary conditions. His successor, Franklin Roosevelt, also found the allure of a balanced budget appealing, but at the same time agonized over what government should do to assist the fast-growing ranks of the unemployed. The answer for Roosevelt was to support public works and employment programs, even if that entailed deficit-spending. Yet he did not abandon his attachment to a balanced budget. Temporary deficits could be justified, in Roosevelt's eyes, as long as the deficit resulted from emergency expenditures. Conceptually, for Roosevelt, government still had an obligation to balance its "normal" budget while it incurred debt to address pressing human needs. Roosevelt and his administration used this distinction to justify deficit-financed support of financial assistance provided by the Federal Emergency Relief Administration, and of work-relief programs such as the Works Projects Administration and the Civilian Conservation Corps.[10] It was not until well into 1938, following a seemingly intractable recession, that FDR came to accept the mounting advice of Keynesians, including the personal entreaties of John Maynard Keynes himself, that the president and Congress turn to increased federal spending "for its own sake" as a means of generating increased purchasing power. In doing so, FDR and his administration raised the indirect, multiplier effects of increased aggregate demand over the palliative effects of direct federal assistance. At the same time, he eschewed tax cuts as a fiscal policy tool.

America's entrance into World War II soon precipitated an increase in federal spending that dwarfed New Deal expenditures. Federal government expenditures more than doubled between 1932 and 1940, but they increased nearly ninefold between 1940 and 1945, rising from $9.4 billion to $97.7 billion. World War II sparked increased aggregate demand well beyond what New Deal programs could have hoped to achieve. It put people back to work, in military uniforms or in industries supporting the war effort. In doing so, it demonstrated the economic fruits of full employment. Aggregate personal income and savings rose markedly during the war years. Savings rose both because patriotic citizens bought Treasury bonds to support the war effort, and because the conversion from a peacetime to a wartime economy presented them with reduced spending options. Nonetheless, this increased pool of savings provided a financial reservoir for the postwar increases in aggregate consumption that followed.[11]

The war also left a legacy of record budget deficits and government debt. With the transition from a wartime to a peacetime economy, federal government expenditures declined precipitously, dropping from $92.7 billion in 1945 to $42.6 billion in 1950. By war's end, the U.S. Treasury had amassed a sizable base level of revenues that, barring a tax cut, could be used to support federal domestic programs aimed at expanding and improving the nation's infrastructure, assisting veterans in their return to civilian life, and accommodating the needs for government services of a growing postwar, "baby-boom" population. Although President Truman successfully led the charge for immediate postwar tax cuts, as a Keynesian he was leery of the potential inflationary effects of subsequent reductions. Like Roosevelt before him, Truman believed in the virtue of a balanced budget, even though he realized the value of debt financing under certain circumstances. Truman might be best described as a "guarded Keynesian," preferring to finance current expenditures out of current revenues, if at all possible.

For Truman, inflation posed America's major postwar economic problem. He worried that growing civilian demand in the postwar economic transformation would outstrip supply and run up prices. For that reason, he steadfastly opposed Republican calls for postwar tax cuts, believing that consumers, whose demands had been suppressed by the austerity associated with war mobilization, would spend their additional disposable income, not save it. Truman, accordingly, vetoed three tax cuts approved by Congress, although Congress overrode the last of Truman's vetoes in April 1948. He saw a balanced budget, combined with private sector productivity improvements, as the best way for America's economy to grow without undue inflation. To dampen inflationary impulses in the short run, Truman called for a tax increase in 1948—an initiative that Congress rejected. An unexpected recession in early 1949 reduced concerns about inflation, and replaced them with worries about rising unemployment. The onset of the Korean War in June 1950 energized demand but soon precipitated renewed fears of inflation. Within a year, inflation approached 8 percent. In that setting, the president and Congress turned to short-lived wartime price controls as a tool of inflationary restraint, which succeeded in dropping inflation below 1 percent during 1952 and 1953.[12]

In the aftermath of the Korean War, the U.S. economy embarked on a period of growth, spurred by domestic, not war-driven, demand. It also provided the beginning of a sustained test of national policymakers' resolve to employ Keynesian tools to manage the American economy, at a time when deficit-financed spending kept an upward pressure on prices. It was also a time when the Republicans, the party of Herbert Hoover, had regained control of both the presidency and the Congress.

Dwight Eisenhower, Truman's successor, shared his predecessor's affinity for a balanced budget. Like Truman, Eisenhower viewed inflation to be the most serious potential problem facing the nation's economy. In comparison, however, Eisenhower appeared more ready to accept somewhat higher unemployment than did Truman in order to keep inflation at low levels when prices were not subject to control. The Eisenhower presidency's dogged pursuit of a balanced budget in an environment of inherited deficits helped to reduce inflation during most of its first term. At the same time, higher-than-expected revenues associated with unexpectedly strong economic growth provided a cushion for expanded spending while still allowing for a balanced budget. By early in his second term, President Eisenhower once again turned his attention to a fledgling reinflation. In January 1957, his budget message highlighted the importance of attaining a budget surplus, particularly as a tool with which to restrain inflation.[13] That stance ruled out any initiative to reduce taxes.

The Eisenhower administration's policy of turning an inherited deficit into a balanced budget, or even a small surplus, was tested by two recessions. The first, in 1954, was of moderate proportions and in large part the product of decreased defense expenditures. The OMB, without much fanfare, ordered the speedup of expenditures as a modest fiscal stimulus late in the 1954 fiscal year. President Eisenhower vowed to provide greater stimulus if necessary, but chose instead a relatively conservative course, as the recession proved to be of short duration.[14] The second, in late 1957 and into 1958, was much deeper—pushing unemployment close to 7 percent and testing the administration's stable policy course.

As the recession deepened, calls for a tax cut intensified. The nation found itself in the midst of a recession, even as President Eisenhower and his top advisors continued to view inflation as the major long-term problem facing the U.S. economy. The dilemma for them was how to deal successfully with the recession they believed to be a short-term problem without creating the groundwork for later sustained inflation, a condition fostered by spending pressures brought by steep population growth and cold war competition. It was those pressures that kept the Eisenhower administration from enthusiastically supporting an economic stimulus package of increased federal spending on public infrastructure, as championed by economist John Kenneth Galbraith and demanded by some in Congress. They argued that the federal government should use increased spending to stimulate the economy, then resort to a tax cut if additional measures were necessary.

Without the president leading the charge, however, Congress approved only a modest package of additional spending, largely including increased highway spending and an acceleration of defense contract obligations, altogether amounting only to a $1 billion increase in annualized spending.[15] Tax cuts never materialized. Inflation remained the administration's privileged economic problem for the remainder of Eisenhower's term. With the revenue growth that accompanied economic recovery in 1959, not only could the 1960 fiscal year budget be balanced; it even yielded a modest surplus. However, unemployment remained relatively high, at 5.6 percent, although that was down from a recession-high of 7.6 percent two years earlier—the political implications of which were not lost on Republican presidential candidate Richard Nixon, Eisenhower's vice president.

Critics, among them economist Paul Samuelson, viewed the Eisenhower presidency's conservative approach to fiscal policy as sacrificing higher potential economic growth to the shibboleth of a budget in balance or in surplus.[16] For Samuelson and others, Eisenhower's fiscal stance allowed economic recovery to lag far short of its possibilities. As a consequence, Americans had to contend with an unemployment rate that was higher than it could have been with greater fiscal stimulus. But for Eisenhower the question remained: Fiscal stimulus at what economic costs?

John F. Kennedy, the Democrats' presidential candidate, promised to improve America's rate of economic growth and lower unemployment while closing the so-called "missile gap" with the Soviet Union. Kennedy came into office predisposed to use the power of the presidency and Keynesian fiscal policy tools to realize his economic agenda. He took the position of those who argued that the Eisenhower administration had passed up an interventionist opportunity to extend economic opportunity and broaden its benefits by not tapping the unused potential in the American economy. The goal for the Kennedy administration was to get back to a full-employment economy and stay there.[17]

Faced with sluggish recovery from the mild 1960 recession, and confronting the prospect of still another recession in 1962, Kennedy at first leaned toward accepting the advice of his advisor, John Kenneth Galbraith, to mount a large program of expansive federal spending. Many in Congress, however, remained wedded to the proposition that a budget surplus would allow for orderly growth while restraining inflation and providing the investment capital to finance sustainable growth. Business leaders added their political weight to that perspective. Although the signals were mixed on inflation, Kennedy calculated that the attractiveness of faster economic growth and reduced unemployment resulting from government intervention outweighed the political risks of any accompanying inflation. Yet faced with opposition in Congress and from the business community to significantly increase federal spending, Kennedy turned his sights on a tax cut as his means of economic pump-priming, acceding to the advice of CEA Chairman Walter Heller and economist Paul Samuelson. For Kennedy, however, it was a second-best alternative, compared to the stimulus of significantly increased federal spending.

Both Kennedy and his advisors saw an opportunity to use tax cuts to close the gap between the economy's actual performance and its potential performance with full employment. In Kennedy's words, "Tax reduction will remove an obstacle to the full development of the forces of growth in a free economy."[18] Not only would tax cuts provide individuals with greater after-tax income that could be spent in the marketplace; they would also leave corporations with increased resources for investment. At the same time, Kennedy recognized that tax cuts would reduce federal revenues in the short run, but held out the expectation that the economic stimulus resulting from them would increase national income and associated income tax revenues. Thus, he argued, it could be possible to stimulate the economy through tax cuts without jeopardizing a balanced budget, foreshadowing the arguments of supply-siders nearly two decades later. In his 1963 economic report to Congress, Kennedy argued that "tax revision, involving both reduction and reform, cannot only provide stimulus for growth and prosperity, but can even, as a result, balance the budget or produce surpluses."[19]

The tax cut proposed by the Kennedy administration was not a small one, a departure from the measured fiscal policy initiatives of the Truman and Eisenhower administrations. It called for sizable personal income tax reductions estimated to cost the Treasury about $14 billion a year, once fully phased in, notwithstanding any offsetting revenue increases resulting from greater economic activity triggered by the cuts.[20] The proposed legislation included across-the-board personal income tax rate reductions averaging about 25 percent. It also reduced the rate of corporate profits taxation and included liberalized capital depreciation schedules. Although Kennedy proposed the tax cut package late in 1962, Congress, after considerable debate, did not approve it until early 1964, following his death.

The economy responded in the expected direction. Aggregate spending and real output rose, and unemployment fell. The gross domestic product (GDP) increased by a record $47 billion in fiscal year (FY) 1965, well above the CEA's optimistic projection. Federal revenues rose, not declined, as economic growth generated tax revenues in excess of the amount foregone by tax cuts.[21] Yet scholars agree that it is problematic to determine how much of the economic growth and resulting revenue increases can be attributed to the stimulative effects of the tax cuts, and how much should be associated with a normal upswing in the business cycle. One student of America's political economy attributes the strong economic performance to the larger collection of government policies. Marc Allan Eisner writes:

> At the same time that the economy was being pushed to full employment by the tax reductions, the increase in social spending via the War on Poverty and the increase in military demands via the war in Vietnam were sufficient to push the demand for goods and services beyond capacity. The result was an unemployment rate that associated with full employment and a growing problem of inflation. This inflation would become one of the major issues of the next 15 years as successive administrations would promote price stability, whatever the cost.[22]

The Johnson administration was quick to take credit for the economic growth of the mid-1960s, but President Johnson himself appeared most interested in leaving his mark on American social policy. With economic growth, Johnson saw an opportunity to finance a major program of increased social spending targeted at improving the lot of America's disadvantaged population. For Johnson, a country's true greatness should be judged on how well it provides for its less fortunate citizens. The War on Poverty would be Johnson's legacy; and its pursuit, along with the United States' growing entanglement in Vietnam, became his preoccupation. Keynesian theory achieved a certain paradigmatic status among policy practitioners and academics alike following its widely perceived successful application in the mid-1960s. President Johnson, however, appeared to be far less motivated by fiscal policy objectives than by social policy goals and his own desire for a treasured place in history.[23]

Greatly expanded social spending and the rising costs of military action in Vietnam led to a growing budget deficit and rising inflation. In response, Johnson's advisors, drawing on the Keynesian recipe, urged him to consider a corrective tax increase. The large Democratic majority in Congress, however, showed no appetite for a tax increase, still basking in the glow of the 1964 tax cut. Johnson demurred, and the job of fighting inflation was left to the Federal Reserve Board's monetary policy, as discussed later in this chapter.

With inflation rising above 4 percent in 1967, up from 1.7 percent in 1965, and with the budget deficit topping $25 billion, compared to less than $2 billion just two years earlier, Johnson felt that he had no choice but to propose a tax increase. After all, America's widening involvement in Vietnam provided little opportunity for expenditure cuts in defense, and Johnson had little enthusiasm for cutting support for his Great Society programs, the biggest part of which received automatic funding given their entitlement status. Accepting the advice of his CEA chairman and OMB director, Johnson proposed a 6 percent personal and corporate income tax surcharge in 1967 as an instrument of economic restraint. Congress balked at raising taxes, following House Ways and Means Chairman Wilbur Mills' insistence that a tax surcharge be accompanied by spending cuts.[24] But facing intensified inflationary pressures nearing the 1968 election, Congress agreed to the surcharge, upping the ante to 10 percent—an action that political observers believe cost the Democratic majority seats in the presidential election year.

The surcharge's injection of additional revenues erased the deficit in 1969, but did little to lower inflation. By the time Richard Nixon assumed the presidency, inflation stood at 5 percent, the highest since the Korean War. Spending pressures, driven by growing entitlement programs, would keep inflation squarely on the policymaking agenda for another decade to come.

Although Richard Nixon proclaimed himself a Keynesian early in his presidency, he relied on the imposition of wage and price controls as inflation-suppressing policy instruments after Congress refused to accept his recommended spending cuts intended to produce an inflation-suppressing balanced budget. The controls once again worked temporarily, and inflation declined, without a corresponding increase in unemployment. An improved economy influenced Nixon to relax price controls, and it contributed to his reelection victory. Yet shortly following the relaxation of controls, the Arab oil cartel's restraint of supply sent the prices of oil and petroleum-based products climbing. Almost simultaneously, a U.S. and international decline in agricultural production drove up food prices. Inflation in 1974 reached post–World War II double-digit highs. Weakened by the Watergate scandal that would force him to resign the presidency, Nixon found himself in a tenuous position to function as the nation's chief economic policymaker.

Shortly after Nixon's resignation, the Ford administration launched a public relations campaign calling for voluntary restraint against inflation. The centerpiece of that campaign was the WIN button, for Whip Inflation Now, worn prominently by the president and his top officials and aides. The symbolic campaign failed to catch on, and it soon became an ineffectual embarrassment to the administration.

What the WIN campaign could not accomplish, a severe recession did. Brought on by oil shortages, related production slowdowns, and restrictive monetary policy, the gathering recession resulted in rising unemployment that coexisted for awhile with still-high inflation. Soon, however, the restraining forces of recession prevailed, subduing inflation, but at the price of increased unemployment. The Ford administration continued to view inflation as the greatest threat to the country's long-term economic health, but both the president and Congress underestimated the recession's depth. Facing rising unemployment that threatened to reach double-digit levels, just as inflation was falling back into single-digit range, President Ford succumbed to his economic advisors' counsel and sent to Congress a stimulus package consisting primarily of temporary tax cuts, including an $8 billion tax rebate and a modest personal income tax reduction of $12 billion. Congressional leaders called for greater stimulus, but Ford demurred, fearing that significant permanent cuts would soon trade employment gains for a renewal of inflation. In May 1975, the unemployment rate rose to 9.2 percent, and it remained at about 8 percent by year's end. In response, Congress approved Ford's proposed extension of the temporary tax cuts. By the end of 1976, the economic numbers had improved. The unemployment rate dropped below 8 percent, still high compared to the 1950s and 1960s, and inflation fell below 6 percent. The recession's dampening of demand cut inflation about in half, even with the modest fiscal stimulus aimed at reducing unemployment.

In contrast with his predecessors, Jimmy Carter defined unemployment, not inflation, as America's privileged economic problem. He found ready support among the Democratic majority in Congress, which had difficulty accepting that unemployment appeared to be leveling off in excess of 7 percent, well above the level traditionally associated with full employment. In fact, Democrats had been working since the mid-decade recession on legislation that would require the federal government to use fiscal policy to keep unemployment low. The original legislation required the federal government to create public service jobs to the extent necessary to bring unemployment within a 3 percent floor. After three years of debate, Congress finally passed a watered-down version in the form of the Full Employment and Balanced Growth Act of 1978, also known as the Humphrey-Hawkins Act. The amended version raised the floor to 4 percent and eliminated the public sector job-creation provisions, essentially leaving 4 percent unemployment as a hopeful goal, but without any accompanying enforcement mechanisms or sanctions. What remained was a largely symbolic statement made in a congressional election year.

Although unemployment stood at a little over 6 percent by the end of 1978, still well above the legislated 4 percent unemployment rate, prices climbed precipitously. For 1979, inflation rose to 11 percent, up from 8 percent in the prior year, while unemployment remained essentially flat. The Carter administration found itself confronting both high unemployment and high inflation, but with inflation looking the most menacing. Carter's heart remained with the unemployed; yet he realized that double-digit inflation posed the greater systemic problem for the economy. At the same time, he shared the growing concern that fiscal policy instruments as tools of economic management had met with checkered success, at best, during the 1970s. With the "misery index" (the sum of inflation and unemployment rates) rising, Carter essentially punted, passing the baton of economic leadership to the Federal Reserve Board, and to its chairman, in particular, with the hope that at least a more restrictive monetary policy could bring down inflation enough to improve his reelection chances—but without triggering even greater unemployment, an outcome that would not be helpful politically. That tightening came too late to rescue Carter from electoral defeat at the hands of an inflation-weary electorate.

With the election of Ronald Reagan in 1980, the Federal Reserve was freed of any compunction about greatly tightening the money supply at the very time that an incumbent president was seeking reelection. The highly restrictive monetary policies of the Volcker-led board that followed did indeed squeeze inflation out of the economy, but at a cost of the steepest recession since the Great Depression. Double-digit inflation gave way to near double-digit unemployment—to an extent unexpected by the president, Congress, or the Federal Reserve Board.

Carter's successor, Ronald Reagan, promised to spur economic recovery by leading the nation away from the federal government's excesses of the 1970s, which he viewed as rooted, to a significant extent, in Johnson's Great Society. Reagan's campaign message was straightforward: Reduce government's reach in the economy and in society by cutting taxes, reducing the growth rate of domestic spending, and paring back government regulation. It is true that a small cadre of presidential advisors cast the tax cut as an instrument of supply-side economics, aimed at inducing a wellspring of savings to finance expanded investment—a theorized outcome that failed to materialize. But for Reagan, despite the intuitive appeal of supply-side theory, the large tax cut of 1981 served primarily as a means to reduce the federal government's penetration, allowing taxpayers to keep more of their hard-earned income, and not so much as an instrument of fiscal policy. At the same time, supply-side theory gave Reagan a justification for avoiding the draconian cuts in domestic spending that would otherwise have been necessary to balance the budget.

Scholars disagree, and the evidence is mixed, about whether the sizable cuts in personal and corporate income taxes contributed significantly to economic recovery and the seven years of growth that followed the early 1980s recession. In contrast, there is wide agreement that the tax cut, coupled with major increases in inflation-adjusted defense spending, led to a ballooning federal budget deficit. Rapid increases in uncontrollable spending—most notably on public assistance entitlement programs and in the form of interest on the public debt—added to the fiscal burden imposed by the conscious policy choices outlined above. Economic recovery carried with it the legacy of record post–World War II budget deficits, even though both inflation and unemployment fell within an acceptable range by the decade's end.

George Bush inherited a growing economy with both inflation and unemployment in check, but right before the 1991 fiscal year the economy fell into recession—an economic downturn that would all but wipe out the deficit-reducing power of the compromise package of tax hikes and budget cuts approved by Congress shortly thereafter. The recession also proved untimely, occurring just as the Bush camp turned its attention to the president's reelection campaign. Economic recovery came too late to help Bush's electoral fortunes, and the recession's timing afforded Bush and his top aides little opportunity to work stimulus legislation through a Congress led by a politically unsympathetic opposition party. Bill Clinton, the Democrats' nominee, wasted little time in making the economy his number one campaign issue.

It was Clinton who got the chance to offer Congress a package of fiscal stimulus. But with Republicans labeling much of the legislation as "pork," and the CBO warning that it could prove inflationary in a recovering economy, the newly elected president could not marshal sufficient votes from within his own party to win passage. He was later successful, however, in convincing enough Democrats in Congress to support reconciliation legislation containing a combination of tax increases and budget reductions aimed at reducing a recession-swelled federal budget deficit. In leading the way, Clinton was motivated by what he viewed to be the political imperative of deficit reduction, not by fiscal policy designs. He intended the tax increases as instruments to raise revenue and thereby reduce the deficit, as well as a means to restore some lost equity between high-income and other taxpayers, rather than as a tool of fiscal restraint.

The upturn in the business cycle started out slowly, but it accelerated quickly by mid-decade. Growth became strong, and the misery index dropped to its lowest point since the mid-1960s, creating a hospitable climate for the president's reelection bid. That strong growth continued well into Clinton's second term, generating unexpectedly high revenues and greatly shrinking the federal budget deficit.

The real story of economic management in the 1990s, however, has not been one of presidential leadership employing fiscal policy tools, but of the Federal Reserve's use of preemptive monetary policy to keep inflation under control in a growing economy. That policy continuity created an environment of confidence and security, spurring investment, creating new jobs in record numbers, and sending U.S. stock markets to a series of new highs in the mid- and late-1990s.

Monetary Policy

The Primacy of the Federal Reserve

Unlike fiscal policy, for which Congress directly exercises its constitutional power to tax and spend, although the president typically sets the national agenda, Congress has vested the authority for monetary policy in an independent government agency, the Federal Reserve. The Fed was established by Congress in 1913 and is governed by a seven-member board, with its members appointed by the president for staggered fourteen-year terms, subject to Senate confirmation. The Board of Governors is augmented in its policymaking functions by the presidents of the twelve Federal Reserve banks, who are appointed by regional governing boards, subject to approval by the Board of Governors. The twelve Federal Reserve banks and their twenty-five branches carry out a wide variety of financial and regulatory functions, including serving as a depository for the banks in their own district, distributing the nation's currency and coin, operating a nationwide payments system (involving interbank check clearing), and regulating member banks and bank holding companies. Federal Reserve banks also serve as fiscal agents of the U.S. government, performing several services for the Department of the Treasury, including maintaining the Treasury's funds account; clearing Treasury checks; and conducting auctions of Treasury securities, as well as issuing, servicing, and redeeming them.[25]

The presidents of the Federal Reserve banks, in addition to providing executive leadership for these functions, also have representation on the Federal Open Market Committee (FOMC). The FOMC is composed of the seven members of the Board of Governors and five of the twelve Reserve bank presidents. The president of the Federal Reserve Bank of New York is a permanent member, and the other presidents serve rotating one-year terms. The FOMC directs the buying and selling of government securities on the open market as a principal instrument of monetary policy. When the Domestic Trading Desk at the Federal Reserve Bank of New York sells Treasury securities through about three-dozen large-volume dealers to the highest bidding banks and other depository institutions, such as savings and loan associations and credit unions, it draws reserves from the banking system, thus shrinking the availability of loanable funds. Conversely, when it buys government securities at the lowest price the market will bear, it pays for them by adding reserves to the banking system, thus increasing the capacity of banks and other depository institutions to make loans (see Figure 2.1).

These market operations, in turn, can affect interest rates charged private borrowers. As the reserves of financial institutions decline, interest rates rise, reflecting the basic factors of supply and demand. Conversely, a rise in reserves decreases interest rates, reflecting the reduced availability of loanable funds. FOMC transactions can also importantly affect the federal funds rate (FFR), the rate of interest

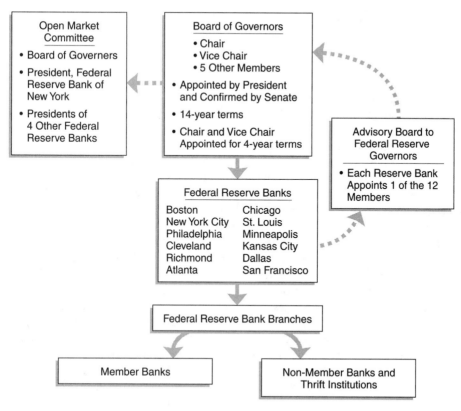

FIGURE 2.1   Federal Reserve System

that depository institutions charge one another for overnight loans. Overnight borrowing allows the borrowing institution to acquire resources beyond its existing reserves to meet the immediate needs of its commercial customers and to meet reserve requirements (the percentage of deposits that depository institutions must keep in cash or as non-interest bearing balances in Federal Reserve banks). When the FFR moves, or is expected to move, short-term interest rates available to borrowers tend to move in the same direction, as commercial lenders typically follow the Fed's lead. However, that association has not been uniform over time; exceptions have existed.

In addition to the FOMC's actions, the Federal Reserve Board possesses two other policy instruments that it can use to effect its monetary policy. First, it can change the *reserve requirement* that it imposes on depository institutions, the requirement that they hold a certain percentage of their deposits—typically between 8 and 14 percent—in reserve, either in vault cash or as balances in Federal Reserve banks.[26] When the Fed raises the reserve requirement, banks have less money available to loan, exerting upward pressure on interest rates. Conversely, when the Fed lowers the reserve requirement, banks have more funds available to loan, depressing interest rates. In practice, the Fed has made increasingly infrequent use of changes in the reserve requirement as an instrument of monetary policy, preferring instead to rely on open market operations and their targeted effects on the FFR. Yet the very existence of reserve requirements provides a stable base on which the Federal Reserve Board can use open market transactions to affect the price of reserves by adjusting their supply.

Second, the Fed can raise or lower the *discount rate*, the rate of interest charged to depository institutions that borrow directly from Federal Reserve banks. Any financial institution subject to reserve requirements is eligible to borrow from the Fed. The economic relationships parallel those of altering the reserve requirement. An increase in the discount rate raises the cost of credit and reduces demand for it. The converse also is true.

Discount borrowing accounts for only a small fraction of total reserves. Depository institutions tend to borrow from the Federal Reserve only after they have drawn from all other available sources of funds, a practice encouraged by the Fed. Given its marginal effect on reserves, a change in the discount rate alone is likely to affect interest rates only in a limited fashion, as open market operations and their effect on the FFR tend to overwhelm the discount rate's effect on commercial interest rates.

Under Chairman Alan Greenspan, the Federal Reserve—through its Open Market Committee—has elected to use induced changes in the FFR as its primary tool of monetary policy.[27] And it has proved to be highly effective, as commercial banks have been quick to reflect changes to the FFR in the rates they charge their borrowers. During the 1990s, the FOMC has followed a strategy of making small, incremental adjustments in the FFR, usually at the 25 basis point (a quarter of 1 percent) level, preferring a series of small adjustments over the shock-therapy strategy employed by the early Volcker-led Federal Reserve, discussed previously, and, to a lesser extent, by the Greenspan-led Federal Reserve during 1988 and the first half of 1989, during which time the FFR rose from just below 7 percent to almost 10 percent.

Both presidents and Congresses over the past two decades have deferred to the Federal Reserve for national economic management; and monetary policy, accordingly, has become the national government's most important macroeconomic policy instrument. With the exception of President Clinton's support in early 1993 of an unsuccessful economic stimulus package of "investment spending," the taxing and spending choices of presidents and successive Congresses have centered on deficit reduction and the policy tradeoffs inherent in attaining it. As they focused on deficit reduction and controlling entitlement spending, both institutions looked to the Fed to keep America's economy on course.

Executive Branch Relationships

Presidents are much better positioned to influence fiscal policy than monetary policy. As discussed earlier, they set the fiscal policy agenda. And facing an upcoming election, many in Congress may see their own reelection prospects linked with the president's to the state of the economy, thus providing an incentive for Congress to support presidential efforts to use fiscal policy to improve economic conditions, unless partisan opponents in Congress believe that they can successfully deflect blame to the president for the economy's woes. In comparison, the institutional influence of presidents on monetary policy is far less marked.

The president appoints members of the Federal Reserve Board, but the length and staggered nature of their terms makes it difficult for a president to appoint a majority of board members, even though high member turnover can at times enable a two-term president to do so. Moreover, as monetary policymaking has shifted to the FOMC, the addition of Federal Reserve bank presidents to the FOMC, joining presidential appointees, further distances the president from the committee. Yet the fact of institutional separation should not lead to the conclusion that the president lacks influence on monetary policy. The president's "bully pulpit" is his greatest nonlegal resource. Presidential statements garner attention, and when presidents highlight their visibility, political actors and the media pay attention to both the message and the political forces behind it. Federal Reserve chairs want presidential support for their board's policies, and do not relish presidential criticism. That does not mean, however, that the Fed does whatever the president wants. Nevertheless, a generalizable pattern of political responsiveness on the part of the Fed to the incumbent president does appear to exist, characterized by increased monetary stimulation prior to a presidential election, followed by a more restrictive policy to dampen inflationary tendencies after the election. At least, time series analysis shows this responsiveness to apply considerably more often than not.[28]

The 1980 election year provides a case in point. Two months after he took over as chairman, Paul Volcker pledged to Congress that the Federal Reserve would significantly tighten the money supply as its primary weapon against inflation, which had hit double-digit proportions. Yet in the six months following the chairman's declaration, the FOMC had increased the monetary base at a rate not much different from the rate of increase before the announcement, prompting observers to question the Fed's resolve to follow through in an election year and to lead the more cynical among them to rename the FOMC the "Committee to Reelect the President." In the twelve-month period preceding the election, the price level increased by almost 13 percent.[29] As the election neared, Carter's Republican challenger, Ronald Reagan, continued to hit inflation hard as a central campaign issue.

The 1980 election not only gave Reagan a landslide victory but also swept conservatives into Congress, giving Republicans control of the Senate for the first time since the Eisenhower years. Political support clearly existed for a more restrictive monetary policy, a mood that the inflation-weary Federal Reserve Board was prepared to embrace. The FOMC followed suit, free of any compunction about jeopardizing the reelectability of a sitting president who appointed many of its members, and its restrictive policies drove growth rates for the monetary base to near zero.[30] The Fed's implementation of monetary shock therapy had begun in earnest.

The Reagan administration supported the tight money policy of the Volcker-led Federal Reserve Board as necessary to bring inflation under control, but as unemployment reached post-Depression record highs toward the middle of Reagan's first term, a number of his economic advisors grumbled that the Federal Reserve was too slow in easing credit restraints to help the economy grow out of the recession as the upcoming reelection campaign drew nearer. Yet apart from a few media stories of presidential discontent, administration officials elected not to take on the Fed directly, probably due in part to the president's own antipathy toward inflation, which was clearly reflected in his August 1983 message announcing Volcker's reappointment as chair. Reagan commented that Volcker "is as dedicated as I am to continuing the fight against inflation. And with him as Chairman of the Fed, I know we'll win that fight."[31]

Nearly a decade later, Richard Darman, George Bush's OMB director, and Nicholas Brady, Bush's Treasury secretary, took issue publicly with Alan Greenspan's unwillingness to urge the Federal Reserve to take actions that would lower interest rates and stimulate recovery to the extent the administration wanted. Both understood the political implications of slow recovery. Greenspan, however, voiced his determination to stay the course and support measured, sustainable, noninflationary recovery.[32] President Clinton and his administration reaped the economic fruits of that approach. In return, President Clinton reappointed Greenspan to another four-year term as chairman.

Beyond the issue of presidential support or lack of support for the policy direction taken by the Federal Reserve, and the public expression thereof by the president or top administration officials, presidents have come to use the position of vice chair as their regularized liaison with the Fed. The vice chair, also appointed by the president, has become the administration's day-to-day point person with the Fed, the board member who tends to be the most attuned to the president's economic philosophy and policy stances, and to his political needs.[33] Clinton's appointment of Alice Rivlin, formerly his OMB director, confirms these expectations.

Congressional Oversight

Federal law not only provides the Federal Reserve with independence in monetary policymaking but also shields it from traditional forms of congressional oversight. Unlike most federal agencies, the Federal Reserve System does not rely on congressional appropriations for its financial support. Instead, it derives its revenue primarily from the interest on U.S. government securities it has acquired through open market operations, along with the interest it earns from the discounted loans it makes to depository institutions. Federal Reserve banks also charge fees for the financial services they provide to banks and other thrift institutions. This financial independence from Congress removes the regularized oversight associated with the annual appropriations process and the scrutiny subcommittees give agencies, which is often linked to agency fulfillment of congressional expectations tied to appropriations. Federal law does, however, require the Federal Reserve chair to report twice a year to the congressional banking committees on the state of the economy and the course of monetary policy followed—occasions that can elicit hard questioning and heated exchanges when the economy is in trouble, especially when a congressional election is forthcoming.

Although Congress has given the Federal Reserve System freedom from the annual appropriations process and the oversight that goes with it, the Fed still is subject to Congress's power to amend the laws that give the Fed its authority and independence. Yet several factors mitigate Congress's inclination to alter present arrangements. First, the Federal Reserve enjoys a high degree of legitimacy in the American political system. Its widely perceived effective performance over the past two decades has strengthened its grip on favorable public opinion. Second, it has a solid foundation of constituency-based support in Congress, drawn from districts that represent major banking interests, traditionally strong supporters of Fed independence.[34] Third, the technical demands of monetary policymaking, with its complex models and seemingly endless data, limit the feasibility of close congressional oversight. Fourth, the Federal Reserve provides a political shield for Congress. Poor economic performance can be blamed on Fed policies and their implementation. Conversely, members of Congress readily share the accolades that follow strong economic performance. Federal Reserve independence allows members of Congress to deflect negative fallout, while basking in economic success.

ISSUES OF ECONOMIC GROWTH AND BENEFIT

Monetary policy in the 1990s became synonymous with Federal Reserve chairman Alan Greenspan. Public confidence in both has been high. Popular publications such as *Business Week* and *U.S. News and World Report* recounted the nation's record of economic successes, and were quick to attribute them to Federal Reserve Board policy under Greenspan's leadership. Both articles and editorials raised the issue of whether economic prosperity could be extended indefinitely. They wondered whether the United States has embarked on an era of "New Economics," in which there need not be a tradeoff between economic growth and inflation. The triumphalists among them mused over whether the grip of the traditional business cycle has been broken. Even President Clinton shared the optimism, stating "I believe it's possible to have more sustained and higher growth without inflation than we previously thought."[35]

For most of the 1990s, as the economy sustained growth off its recovery from recession, the FOMC proved willing, under Greenspan's leadership, to employ open market transactions to raise the federal funds rate incrementally at early signs of rising inflation. But by 1997 the FOMC appeared to be more willing to leave economic incentives unaltered for a time, but with the chairman's promise that rate hikes could be expected if indicators pointed to renewed inflation. Greenspan's newfound optimism was rooted in what he believed to be the sound fundamentals of the U.S. economy. They include low inflation and unemployment, heightened global competition restraining wage growth and limiting companies' ability to pass along higher costs to consumers, corporate restructuring and downsizing that have improved business efficiency, signs of rising productivity associated with new technological applications involving recent advances in computers, and a fiscal policy of deficit reduction embraced by both the president and Congress.[36] For Greenspan, these factors held out a higher prospect of sustainable growth. As the chairman told Congress, "The Federal Reserve is intent on gearing its policy to facilitate the maximum sustainable growth of the economy, but it is not, as some commentators have suggested, involved in an experiment that deliberately prods the economy to see how fast it can grow."[37] While a number of his colleagues on the FOMC have not shared their chairman's sanguine scenario, they have been willing to follow his lead because of the demonstrated success of his judgments.[38]

Most economists are not prepared to embrace a new economics of indefinitely sustainable growth with price stability. They see strong economic growth and falling unemployment as signals for government-imposed restraint lest inflation once again become a problem. The trick for them is to assess the appropriate timing for restraint. Alan Binder of Princeton University, and a former Federal Reserve vice chair, is one who believes that growth must be managed if it is to be sustainable. For him and other mainline economists, much faster growth will inevitably lead to unacceptably high inflation and to the inevitable corrective policies that will cause unemployment to rise to unacceptable levels. Binder relies on the historical relationship between inflation and unemployment, using unemployment as an indicator of aggregate pressure on capacity. He also questions the premise that the U.S. economy can expect significant productivity gains that will keep inflation in check during high growth, asking why we now should expect computer technology to raise worker productivity significantly when the trend line, which covers periods of vastly expanded computing power and technological innovation, points to continued marginal growth in worker productivity overall, despite recent gains in the manufacturing sector (which by 1998 accounted for only 20 percent of the GDP).[39]

Others—among them economists, politicians, and popular writers—argue that the economy could grow even faster if government were willing to pursue more growth-oriented policies. These critics fall into two camps: those who see government policies as getting in the way of faster growth, and those who believe that government should do more to promote growth in areas of highest potential return. The former point to Alan Greenspan and the FOMC as culprits, whom they believe have been all too eager to slow economic growth by prematurely raising interest rates during a good part of the 1990s, even though Greenspan by 1997 had shown a greater willingness to allow a somewhat higher rate of growth, as discussed above. Proponents of even faster growth come from a distinct normative perspective; they are willing to support more stimulative economic policies even if that entails higher inflation as the price to be paid for lower unemployment and broadened economic benefits across the population.

Robert Eisner, Lester Thurow, James K. Galbraith, Barry Bluestone, and Bennett Harrison are among economists who take this position in varying degrees.[40]

Thurow is its most adamant proponent, stating boldly that "rising inequality and falling wages (discussed in Chapter 1) are more important problems than the ghost of inflation."[41] Galbraith points to economic policymakers' inability to predict the economic future, yet recognizes that high growth rates without rising inflation cannot be sustained indefinitely. Nevertheless, he, like Bluestone and Harrison, sees signs in current fundamentals that spark optimism in the short run, among them expected productivity increases associated with the maturing of the information age—favorable signs that should lead economic policymakers to do nothing to slow economic growth. Galbraith's prescription is to test the limits, for, like Bluestone and Harrison, he views the employment and income gains brought by growth as outweighing the risk of price-level increases. Bluestone and Harrison emphasize the social value of faster growth, arguing that, if used wisely, it holds the only realistic hope of raising living standards, reducing the gap between the rich and poor, and helping to solve many of America's social problems.

With growth comes increased tax revenue. The question for both policymakers and interested observers becomes: How should government use that increased revenue? Here we get back into issues of fiscal policy. Several nonexclusive options are available to policymakers: Apply some or all of the added revenue to reduce the nation's budget deficit; return some or all of it to taxpayers in the form of tax cuts; and spend some or all of it on priority governmental programs. The first increases national savings and may contribute to lower interest rates; the second can stimulate increased aggregate demand, assuming that the tax savings are spent; and the third can also increase aggregate demand, although its effect is in part a product of the nature of that government spending.

Policymakers do not make these choices based on their fiscal-policy effects alone. In fact, fiscal-policy considerations may be far down the list of influences on choice. Policymakers act for a number of sometimes competing reasons, including their sense of what is in the public interest, how decisions affect important constituencies, and the partisan political implications of choice. Those who advocate testing the limits of growth typically have a social agenda to pursue as well. And that agenda often includes using the added revenues produced by growth to reduce income inequality and to invest in infrastructure—both human and physical.

Others urge government to support targeted growth by implementing what has been referred to as industrial policy. Industrial policy involves the national government adopting a conscious policy strategy that provides incentives to attract capital from declining industries and into those that offer higher prospects of growth. In a real sense, policymakers use financial incentives and regulatory devices to bias the options of industrialists so that they are in line with, and supportive of, national industrial policy directions. Elements of that strategy commonly include direct government subsidies and government channeling of capital (potentially at discounted rates) to targeted industries, special tax treatment, low-interest loans and loan guarantees, government financing of research and development and labor training, relief from government regulations, and government support of exports and new market creation.

Although the U.S. federal government has supported a loose, ad hoc panoply of subsidies, tax deductions and credits, labor training programs, and loans and loan guarantees over time, it never has pursued a comprehensive and coherent industrial policy outside of wartime, when the federal government created special institutions to coordinate resource use, shift production priorities, allocate capital, and train workers.[42] Americans' devotion to the market economy and to restraint of government intervention has mitigated support for industrial policy in this country. Moreover, the U.S. economy's sustained success for most of the 1990s, despite the intrusions of foreign economic crises, reinforced Americans' predilection to let the market work and pretty much limit government's intervention in the economy to fine-tuning through monetary and fiscal policy. Whether that sentiment will be sustained should foreign economic difficulties drag down the U.S. economy is an open question as America nears the twenty-first century.

NOTES

1. Stephen L. Robertson, "The Executive Office of the President: White House Office," in *Cabinets and Counselors: The President and the Executive Branch*, 2d ed., ed. W. Craig Bledsoe, et al. (Washington, DC: Congressional Quarterly, Inc., 1997), 3.

2. Herbert Stein, *The Fiscal Revolution in America* (Washington, DC: The AEI Press, 1996), 108–120.

3. Herbert Stein, *Presidential Economics*, 3d ed. (Washington, DC: The AEI Press, 1994), 34–46.

4. Roger Porter, "Economic Advice to the President, from Eisenhower to Reagan," *Political Science Quarterly* 98 (Fall 1983), 403–426; Edwin C. Hargrove and Samuel A. Moorley, eds., *The President and the Council of Economic Advisors: Interviews with CEA Chairmen* (Boulder, CO: Westview Press, 1984).

5. James J. Gosling, *Budgetary Politics in American Governments*, 2d ed. (New York: Garland Publishing, 1997), 100.

6. Jeffrey E. Cohen, *Politics and Economic Policy in the United States* (Boston: Houghton Mifflin Co., 1997), 144–145.

7. Aaron Wildavsky, *The Politics of the Budgetary Process* (Boston: Little, Brown, 1964), 58.

8. Office of Management and Budget, *The Budget of the United States Government*, Fiscal Years 1961 and 1975.

9. Committee on the Budget, United States Senate, *Congressional Budget Reform* (Washington, DC: Government Printing Office, 1976), 8.

10. Herbert Stein, *The Fiscal Revolution in America*, 49–63.

11. Ibid., 170–175.

12. Marc Allan Eisner, *The State in the American Political Economy* (Englewood Cliffs, NJ: Prentice-Hall, 1995), 246–249; Daniel C. Diller and Dean J. Peterson, "Chief Economist," in *Powers of the Presidency*, 2d ed. (Washington, DC: Congressional Quarterly, Inc., 1997), 248.

13. Herbert Stein, *The Fiscal Revolution in America*, 314.

14. Ibid., 299–308.

15. Ibid., 329.

16. Arthur F. Burns and Paul A. Samuelson, *Full Employment, Guideposts and Economic Stability* (Washington, DC: American Enterprise Institute for Public Policy Research, 1967), 86–88.

17. Herbert Stein, *Presidential Economics*, 89–101.

18. Council of Economic Advisors, *Economic Report of the President*, 1963, xxiv.

19. Ibid., 74.

20. Herbert Stein, *Presidential Economics*, 107.

21. Ibid., 111–112; *Economic Report of the President*, 1966, 38.

22. Marc Allan Eisner, *The State in the American Political Economy*, 254.

23. Norman C. Thomas and Joseph A. Pika, *The Politics of the Presidency*, 4th ed. (Washington, DC: Congressional Quarterly Press, 1996), 40–42.

24. Marc Allan Eisner, *The State in the American Political Economy*, 256.

25. This section on monetary policy draws on information and analysis found in *The Federal Reserve System: Purposes and Functions* (Washington, DC: Board of Governors of the Federal Reserve System, 1994), especially Chapters 1–3.

26. Before 1980, only banks that were members of the Federal Reserve System were subject to reserve requirements. However, the Monetary Control Act of 1980 extended the requirement to all depository institutions.

27. Glenn Rudebusch, "Interest Rates and Monetary Policy," *FRBSF Economic Letter*, No. 97–18 (June 13, 1997).

28. Richard H. Timberlake, *Monetary Policy in the United States: An Intellectual and Institutional History* (Chicago: University of Chicago Press, 1993), 356–357; Thomas D. Willett, *Political Business Cycles* (Durham, NC: Duke University Press, 1988).

29. Richard H. Timberlake, *Monetary Policy in the United States: An Intellectual and Institutional History*, 350.

30. Ibid., 357.

31. Quoted in Ibid., 379.

32. Clyde H. Farnsworth, "Brady Warns That Fed Could Delay Recovery," *New York Times*, June 2, 1992; Richard H. Timberlake, *Monetary Policy in the United States: An Intellectual and Institutional History*, 390–401.

33. Thomas Havrilesky, "The Politicization of Monetary Policy: The Vice Chairman as the Administration's Point Man," *Cato Journal* 13 (Spring/Summer 1993), 137–142.

34. John T. Wooley, "The Politics of Monetary Policy: A Critical Review," *Journal of Public Policy* 14 (1994) 57–85.

35. Quoted in *Business Week*, July 7, 1997, 48.

36. Alan Greenspan, *Testimony Before the Subcommittee on Domestic and International Monetary Policy of the House Committee on Banking and Financial Services*, July 22, 1997.

37. Ibid., 7

38. Dean Foust, "Alan Greenspan's Brave New World," *Business Week*, July 14, 1997, 45–50.

39. Alan Binder, "The Speed Limit: Fact and Fancy in the Growth Debate," *The American Prospect* 34 (September-October 1997), 57–62.

40. Robert Eisner, *The Misunderstood Economy* (Cambridge, MA: Harvard Business School Press, 1995), 145–213; Lester Thurow, "The Crusade That's Killing Prosperity," *The American Prospect* 25 (March-April 1996), 54–59; James K. Galbraith, "The Surrender of Economic Policy," *The American Prospect* 25 (March-April 1996), 60–67; James K. Galbraith, "Test the Limit," *The American Prospect* 34 (September-October 1997), 66–67; Barry Bluestone and Bennett Harrison, "Why We Can Grow Faster," *The American Prospect* 34 (September-October 1997), 63–70.

41. Lester Thurow, "The Crusade That's Killing Prosperity," 59.

42. Marc Allan Eisner, *The State in the American Political Economy*, 319–320.

CHAPTER 3

Deficits and Debt

The federal budget deficit was at the forefront of America's national political debate during the 1980s and for most of the 1990s. No other political issue came close to matching its share of news media coverage or its absorption of policymakers' attention and time. Presidents and Congresses alike have been preoccupied with the question of how best to reduce a deficit that in the early 1980s reached postwar highs as a percentage of the gross domestic product (GDP), and that stubbornly persisted well into the next decade. As the deficit skyrocketed in the early- to mid-1980s, the result of substantive policy choices and a monetary policy–induced recession, so did partisan rhetoric. Placing blame for the rising deficit and government's inability to pare it down became the centerpiece of deficit politics. Partisan positions became entrenched, and presidential budget recommendations were treated as "dead on arrival" by congressional budgeteers. Even Congress's passage of deficit-reduction targets, and its creation of so-called sequestration controls to cancel spending authority that pushed the deficit in excess of those targets, seemed impotent to turn the deficit around significantly.

It was not until late in 1990, well after the beginning of a new fiscal year, that mounting editorial and public pressure prodded President Bush and Democratic congressional leaders to forge an eleventh-hour bipartisan deficit-reduction package that contained both spending cuts and tax increases. It soon became apparent, however, that still another recession would all but cancel out the legislation's deficit-reduction gains. As the budget deficit[1] approached $300 billion at the end of Bush's presidential term, it appeared as if a large budget deficit would remain a permanent fixture of America's political landscape. Oh, how different the scene looked toward decade's end! By the end of the 1997 fiscal year, the federal budget deficit had fallen to $22 billion, the smallest since 1974, both in dollar terms and as a share of the GDP. Moreover, both the Office of Management and Budget (OMB) and the Congressional Budget Office (CBO) projected a growing federal unified-budget surplus by 2002, occurring earlier if the economy continued to grow toward the turn of the century at its 1996–1997 pace. That indeed happened, and President Clinton happily announced in September 1998 that Americans should expect to find a unified-budget surplus of about $70 billion by the official close of the 1998 fiscal year—the first surplus since 1969, and only the ninth since World War II.

What changed the budget picture so dramatically? The answer includes a combination of tough policy choices and budgetary actions, sound monetary policy, and just plain luck—or, as economists might put it, the absence of any economically dislocating external shocks (although the financial crisis in East Asia began in 1997 to raise concerns about how long that luck would hold out).

Unlike the end of Bush's term, when a sagging economy undermined attempted deficit reduction, President Clinton inherited an economy already recovering from recession. He also found himself working with a Democratic majority in Congress, ending twelve years of divided partisan government—a majority eager to show that they and their chief executive colleague could govern effectively. The mounting budget deficit—then projected by the CBO to reach $350 billion by 1997, rising to over a half-billion by 2002—provided a natural target of action. For both the president and most congressional Democrats, tax increases appeared to be a necessary part of any package of deficit reduction.

Not far removed in time from President Bush's admission to the nation that his support for the comparatively modest tax increases of 1990 was a mistake he would not repeat, Republicans in Congress showed no enthusiasm for additional tax increases. Democrats, without any Republican support, passed legislation in 1993 projected to reduce the budget deficit by $433 billion over five years. Increased tax revenues, derived primarily from increases in the personal income tax, were projected to account for $240 billion of the total. In fact, the actual deficit reduction over that period amounted to nearly $1 trillion, with the difference largely the product of much higher-than-projected national economic growth. Continued strong economic growth and the subsequent deficit-reduction legislation enacted in 1997 charted the way toward a budget surplus at the end of fiscal year (FY) 1998 (see Table 3.1).

The 1997 legislation was especially notable for the overwhelming bipartisan support it received in both congressional chambers. The rising tide of economic growth lifted the political fortunes of incumbents in the 1996 national election and provided an environment of unexpectedly high revenues that gave both the Clinton administration and congressional budgetmakers added leeway in crafting their plan of further deficit reduction and packaging tax cuts with spending reductions in a way that created what both political parties perceived as a win-win outcome.

The nation in the late 1990s seemed to breathe a collective sigh of relief over deficit reduction, except for those relatively few spoilers who failed to share in the euphoria and pointed to the longer-term fiscal implications of demographically driven pressures on Social Security and health care spending. Other detractors argued that even though we can be heartened by the recent deficit reduction, Americans should be greatly concerned about the large accumulated debt that their national government owes to its creditors—an obligation that topped $5.4 trillion at the end of the 1998 fiscal year and that the OMB estimated will rise to $5.8 trillion by the end of FY 2002, even with projected budget surpluses through the end of the decade and into the next.[2] This chapter assesses both concerns; but, first, it is necessary to explore the relationship between deficits and debt.

TABLE 3.1   The Changing Budget Deficit: Selected Years, 1969–2002 (in $ billions)

Fiscal Year	Receipts	Outlays	Deficit/Surplus
1969	186.9	183.6	3.2
1972	207.3	230.7	−23.4
1974	263.2	269.4	−6.1
1976	298.1	371.8	−73.7
1977	355.6	409.2	−53.7
1978	399.6	458.7	−59.2
1979	463.3	504.0	−40.8
1980	517.1	590.9	−73.8
1981	599.3	678.2	−79.0
1982	617.8	745.8	−128.0
1983	600.6	808.3	−207.8
1984	666.5	851.9	−185.4
1985	734.1	946.4	−212.3
1986	769.2	990.5	−221.2
1987	854.4	1,004.1	−149.8
1988	909.3	1,064.5	−155.2
1989	991.2	1,143.7	−152.5
1990	1,032.0	1,253.2	−221.2
1991	1,055.0	1,324.4	−269.4
1992	1,091.3	1,381.7	−290.4
1993	1,154.4	1,409.4	−255.0
1994	1,258.6	1,461.7	−203.1
1995	1,351.8	1,515.7	−163.9
1996	1,453.1	1,560.1	−107.5
1997	1,579.3	1,601.2	−22.0
1998	1,721.8	1,652.6	69.2
1999e	1,806.3	1,727.0	79.3
2000e	1,883.0	1,765.7	117.3
2001e	1,933.3	1,799.2	134.1
2002e	2,007.1	1,820.3	186.8

e = Estimate.
SOURCE: U.S. Office of Management and Budget, *The Budget of the United States Government, FY 2000, Historical Tables*, Table 1.1, 19–20.

THE RELATIONSHIP BETWEEN DEFICITS AND DEBT

Governments incur deficits because they spend more in a given fiscal year than they collect in revenues from taxes and other receipts. When that occurs, governments must borrow to make up the difference. But governments' authority to borrow can be constrained by constitutional prohibitions or by statutory law. As noted in Chapter 1, budgets must be balanced in virtually all state and local governments in the United States. They are prohibited from running operating budget deficits and borrowing to obtain the resources to pay for spending in excess of revenues. Yet a qualification is in order here. States and most local governments possess the authority to use borrowing to finance capital acquisitions, such as the construction of courthouses and schools or highways and bridges. Following a separate capital budgeting process, state and local governments finance these projects by selling bonds to the public, paying back the amount of indebtedness over the lives of the bonds. In that way, future users of these capital projects contribute to their financing over time.

In contrast, no separate capital budget exists at the federal level. Capital expenses are budgeted within the operating budget. When revenues fall short of budgeted expenditures (called outlays in federal budgetary terminology) during any fiscal year, the federal government borrows to fill in the gap, irrespective of the capital expenses that exist in the mix. The federal government borrows money by selling Treasury securities of varying denominations and durations of maturity, including Treasury bills, issued with three-, six-, or twelve-month maturities; notes that come due in two to ten years; and bonds, which mature in more than ten years.

The Federal Reserve acts as the Department of the Treasury's agent, auctioning the securities to the highest bidders. The bidders are financial intermediaries typically acting on behalf of large purchasers such as banks, corporations, and pension funds, both domestic and foreign. In auctions, buyers seek the highest rate of return possible, while the Treasury tries to acquire capital at the lowest obtainable interest costs. Once acquired, the holder can resell them on the secondary market, and it is not unusual for the same security to be traded many times prior to its maturity.

The federal government even borrows from itself. Several large federal programs draw their financial support from trust funds—into which revenues are deposited, and from which expenditures are debited. They include trust funds for civil service retirement, highway and bridge construction, airport construction, Medicare, and Social Security, among the largest. Federal law requires that any surpluses in trust funds be invested in Treasury securities, providing resources that can be used to help finance any annual deficit that exists. In addition to trust fund holdings, the Federal Reserve maintains a reservoir of Treasury securities that it uses to effect monetary policy—buying securities on the open market when it wants to expand the money supply and lower interest rates, and selling them when it wishes to contract the money supply and raise interest rates.

TRENDS IN FEDERAL DEBT

Before examining trends in federal debt, we must decide what federal debt to look at. Do we want to look at gross federal debt, or does it make more sense to limit our analysis to debt held by the public? A strong argument can be made for following the latter approach. True, it excludes debt held in government accounts, but should that debt be treated the same as debt held by the public? The Treasury pays no *net* interest on debt held in government accounts, since interest earnings are repaid to the Treasury by law. The same is true for debt held by the Federal Reserve. Since the federal government incurs no *net* interest obligation, Federal Reserve–held debt imposes no claim on the federal budget. It makes most sense, therefore, to look at publicly held debt *exclusive of* that held by the Federal Reserve, which subsequently will be referred to as net publicly held debt or *debt held outside the federal government*, treating the Federal Reserve as a quasi-governmental agency.

An argument can also be made that debt service payments to state and local governments, treated as part of the repayment of publicly held debt, represent a wash of sorts if we are concerned most with the condition of total government debt in the United States, including that of state and local governments. However, the traditional focus looks at federal debt alone and treats it and the national debt as synonymous.

With net publicly held debt, interest payments flow out of the Treasury, to be held and used by others. Interest payments on domestically held federal debt remain within the economy and become part of the aggregate income from which government gets its own revenues, whether through taxes or borrowing. Moreover, a portion of the interest paid on foreign-held federal debt also finds its way into national income flows, as some of the dollar-denominated interest payments are reinvested or spent in the United States and are subject to federal tax. Even some of the earnings that leave the country will return in exchange for U.S. exports and assets such as financial securities and real estate.

As Table 3.2 shows, approximately 32 percent of the gross debt of the federal government is held in federal government accounts. The Federal Reserve holds Treasury securities equal to another 8 percent. The remaining 60 percent is owned by a broad assortment of financial institutions, corporations, state and local government investment funds, foreign governments, and individuals, among others. In accounting terms, all debt not held in federal government accounts is considered debt held by the public, even debt held temporarily by the Federal Reserve. Yet for our purposes, as discussed above, it makes the most sense to focus on debt held outside of the federal government, excluding that held by the Federal Reserve, of which about 37 percent is owned by foreign institutions and individuals.

T A B L E 3 . 2   Who Holds the Federal Debt? (1998)

Holder	Amount (in $ billions)	Percentage of Total
Federal government accounts	1,759	32.1
The Federal Reserve	458	8.4
Others outside the federal government	3,262	59.5
	5,479	100.0
Debt Held Outside the Federal Government,* Domestic and Foreign		
Domestic holders	2,045	62.7
Foreign holders	1,217	37.3
	3,262	100.0

*Excluding that held by the Federal Reserve.
SOURCE: U.S. Office of Management and Budget, *The Budget of the United States Government, FY 2000, Analytical Perspectives*, 270; *Historical Tables*, Table 7.1, 110–111.

Putting Debt Levels in Perspective

To help put debt levels in perspective, it is useful to compare them to historical debt patterns and to the debt obligations of other industrial nations. Table 3.3 shows trends in federal debt dating back to World War II. At the end of World War II, debt held outside the federal government approached 100 percent of the GDP. In other words, the federal debt in 1946 almost equaled the economy's entire output for that year. But as should be expected based on historical experience, America's debt load declined significantly in the postwar years, as defense spending's share of the federal budget shrank during peacetime, despite cold war tensions with the Soviet Union. A string of balanced or near-balanced budgets and solid economic growth during the late 1940s, 1950s, and a good part of the 1960s allowed the federal debt to drop precipitously as a percentage of America's economic output, falling to 24 percent in 1969, the last year of federal budget surplus before 1998. It continued to fall, but at a much slower rate during the 1970s, reversing course in the early 1980s and rising sharply through the early and mid-1980s, and again in the early 1990s, reaching a post-1956 peak of 45 percent in 1993. By 1998, debt held outside the federal government as a percentage of the GDP had fallen 6 percentage points

TABLE 3.3   Trends in Federal Debt: Selected Years, 1940–2002

End of Fiscal Year	Debt Held Outside the Federal Government* (in $ billions)	Percentage of GDP
1940	40.3	41.8
1946	218.1	97.8
1952	191.9	55.0
1956	198.4	46.4
1962	218.3	38.5
1966	221.5	29.4
1969	224.0	23.6
1972	251.0	21.3
1976	398.8	21.9
1982	785.3	24.5
1986	1,545.9	35.3
1992	2,702.4	44.0
1993	2,921.8	45.1
1996	3,342.0	44.3
1998	3,261.7	38.8
2000e	3,092.0	33.6
2002e	2,796.0	27.9

*Excluding debt held by the Federal Reserve.
e = Estimate, assuming that debt held by the Federal Reserve remains constant as a percentage of publicly held debt.
SOURCE: U.S. Office of Management and Budget, *The Budget of the United States Government, FY 2000, Historical Tables*, Table7.1, 110–111.

from its 1993 level. The OMB projects it to decline even further by 2002, to 28 percent, taking into account projected budget surpluses and projections of continued moderately strong economic growth.

Although debt held outside the federal government has declined as a percentage of America's productive output, the federal government's reliance on foreign borrowing, as a component of that debt, has increased greatly. As recently as 1969, foreign holdings counted for 5 percent of the debt held outside the federal government. Twenty years later, their claim increased to 20 percent. By the end of 1998, foreign holdings ballooned to 37 percent of debt held outside the federal government.[3] Despite that seemingly dramatic increase, it should be recognized that foreign purchases of federal debt are only a modest part of the annual gross capital inflow from abroad. They are overwhelmed by foreign purchases of assets in the United States and by foreign investments in U.S. corporations. It is nonetheless true that the federal government has become increasingly dependent on foreign institutions and individuals to finance its debt. Historically, the federal government has not been nearly as reliant on foreign capital to finance its debt. During most of American history, individuals and institutions within the United States held nearly all of the federal debt.

The recent decline in outside federal debt as a percentage of the economy's productive output should not mislead anyone into believing that the federal government's gross debt is declining in current dollars. It clearly is not. In fact, the federal government added slightly over a $1.1 trillion of gross debt between 1993 and 1998 alone. The comparable figure for debt held outside the federal government is $340 billion. The OMB projects gross debt to grow by another $337 billion by 2002, while debt held outside the federal government is projected to *decline* by $466 billion over those years, reflecting the projected budget surpluses that eliminate the federal government's need to borrow from the public to finance deficit spending. The estimated growth in gross federal debt is exclusively a product of the debt held by government accounts, primarily accounted for by rising trust fund balances through 2002.[4]

Another way of putting America's debt load in perspective is to compare the federal government's debt with that of other advanced, industrial nations. The trick here is to make valid comparisons, comparing apples to apples, as the adage goes. Ideally, following the analytical approach pursued above, it would be best to compare nongovernment-held debt as a percentage of a nation's economic output. However, due to data inconsistencies, we are left to rely on comparisons of *gross* national government debt as a percentage of the GDP. Table 3.4 shows the results of that comparison for 1997, the most recent year for which comparable data are available. Clearly, the national debt burden of the United States fell below that of most of the industrial nations with which it is usually compared. We can realistically expect that its position has improved since 1997, given comparative rates of national economic growth and the United States' comparative success in deficit reduction.

Interest Obligation on the Debt

The fiscal implications of the federal government's debt hits home in the federal budget. Net interest payments on the debt have comprised a growing share of federal budget outlays. Although net interest on the debt is not treated as an entitle-

TABLE 3.4   Comparative National Government Public Debt:
Gross Debt as a Percentage of GDP, 1997

Nation	Debt/GDP
Italy	122
Belgium	122
Greece	110
Canada	94
Japan	87
Sweden	77
Spain	74
Netherlands	71
Ireland	67
France	65
Germany	64
United Kingdom	56
United States	56
Finland	55
Australia	41
Norway	36

SOURCE: Organization for Economic Cooperation and Development, *Analytical Databank,*
December 1998, Table 6.

ment program, per se, budgeteers treat it as a form of uncontrollable spending, since
it is highly unlikely that the U.S. government would fail to honor its interest obligations. Rising net interest costs tend to crowd out other federal discretionary
spending, particularly in the constrained environment of deficit reduction.

Beyond crediting interest to the holders of Treasury securities, the federal government also has the obligation to pay back principal when securities are redeemed.
However, Congress does not appropriate funds for principal repayment. Instead, the
Federal Reserve uses the proceeds of new borrowing to repay principal in a continuous process of selling and redeeming securities, borrowing enough to plug the deficit
gap and honor redemptions.

Deficit reduction decreases the federal government's reliance on borrowing, and
slows the growth rate of its debt. Balanced budgets eliminate the federal government's
need to borrow to finance annual spending, adding no debt burden. Budget surpluses
actually reduce the federal debt, shrinking net interest's share of federal outlays.

Table 3.5 illustrates the changing claim that interest has made on the federal
budget. Net interest outlays grew dramatically between 1947 and 1998, rising from
$4.2 billion to $243 billion. Although the cost of net interest payments in 1947
looks small in relation to their cost fifty-one years later, their respective shares of
federal outlays do not differ all that much. In fact, it was not until 1984 that net interest exceeded its 1947 share of total outlays. Yet that is not at all surprising. In
1947, the Treasury was on the front end of paying interest on the large federal debt
accumulated during World War II. The greatest explosion in interest spending,
however, occurred from the late 1970s through the early 1990s. Net interest's share
of total budget outlays increased from 7.3 percent in 1977 to 14.4 percent in 1992.

TABLE 3.5 Net Interest: Selected Years, 1947–2002

Fiscal Year	$ Billions	Percentage of Outlays	Percentage of GDP
1947	4.2	12.2	1.8
1957	5.4	7.0	1.2
1967	10.3	6.5	1.3
1977	29.9	7.3	1.5
1982	85.0	11.4	2.6
1987	138.7	13.8	3.0
1992	199.4	14.4	3.2
1997	244.0	15.2	3.1
1998	243.4	14.7	2.9
2000e	215.2	12.2	2.4
2002e	194.7	10.7	2.0

e = Estimate.
SOURCES: U.S. Office of Management and Budget, *The Budget of the United States Government, FY 1998, Historical Tables*, Tables 8.1, 8.3, and 8.4; *The Budget of the United States Government, FY 2000, Historical Tables*, Tables 8.1, 8.3, and 8.4.

It was also during that period that net interest took its biggest bite out of national income. The OMB projects that, with the deficit-reduction package approved in 1997 and continued moderately strong economic growth, net interest outlays will fall in current dollars by 2002, a marked reversal of course. So will the share of the budget devoted to net interest. Net interest will also take a much smaller slice of national income, returning its claim to the 1980 level. Budget surpluses, should they grow beyond 2002, will reduce federal debt held outside the federal government and further cut the federal government's interest obligations.

WHY THE DEFICIT ROSE SO STEEPLY, PUTTING AMERICA DEEPER IN DEBT

As discussed earlier, the federal government runs a deficit in a given fiscal year when revenues fall short of outlays. That can happen for two reasons: one under Congress's direct control, and the other a product of exogenous economic forces. First, let's look at the part that Congress can control.

Congress authorizes federal agencies to spend money for public purposes. In some cases, that authorization allows agencies to spend whatever is necessary to accomplish the purpose of a particular federal program. Typically, such open-ended authority is tied to statutory requirements that an agency make payments or provide services to anyone who meets the program's eligibility criteria, as set by law. So, in a very real sense, it does not matter what estimates of outlays appear in the budget; the Treasury must cover the actual costs of the cash payments or services provided. Spending on Social Security, Medicare, Medicaid, and civilian and military retirement constitutes the bulk of federal entitlement expenditures. It is true that Congress can change an entitlement and reduce related spending by amending the statutory authorization itself, for example, toughening the eligibility requirements for federally funded medical assistance. In other cases, Congress must appropriate funding in order for agencies to spend it for authorized purposes. That provision not only gives Congress the flexibility to change the amounts appropriated from year to year but also places a lid on how much can be spent during the fiscal year. With so-called discretionary spending, agencies have no authority to overspend the amounts appropriated. It does not matter, for example, how many people qualify for services.

Congress, then, can exercise choice with both entitlement and discretionary spending. With entitlement programs, Congress can restrict or broaden eligibility for entitlements, and it can increase or decrease benefits. With discretionary spending, Congress can increase or decrease appropriations. It has the authority to act in both cases, but it may choose not to do so; or it may not be able to muster enough votes to override a presidential veto.

Altering entitlements presents the greatest political obstacles. It is one thing to get a majority in Congress to cut a program's annual appropriation, and quite a different matter to change an entitlement significantly or to eliminate it altogether. The political consequences of the latter may be far greater, and congressional leaders and rank-and-file members may not be willing to take the risk; nor may presidents be willing to take the lead. Congress's caution may be accentuated when the president's position on the proposed entitlement change is at odds with its own. The credible threat of a presidential veto can be enough to prevent majority support from developing.

Beyond considerations of political choice, the condition of the economy can affect relative budget balance. A strong, growing economy increases national income, which is subject to taxation. Rising revenues make it easier for policymakers to balance the budget; that is, unless spending follows apace. Significant revenue growth gives policymakers leeway to meet political needs and keep spending at a level that reduces the budget deficit or attains balance or even a surplus.

On the political downside, a recessionary economy pushes up the aggregate costs of government programs, hitting entitlement-based social welfare programs the hardest. As unemployment rises, so do the costs of providing cash benefits or services to the growing ranks of the needy. Rising unemployment also reduces personal income, resulting in lower tax revenues. Those very conditions, in turn, can affect fiscal policy, prompting policymakers, perhaps, to increase government spending as a fiscal policy tool to raise aggregate demand and reduce unemployment.

As we shall soon see, both downward swings in the business cycle and conscious policy choice contributed to the large budget deficits of the 1980s and early 1990s. In contrast, most large changes in the federal deficit and debt before the 1980s were a product of the business cycle. In the 1980s, the Reagan policy agenda and inflation-fighting actions of the Volcker-led Federal Reserve combined to set the deficit on its upward spiral.

The Volcker and Reagan Legacies

As was discussed more fully in Chapter 2, inflation appeared to be out of control in the closing months of 1979. President Jimmy Carter, facing reelection with slumping popularity, vacillated in his response to the problem. He could have fashioned an aggressive fiscal policy designed to dampen demand, but that would have further driven unemployment up. After sending Congress a 1980 fiscal year budget calling for restrained spending, Carter reversed course later in the year and advocated a moderate package of fiscal stimulus. With the election nearing, Paul Volcker, the recently appointed Federal Reserve chairman, and his fellow board members awaited the election's outcome before weighing in with corrective monetary policy. After the election of Ronald Reagan and big Republican gains in Congress, the political path was clear for the Federal Reserve to clamp down on the money supply and drive up interest rates, launching a battle against inflation with which the new president was clearly sympathetic. Both the prime rate and the rate on short-term business credit rose above 20 percent in 1981, that is, when credit was available at all.[5] In response, unemployment rose to double-digit, post-Depression highs, gathering momentum that surprised both the Fed and the Reagan administration. A sharp decline in inflation quickly followed. By 1982, the inflation rate had dropped to just above 6 percent, then fell below 4 percent in the next year. Recovery was underway; inflation had been beaten, and employment was starting to grow once again.

As expected, the recession lowered federal revenues and increased federal outlays. Revenues remained essentially flat between 1981 and 1982, and actually declined from 1982 to 1983. Outlays rose by 16 percent between 1981 and 1983 alone, generating a deficit topping $207.8 billion by the end of the 1983 fiscal year.[6]

The economic growth that began in 1983 strengthened in 1984, as real GDP grew by a staggering 7 percent from a solid 4 percent gain the year before—both years in sharp contrast to a real decline of 2.1 percent in 1982. Real GDP continued to grow steadily at an average annual rate of 3.4 percent during the following five years, before flattening out in 1990 and then dropping in 1991, the victim of yet another recession.[7] This one, however, could primarily be attributed to the business cycle, being far less a product of policy choice than was the recession of the early 1980s.

With the economy's strong performance between 1983 and 1989, a period Robert Bartley refers to as the seven fat years,[8] one could have reasonably expected to see the federal budget deficit decline significantly and the national debt shrink. Yet that did not happen. As Table 3.1 shows, the deficit actually rose in current dollars between 1983 and 1986, the years of steepest economic growth. It fell the following year, then leveled out through the remainder of the decade.

Why didn't America's economic growth cut into the deficit more sharply? The answer lies in policy choice. True to his campaign promises, Reagan championed major income tax relief and large increases in defense spending. Congress followed his lead in these areas, for the most part. The Economic Recovery Tax Act of 1981, passed during Reagan's first year in office, cut income tax rates across the board by 25 percent. And although Congress subsequently enacted a dozen tax increases between the 1982 and 1990 fiscal years, largely through increased Social Security taxes, motor fuel taxes, and other nonincome taxes, those increases were not large enough to offset the amount of revenue lost due to the 1981 rate reductions.[9]

At the same time that Reagan set out to reduce the income tax bite, he also sought to return real-dollar defense spending to its 1970 level. Reagan believed that defense spending's purchasing power had dropped during the 1970s to a dangerous low, even though it began a modest climb in the late Carter years. For Reagan, the Soviet Union remained a threat that could only be countered by military

TABLE 3.6   Changing National Defense Spending: Selected Years, 1965–2002

Fiscal Year	Constant Dollars (FY 1992) (in $ billions)	As Percentage of Outlays
1965	250.8	43.2
1970	316.3	41.9
1975	227.0	26.4
1980	230.5	22.8
1985	306.6	26.7
1988	334.5	27.3
1990	325.5	24.0
1995	258.2	18.0
1998	238.1	16.4
2002e	239.6	16.1

e = Estimate.
SOURCE: U.S. Office of Management and Budget, *The Budget of the United States Government*, FY 2000, *Historical Tables*, Tables 8.2 and 8.3.

strength, and he saw America's military capability falling short of the mark—in military personnel, equipment, and weapons development. A turnaround would be costly, and Reagan called for budget increases of 5 to 6 percent in excess of inflation. Here, again, Congress complied, at least through the 1986 fiscal year, as constant-dollar defense spending grew by 40 percent between 1980 and 1986. Constant-dollar defense spending flattened out for the remainder of the decade, although defense spending's share of total federal spending actually fell during the last two years of Reagan's second term and continued to do so during the Bush administration. That slide accelerated during the 1990s following the breakup of the Soviet Union and the thawing of cold war tensions in Eastern Europe (see Table 3.6).

To offset the added costs associated with net tax cuts and defense buildup, Reagan sought to decrease domestic spending. Here he realized mixed success. As Table 3.7 shows, discretionary domestic spending declined in both constant dollars and as a share of outlays during Reagan's presidency, although the rate of decline slowed during his second term. In contrast, constant-dollar, means-tested entitlement spending rose during all of his administration, yet constituted a fairly consistent share of federal outlays over that period. Its relative share would have been larger had net interest not increased its share as starkly as it did during the Reagan years.

Since the growth of defense and entitlement spending outstripped inflation, and reductions in domestic discretionary spending were insufficient to offset any more than a small part of those spending increases, spending pressures alone were enough to produce a rising budget deficit. Add to the mix revenue loss from net tax cuts, and the ingredients were in place for mounting deficits, that is, unless economic growth would have generated sufficient other revenue gain to replace the foregone revenue and cover the costs of higher spending. That did not happen, despite supply-siders' most fervent hopes. Revenues did rise with economic recovery

T A B L E 3 . 7   Changing Domestic Spending: Selected Years,
1965–2002

| | *Discretionary Spending* | | *Means-Tested Entitlement and Spending* | |
Fiscal Year	Constant Dollars (FY 1992)	Percentage of Outlays	Constant Dollars (FY 1992)	Percentage of Outlays
1965	97.7	18.7	21.2	4.4
1970	122.8	17.5	34.7	5.2
1975	156.6	18.7	65.8	7.7
1980	219.9	21.8	78.2	7.6
1985	185.9	15.3	82.1	6.6
1988	183.0	14.8	91.6	7.2
1990	194.7	14.5	101.8	7.5
1995	231.3	16.6	168.3	12.0
1998	229.7	16.1	175.5	12.1
2002e	248.5	16.9	204.5	14.0

e = Estimate.
SOURCE: U.S. Office of Management and Budget, *Budget of the United States Government*, FY *2000, Historical Tables*, Tables 8.2 and 8.3.

and growth, but not enough to finance spending increases *and* fill the revenue hole created by the deep income tax cut of 1981.

The recession of 1990 made matters worse, producing a deficit of $290 billion by the end of the 1992 fiscal year, the deficit's high point in current dollars. (The deficit was higher at the end of the 1982 fiscal year as a percentage of the GDP.) It took a sizable 1993 deficit-reduction package, which contained both tax increases and spending cuts that did not rely on gimmicks, to begin to turn the budget picture around. An improving economy, leading to solid growth after mid-decade, brought the deficit steadily down. With Congress approving further, but more modest, deficit-reduction legislation in 1997, and with economic growth exceeding earlier expectations, the deficit turned into surplus at the end of the 1998 fiscal year, as previously noted.

But does that mean that Americans can expect their national government to be deficit-free for the foreseeable future? Well, history shows that it is unlikely the economy can escape recession. Even if moderate economic growth with low inflation can be sustained, despite the danger signs emanating from East Asia as the century nears an end, there are those who worry about the fiscal pressures that will accompany the retirement of the successive waves of "baby boomers" that can be expected starting in 2010.

Unless Congress makes changes to the Social Security and Medicare programs, any respite from budget deficits that might well be enjoyed in the early years of the twenty-first century will likely be short-lived. If benefits are not reduced and costs controlled in these entitlement programs, dedicated revenues will be inadequate to finance the expected increased expenditures. As the gap grows, and it will without legislative change, so will deficit pressures on the budget. If, however, Congress elects not to reduce benefits and cut costs, then employers and younger workers, through increased payroll taxes, will have to pay the higher bills that can certainly be expected. Yet if that prospect appears too burdensome, Congress could shift some of the burden to general-purpose taxation; but it still is workers, not retirees, who disproportionately pay those taxes. Either way, that increased taxation can be expected to dampen aggregate demand and restrain national economic growth. Neither the prospect of renewed budget deficits and their contribution to national debt, nor that of inhibited economic growth, is attractive to policymakers and citizens alike.

WHY WORRY ABOUT DEFICITS AND DEBT?

The effects of a slumping economy are obvious, but why worry about deficits and debt? That question evokes considerable debate and argument. Popular opinion pieces in magazines and newspapers typically paint both as serious problems that the American public should be greatly concerned about. In comparison, economists differ on the extent to which they view deficits and debt as problematical. This section reviews and evaluates the most widely held concerns, ranging from the unduly alarmist to those having the most substantive merit.

America's Path Toward Insolvency

Some people worry that a long string of budget deficits and the need to finance them through debt accumulation will lead the federal government on a path toward fiscal insolvency. They reason that the rising burden of deficit finance will so strain the government's ability to honor its interest and principal repayment obligations that investors, both domestic and foreign, will shy away from acquiring Treasury securities, threatening the U.S. government's ability to raise the capital it needs to make fiscal ends meet. However, that concern is more visceral than substantively grounded.

Since America's debt is denominated in dollars, any fear that the federal government would default on its obligations is groundless. As a last resort, the Federal Reserve could "monetize" the debt by selling Treasury bonds to the public, using the proceeds to finance the debt. Any reluctance to invest in U.S. securities would be offset by the higher rates of return that buyers could expect from the market. Moreover, prospective buyers recognize that the full faith and credit of the U.S. government stands behind its obligations, including its ability to raise tax revenue, in addition to its ability to create money. Thus concerns about insolvency are misplaced, although they make for good rhetoric.

Net Interest's Budgetary Squeeze

Net interest's claim on federal spending skyrocketed during the 1980s and continued largely unchecked for much of the 1990s, until deficit reduction and subsequent budget surpluses late in the decade drove down its share. Future surpluses would drop its claim even further. Although that apparent turnaround is comforting to those who have watched net interest take over 15 percent of federal spending, projected annual interest payments still in excess of $200 billion by the twentieth century's end provide little solace to most Americans.

Should we be concerned? Yes, we should, but not because interest obligations are pushing the country to the brink of bankruptcy. We should be concerned, instead, because interest payments on the debt represent foregone opportunity. The Treasury, through the Federal Reserve's sale of securities, has already captured the funds it needs to cover the spending commitments it has already made. Now it is simply paying off that indebtedness. It gets nothing new for that spending. In fact, that spending squeezes other potential spending, since interest payments exert a priority claim on federal budgeting. To the extent that 15 percent or so of federal budgetary outlays go to pay interest on the debt, they are not available for other important purposes, such as reducing the deficit or investing in America's physical and human infrastructure. Although it is true that borrowing may have provided the wherewithal to make those investments in prior years, by financing spending that outstripped available revenues, the interest obligation incurred by that borrowing crowds out current spending. Reduced borrowing is the only way to pare down net interest's share of budgeted outlays.

Mortgaging Our Children's Future

Critics point to high interest obligations as mortgaging our children's future. As their argument goes, America's budgetmakers, by regularly allowing spending to exceed revenues, have been throwing a continuous party and leaving the bill for future generations to pay. Although it is true that net interest's future claims will fall with a balanced budget, they would still constitute a sizable share of federal spending—an obligation that will extend well into the future. If the economy does not perform as well as projected, and a slowdown pushes the federal budget back into deficit, interest obligations will again rise rather than fall.

It is true that future taxpayers will annually have to foot the interest bill. Many of them, however, will also receive those interest payments. Since almost two-thirds of the debt held outside the federal government is owned by Americans, the vast majority of interest paid augments their income. Even part of the interest income paid to foreign institutions and individuals makes its way back into the U.S. economy in the form of investments or the purchase of American goods and services, thereby increasing national income.

Obviously, not all who contribute their taxes to pay interest on the debt receive interest income in return. Some redistribution of income does occur. Yet even though upper-income individuals disproportionately receive that interest income, while all taxpayers pay the bill, many middle- and lower-income taxpayers benefit via pension funds, insurance, and small savings bond holdings.[10] Moreover, those at the lowest end of the income spectrum pay no federal income taxes at all, and therefore incur no burden.

Crowding Out Credit

The federal government competes with private interests in credit markets. Many economists worry that government borrowing will crowd out or displace private borrowing. Their thesis is that deficit spending adds a government demand for credit to an existing private demand, thus forcing up the interest rates that both government and private interests must pay. In that competition for scarce savings, government has the advantage. Not only must it borrow to fill the gap between revenues and expenditures, but it has the fiscal and monetary resources to meet the higher interest costs. The private sector, in contrast, is more likely to withdraw from the market, awaiting more favorable conditions.

Practice, however, failed to follow theory during the deficit's big run in the 1980s and early 1990s. No observable crowding out occurred. Interest rates fell after 1982, not rose, even though *real* interest rates remained high. The key factor was not the extent of borrowing by the federal government, but the monetary policy employed by the Federal Reserve. Investment demand strengthened with post-recessionary recovery, and interest rates proved acceptable enough to attract investors into domestic capital markets, despite competition from the federal government. At the same time, high federal budget deficits reduced national savings, which accompanied a growing decline in the saving of households. These parallel forces alone could have been expected to push interest rates up, had not the United States had access to foreign savings. Foreign savings filled the gap between available U.S. national savings and investment demand, as the United States sold increasingly large quantities of its assets to foreigners, thus moderating what would have been much stronger upward pressure on interest rates.[11]

The Deficit, National Saving, and America's Reliance on Foreign Capital

The federal government's borrowing to finance deficit spending drains off part of national savings that would otherwise be available to support domestic investment. National saving is the product of both private and government saving. But when the federal government runs a deficit, it dissaves rather than saves. The federal government's dissaving has been only marginally offset by budget surpluses existing at the state and local levels. The large aggregate deficits experienced in the 1980s and early 1990s have taken a big bite out of national savings. Benjamin Friedman shows that the federal government's borrowing in the 1980s absorbed an amount equal to nearly three-fourths of all net saving done by individuals and businesses in this country (i.e., the percentage of the nation's income that individuals and businesses manage to save after spending for consumption and the replacement of physical assets that reach their useful lives).[12] Friedman likens that outcome to a society eating its seed corn instead of planting it. Once done, its people have no recourse but to turn to other societies for some of theirs.

National saving as a percentage of gross national product (GNP) plunged during the 1980s and early 1990s, falling from 20.7 percent in 1981 to 14.4 percent in 1993. From that low, it recovered to push above 17 percent in 1997—a product of deficit reduction (see Figure 3.1). Personal saving continued its downward slide.

As national saving declined, the United States turned to the savings of foreigners to finance its investments, increasing their net claims on American assets. Fortunately for the United States, the higher saving rates of most other industrial nations put them in a favorable position to pick up the slack. And the U.S. economy's reasonably strong fundamentals provided an attractive lure for foreign capital. Since

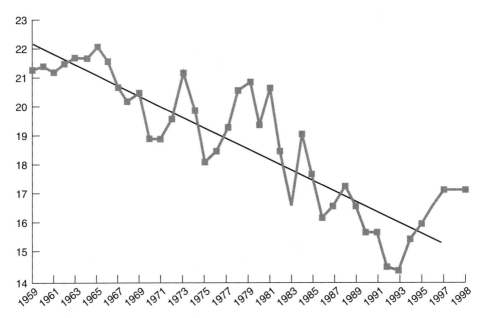

FIGURE 3.1 National Saving as a Percentage of the Gross National Product, 1959–1998

SOURCE: *Economic Report of the President*, February 1999, 315.

the flip side of saving is spending, it should not be surprising that aggregate spending grew faster than national income; and that is significant because the only way for an economy to spend more than it earns is to import more than its exports, to run a trade deficit. Thus, as Paul Krugman reminds us, "It was inevitable that the United States would develop a large trade deficit."[13] Figure 3.2 illustrates the relationship among domestic saving, domestic investment, and America's current (international) accounts deficit as a percentage of the economy's output.

It is readily apparent that a key to improving America's current account deficit, the broadest statement of the trade deficit, is to increase national saving. By increasing its rate of saving, the United States becomes less dependent on foreign capital to finance its investment. As saving grows as a percentage of income, the trick becomes to switch the relatively reduced spending from imported goods to American-made products. Yet American consumer behavior overall shows few signs of altering its appetite or tastes.

The surest way, therefore, to reduce America's trade deficit is to increase its rate of saving. And the surest way to do that over time is to eliminate the budget deficit. Of course, the federal government could attempt to use policy inducements, such as tax deductions and credits, to encourage its citizens to save more of their income, but prior attempts have fallen far short of expectations. Witness the experience of investors with individual retirement accounts (IRAs) in the 1980s. Ample evidence shows that a large proportion of investors merely moved money from less favorably treated investment vehicles into IRAs, substituting within the savings pool rather than augmenting it.[14]

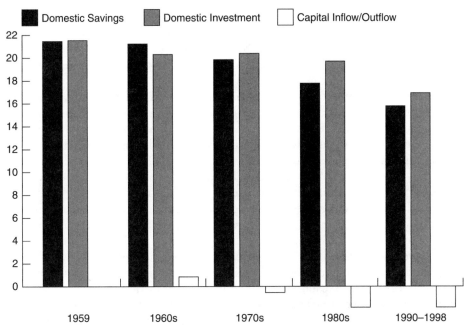

F I G U R E   3 . 2   U.S. Saving and Investment as a Percentage of the GDP,
1959–1998

SOURCE: *Economic Report of the President*, February 1999, 364–365.

THE BENIGN SIDE OF DEFICITS AND THE DEBT

Not all economists and critical observers worry that much about deficits and debt. Some see them as far less problematical than do those in the mainstream, while others view deficits and debt, within limits, to be functional rather than dysfunctional for the economy. Those in the first camp argue that deficits and debt look different when put in the proper perspective, or that their magnitude is far less ominous when they are measured differently. Those in the second, putting on their Keynesian spectacles, emphasize the contribution of deficits to economic growth, focusing on what they add to aggregate demand. This section explores both schools of thought.

One way of putting deficits and the debt into perspective is to look at them in relation to the size of the economy. A large economy that generates a sizable national income has more room to run deficits and incur debt than does a much smaller economy. A rapidly growing economy is better positioned to take on rising deficit and debt levels than is a static or declining economy. One way of putting deficits and debt in perspective is to look at them as a percentage of the GDP. A declining percentage, for example, indicates that the deficit or the debt is placing a lessening burden on an economy's ability to support it, as measured by its economic output and the national income generated by it. These ratios of deficit and debt to the GDP provide a measure of whether the relative burden of each is increasing, decreasing, or remaining about the same.

Beyond viewing deficits and debt in relation to the size of the economy and its relative growth, several prominent economists suggest that we should rethink the way in which the deficit, and its contribution to debt, is measured. Robert Eisner, a past president of the American Economics Association, argues that several adjustments should be made to the gross deficit.

The first adjustment takes into account the surpluses or deficits of state and local governments in the United States. Since laws require nearly all state and local governments to balance their budgets, both tend to underestimate revenues and build some leeway into budgeted expenditures, commonly leading to year-end surpluses. State and local budget surpluses can either offset a federal budget deficit when that deficit exceeds their aggregate level, or they can contribute to a national budget surplus. Eisner argues that if we are interested in the total impact of government on the economy, it makes the most sense to figure in the year-end conditions of state and local governments, together with that of the federal government.[15]

The second adjustment separates out the amount of federal outlays devoted to capital investment, treating them the way state and local governments budget and account for them, to arrive at the federal equivalent of state and local government operating budget balances. Recall that state and local governments enact capital budgets, distinct from their operating budgets, which provide them the authority to borrow up to approved levels to finance capital projects. The federal government has no such discretion. Capital expenditures are financed by operating revenues just as are all other expenditures. Yet it makes good economic sense to finance those projects using debt and requiring future users to contribute to debt retirement. This adjustment, then, relieves the federal operating budget from meeting the costs of capital investment.

The third adjustment corrects for the decrease in the real value of the debt due to inflation, on which a reduced amount of interest must be paid. Subtracting real interest savings, Eisner refers to this adjustment as an "inflation tax," one he argues that is just as real in its impact on people's behavior as a revenue-generating tax increase.[16]

Although Eisner's colleagues such as Robert Heilbroner and Peter Bernstein[17] embrace these adjustments, the vast majority of economists prefer the traditional way of measuring the deficit. Paul Krugman is one of them. The deficit, for Krugman, is no statistical illusion. He is not interested in making the deficit appear less imposing. For him, the important fact is that the borrowing occasioned by deficits contributes to a decline in national savings and helps to cause a trade deficit.[18]

SHOULD THE FEDERAL GOVERNMENT DO WHATEVER IS NECESSARY TO BALANCE THE BUDGET?

Because deficits sap national savings, contribute to trade deficits, and create interest obligations that squeeze other would-be spending, should the president and Congress do whatever is necessary to balance the budget? While there are many who maintain that they should, others are far less sanguine about the idea. Critics voice both political and economic concerns.

On the political side, detractors worry that a political climate which greatly constrains tax increases, or which rewards tax cuts, will prompt policymakers to reach a balanced budget exclusively through spending cuts. Such a tack, critics argue, plays right into the hands of those who want to use deficit reduction as a means of reducing the size of the federal government. For them, the primary problem is big government, not the economic consequences of the deficit. In contrast, those who are concerned about following the path of spending cuts toward budget balance point out the programmatic implications of budget cuts—reductions that can erode government's ability to provide assistance to the needy, support education and training, modernize the highway system, and protect the environment. Here is where critics of balancing the budget connect the political and the economic. They remind us that all spending is not the same. Some government spending improves and expands our nation's physical infrastructure; other spending advances human capital. Broad-based spending cuts can jeopardize these forms of public investment. Although it is true that savings finance investment, so too can public borrowing; and borrowing that improves and expands infrastructure can also help to improve productivity.[19] Some evidence exists that nonmilitary *public* investment contributes more to productivity than does private investment.[20]

Of course, the most commonly voiced reservation about reaching a balanced budget concerns its effects on aggregate demand. Deficit spending adds to aggregate demand—demand for goods and services that will raise national output as long as some slack exists in the economy. Take that increment of demand away, and economic growth can suffer. As Robert Eisner is fond of saying, "The public deficit is the private sector's surplus."[21] Eliminate the public deficit, and you will wipe out the private sector's surplus, potentially threatening prosperity.

To minimize this dampening effect and still make progress toward reducing the deficit's contribution to debt, some critics of a balanced budget suggest that the president and Congress need only keep the deficit's annual contribution to debt below the rate of real economic growth, and thereby reduce debt as a percentage of the GDP over time. Yet until the budget is balanced, the fact is that debt continues to build, squeezing national savings and requiring foreign capital to fill the gap, even though the debt takes a declining share of national income.[22]

Constitutionally Requiring a Balanced Budget

With a sound economy growing America out of its budget deficit in the late 1990s, calls for amending the U.S. Constitution to require a balanced budget have subsided after fifteen years of nearly continuous legislative initiatives and congressional debate. The most recent attempt failed in 1997, as the Senate came up one vote short of the two-thirds majority required for passage. President Clinton's energetic last-minute lobbying proved to be the deciding factor in the amendment's defeat, despite the efforts of Senate Majority Leader Trent Lott (R-Miss.), who actively used the prerogatives of his office in hopes of eking out a narrow victory. The legislation required the budget to be balanced starting in 2002 or two years after the amendment's ratification by the states, unless three-fifths of both chambers vote to allow a deficit in a given year. The bill also provided that deficits could be legally incurred in times of war or serious military threats. The amendment's defeat marked the sixth time since the first election of Ronald Reagan as president that a proposed constitutional amendment made it to the floor and was voted down.

From the vantage point of the late 1990s, a constitutionally required balanced budget seems superfluous, given the policy choices and economic forces that have led to a budget surplus. But, as is discussed in the following section, budget surpluses may well prove to be transitory. Deficit pressures will likely reappear early in the second decade of the coming century and gain strength in the decades to follow. A massive wave of retirees will put overwhelming pressure on the expenditure side of the budget in the absence of legislated changes to the Social Security and Medicare programs. That pressure could once again turn Congress's attention back to a consideration of mechanisms designed to compel a balanced budget.

Public opinion polls indicate that the American public has consistently supported requiring budget balance by constitutional amendment. Most people support the concept of the federal government living within its means, even though they, as individuals, may resort to deficit finance in their own lives. Support for balanced budget amendment dissipates, however, when pollsters tell citizens that cuts in Social Security, Medicaid, and education might be required. In one poll conducted for CBS News and the *New York Times,* support fell from 80 percent to 30 percent when poll designers attached that condition.[23]

WHAT SHOULD BE DONE WITH ANY SURPLUSES?

In contemplating surpluses continuing into the twenty-first century, both policy-makers and opinion leaders are positioning themselves on how they should be used. The voiced options are many: buy back debt, resulting in increased national savings; finance tax cuts; support expanded spending in the near term, especially investments in infrastructure; or save surplus revenues to help pay the rising entitlement costs that are certain to accompany the massive baby-boomer retirements. Republicans, particularly conservatives, tend to opt first for tax cuts, seizing the opportunity to further transfer public resources back into private hands. Retiring debt appears to be their second choice. Democrats lean more toward using surplus revenues to make infrastructural investments, giving investments in human capital top priority. Few politicians seem willing to set aside surpluses to stem a problem with Social Security that is over a decade away. Instead, they appear content to rely on commissions to study the problem and recommend what should be done some time in the future. In the meantime, economic signs are favorable. Baby-boomers in the late 1990s are at or near the height of their earning power, maximizing tax revenues, while a much smaller Depression-era generation is retiring. Welfare reform has set public assistance spending on a downward slope.

Yet historians may come to look at the turn of the century as the calm before the storm. Social Security trustees project that as early as 2013, when baby-boomers will be retiring en masse, the thirty-year string of positive balances in the Social Security Trust Fund will turn negative. By 2030, they project a staggering annual cash deficit of $766 billion if no changes are made to contribution and benefit levels. If Medicare hospital insurance is included, and it too continues under current law, the combined cash deficit will reach an almost unbelievable $1.7 trillion.[24] Such is the power of demography. Demographers estimate that there will be only two contributors to Social Security for every recipient in 2030. That compares to a ratio of 3.3 to 1 in 1997.[25] If policymakers wait until Social Security revenues begin to fall short of expenditures, the demographics of aging will rapidly widen that fiscal gap, necessitating large and growing tax increases in the absence of any changes in benefit schedules—rate increases that could approach 50 percent.[26]

Not all scholars agree with this dark scenario. Jerry Mashaw and Ted Marmor, two distinguished health policy researchers from Yale University, see "the great Social Security scare" as overblown. Although they recognize it as a serious policy problem that belongs on the national agenda, they view it as one requiring "prudent adjustment, but not major revision."[27] They also criticize the financial industry for whipping up hysteria and promoting the message that only radical reform can repair the broken system, a reform that industry leaders and lobbyists want centered around privatization. Privatizing part or all of Social Security would prove to be a boon for mutual funds and other equity securities.

For Mashaw and Marmor, the real issues of Social Security reform involve political choice, not technical repair work. The key political question, as they see it, is whether Americans want a society that insures all workers and their families against the dual risks of dying too young and outliving their private retirement savings, or whether they want a society that merely mandates savings and investment for retirement, while leaving the security of workers and their families to be determined by their choices in financial markets. Mashaw and Marmor believe that most Americans want the former, and argue that collective social insurance is the only sound way to guarantee it. They view the structure of the present system of Social Security as sound, but also acknowledge the need to strengthen its financial foundation. However, they see graduated measures as doing the job, including extending Social Security coverage to currently excluded state and local employees, increasing the length of the computation period for workers' average earnings from 35 to 38 years, revising the consumer price index to lower the cost of inflationary adjustments, and allowing the Social Security Administration, not beneficiaries themselves, to move a portion (less than half) of trust funds from Treasury securities into equity investments.[28] Depending on yields, future modest increases in the Social Security tax rate might be necessary to close any remaining gap between contributions and benefits. Yet those required increases should be far less than the amounts estimated in the gloomier forecasts.

Irrespective of which scenario proves to be correct, it is clear that Social Security will have to be squarely on the national policy agenda in the early part of the twenty-first century, regardless of the performance of the economy. A strongly growing economy, generating solid growth in personal income, will reduce the magnitude of the problem but not avert it, by any means. It seems clear from the vantage point of the end of the twentieth century that without reform of Social Security and Medicare, whatever budget surpluses emerge in the near term will disappear when the baby-boom generation retires in large numbers. Unless Congress puts Social Security and Medicare on a sound financial footing, deficit reduction will surely return to center stage of American politics.

THE POLITICAL IMPLICATIONS OF SURPLUSES

Notwithstanding the specter of big, demographically driven future deficits, the near-term likelihood of a string of balanced budgets or budget surpluses has political implications for national budgetary policymakers. The specter of large deficits hung over national policymakers' heads for nearly two decades. Although a large part of the big deficits of the 1980s was the result of policy choice, once produced, the deficits conditioned budgetary decision making. Widespread opposition to large deficits created a political climate unconducive to program expansion or new program development. Congress's imposition of lids on discretionary spending and PAYGO[29] restrictions on entitlement spending slowed the growth rate of federal spending during the 1990s. With the federal budget in balance or in surplus, a significant political constraint on spending will be removed. In addition, Congress might well be sorely tempted to weaken or remove its restrictions on spending increases, thus eliminating institutionalized roadblocks to accelerating spending. It will need to decide how to order its calendar and priorities without its perennial preoccupation with the deficit.

Balanced budgets could also affect partisan politics, particularly the partisan positioning of the Republican party on the national scene. Deficit reduction gave Republicans, both in and out of Congress, a central issue to rally around. They were able to present themselves as the champions of spending cuts on the road to a balanced budget while labeling Democrats, who controlled Congress during the deficit's rise, as taxers and spenders. Coupled with the demise of the cold war, a traditional focal point of Republican partisan posturing, Republicans may find themselves searching for defining political issues.[30] We can expect to find pressure mounting from the Republican right for the party to turn more toward moral issues as its distinguishing mantle. Factionalism could well be on the rise. Should the economy continue to perform well, however—producing moderate to strong growth with low inflation—both parties in Congress may elect to keep a low policy profile and bask in the glow of prosperity.

That tack might work effectively for congressional incumbents, but it would not seem to advantage the Republican challenger for the presidency in 2000. If the electorate is of the mood to reward incumbents for the country's economic health, that could tend to help the Democratic nominee, especially if that person had close ties with the Clinton presidency.

Sound economic performance has greatly helped to drive out the deficit and make progress toward debt reduction, but, as was illustrated in Chapter 1, the fruits of that success have not been widely shared. That reality could provide a wedge issue for Democrats, as they point to tax and international trade policy as the culprits that need fixing. Yet both can be double-edged swords, so to speak. Congressional Democrats joined their Republican colleagues in overwhelmingly supporting the 1997 tax cuts, including significant reductions in the capital gains tax. Moreover, opinion leaders and voters view the president as the key player shaping America's trade policy. It thus becomes difficult for Democrats to carp on perceived weaknesses in advancing the U.S. interests in international trade without casting a shadow on Democratic leadership.

Democrats are more likely than Republicans to be squeezed by the challenge of how to keep America deficit free and make continued progress in reducing the national debt while facing constituent demands for increased spending. With the deficit temporarily relegated to the status of a historical problem, America's spending shield has been penetrated. We can expect spending pressures to intensify. If that occurs, Republicans could cast themselves as the party of budget balance preservation and debt reduction, once again countering the stereotypical tax-and-spend Democrats. At the same time, Republicans' inclination to cut taxes further and reform the tax system could lead to revenue shortfalls which, in turn, could contribute to future deficits, thereby calling into question their commitment to balanced budgets and debt reduction. Overall, though, the near-term fiscal future looks relatively settled, save uncertainties associated with East Asia. Massive spending pressures will break that relative calm well into the twenty-first century's second decade, unless Congress makes changes to the Social Security and Medicare programs. Retention of the existing tax effort and benefit schedule, coupled with consecutive waves of retirees, will surely energize dark fiscal storm clouds on the horizon.

NOTES

1. This refers to the unified-budget deficit, which includes the relationship between receipts and outlays in the federal trust funds, such as the Social Security and Highway trust funds. Positive aggregate trust fund balances reduce what, in their absence, would be even bigger budget deficits—referred to as the federal fund deficit. The public debate has traditionally centered around the unified-budget deficit. More will be said about this distinction and its implications in Chapters 6 and 7.

2. U.S. Office of Management and Budget, *The Budget of the United States Government, FY 2000, Historical Tables*, Table 7.1, 110–111.

3. *The Budget of the United States Government, FY 2000, Analytical Perspectives*, 270. Calculated as a percentage of the debt held outside the federal government, excluding debt held by the Federal Reserve.

4. *The Budget of the United States Government, FY 2000, Historical Tables*, Table 7.1, 110–111.

5. Robert Heilbroner and Peter Bernstein, *The Debt and the Deficit* (New York: W.W. Norton & Co., 1989), 22–23.

6. *The Budget of the United States Government, FY 2000, Historical Tables*, Table 1.1, 19–20.

7. Council of Economic Advisors, *Economic Report of the President*, February 1999, 331.

8. Robert L. Bartley, *The Seven Fat Years and How to Do It Again* (New York: The Free Press, 1992).

9. Allen Schick, *The Federal Budget: Politics, Policy, Process* (Washington, DC: The Brookings Institution, 1995), 4–6.

10. Robert Eisner, *The Misunderstood Economy: What Counts and How to Count It* (Boston: Harvard Business School Press, 1994), 101.

11. Paul Krugman, *The Age of Diminished Expectations* (Cambridge, MA: The MIT Press, 1994), 51–52.

12. Benjamin M. Friedman, "U.S. Fiscal Policy in the 1980s: Consequences of Large Budget Deficits at Full Employment," in *Debt and the Twin Deficits Debate*, ed. James M. Rock (Mountain View, CA: Mayfield Publishing Co., 1991), 149.

13. Paul Krugman, *The Age of Diminished Expectations*, 54.

14. Benjamin M. Friedman, "U.S. Fiscal Policy in the 1980s: Consequences of Large Budget Deficits at Full Employment," 163–164; Robert Eisner, *The Misunderstood Economy: What Counts and How to Count It*, 41.

15. Robert Eisner, "Deficits for Us and Our Grandchildren," in *Debt and the Twin Deficits Debate*, ed. James M. Rock, 82.

16. Ibid.

17. Robert Heilbroner and Peter Bernstein, *The Debt and the Deficit*, 71–81.

18. Paul Krugman, *The Age of Diminished Expectations*, 91–93.

19. Robert Eisner, *The Misunderstood Economy: What Counts and How to Count It*, 196–199.

20. David Alan Aschauer, "Is Public Expenditure Productive," *Journal of Monetary Economics* 23 (March 1989), 177–200; Robert Eisner, "Extended Measures of National Income and Product Account," *Journal of Economic Literature* 26 (December 1988), 1611–1684.

21. Robert Eisner, "Deficits for Us and Our Grandchildren," 85.

22. Karen M. Paget, "The Balanced Budget Trap," *The American Prospect* 29 (December 1996), 21–29.

23. Reported in *Congressional Quarterly Weekly Report* 53, no. 2 (January 14, 1995), 144.

24. Peter G. Peterson, "Will America Grow Up Before It Grows Old?, *The Atlantic Monthly* 277 (May 1996), 55–86; Joseph F. Quinn and Oliva S. Mitchell, "Social Security on the Table," *The American Prospect* 26 (May-June 1996), 76–81.

25. Joseph F. Quinn and Oliva S. Mitchell, "Social Security on the Table," 77.

26. Sam Beard, "Is There a Social Security Crisis?" *The American Prospect* 30 (January-February 1997), 17.

27. Jerry L. Mashaw and Theodore R. Marmor, The Great Social Security Scare," *The American Prospect* 29 (Novermber-December 1996), 30.

28. Ibid., 31.

29. PAYGO provisions require Congress to pay for new entitlement authorization by either legislated tax increases or offsetting reductions in other existing entitlements.

30. Ronald D. Elving and Andrew Taylor, "A Balanced-Budget Deal Won, A Defining Issue Lost," *Congressional Quarterly Weekly Report* 55, no. 31 (August 2, 1997), 1831–1836.

CHAPTER 4

America and the International Political Economy

R iding the tide of eight years of sustained growth, Americans found their economy in stellar shape as the 1998 calendar year began. Inflation was at a 30-year low, employment reached a record high, and unemployment had fallen to its lowest level since 1970. And that strong economic performance pointed to a balanced federal budget at fiscal year's end. Economic optimists abounded. Federal Reserve Chairman Alan Greenspan had just recently raised the prospect of America embarking on a "New Economy," in which both low inflation and high employment can accompany productivity-led economic growth.[1] Mortimer Zuckerman, Chairman and Editor-in-Chief of *U.S. News and World Report,* placed the contemporary economic record above that of the post–World War II German and Japanese economic "miracles." Summing up his enthusiastic appraisal, Zuckerman noted that "Everything that should be up is up—GDP, capital spending, incomes, the stock market, employment, exports, consumer and business confidence. Everything that should be down is down—unemployment, inflation, and interest rates."[2] Based on what he saw as strong structural fundamentals in the U.S. economy, particularly America's cutting-edge productive use of computer-based technology and its dominance in emerging knowledge industries, along with corporate America's demonstrated willingness to restructure and downsize its operations, Zuckerman was quick to project that the coming century will go down in history as "a second American century."

Others questioned the sustainability of the United States' good economic fortunes. Some pointed to the inevitability of a downturn in the business cycle—whether driven by restrictive governmental economic policies in response to rekindled inflation, or in response to dampening economic forces originating outside the

United States. MIT economist Paul Krugman saw either scenario as possible. Although he readily acknowledged America's record of economic success in the 1990s, Krugman pointed to serendipitous "special and temporary factors" that allowed the U.S. economy to grow with little inflation, most important among them a squeeze on worker benefits, mainly due to the widespread switch to managed health care, and a strengthened dollar, reflective of the economic strength at home and the economic disarray in most of Asia. Other factors, according to Krugman, included reluctance on the part of workers to demand wage increases in an era of downsizing, and the reluctance of employers to grant sizable increases in an environment of heightened competition.[3]

Although the Asian economic crisis helped to keep U.S. inflation in check, it also engendered concern that a broad-based Asian recession would significantly pull down economic growth in the United States. Faced with a plethora of speculative investments, a growing number of failed financial institutions and a near collapse of credit, greatly devalued currencies that render foreign debt repayment difficult to impossible, and depressed economic activity at home, many Asian leaders saw little room for optimism. Although Indonesia, Malaysia, Korea, and Thailand were hardest hit, no Asian nation remained immune. Policymakers fretted that China would be sorely tempted to devalue the yuan in order to remain competitive in exports with those nations that have seen the value of their currencies fall by between a third and 80 percent—an action that would further disstabilize financial markets.

Even Japan stood not far from the brink of financial crisis, having lent large sums of money to finance risky ventures in a number of Southeast Asian countries. Just as Asian political and industrial leaders looked to Japan to provide both transfusions of capital and demand for their countries' exports, the Japanese economy found itself in no position to extend such help. Experiencing continued sluggish economic growth, rising unemployment, weak consumer confidence, falling land prices and equity values, and a steady decline in the value of the yen, Japanese officials were preoccupied with how they could best get their own economic house in order. An improving Japanese economy would indeed benefit its Asian neighbors, by restoring demand for their products and potentially providing necessary infusions of capital from the world's biggest creditor nation. Yet Japanese policymakers demonstrated scant willingness to stimulate their economy through expansive fiscal policy. And with interest rates below 1 percent, not much more could be done with monetary policy.

By mid-year, several emerging Asian economies were in recession, with Indonesia, Malaysia, and Korea in the deepest troughs, but joined by the perennial economic powerhouse, Hong Kong. The Japanese economy, too, fell into recession, following eight years of sluggish growth. With the prospects for a swift reversal looking anything but bright, what are the implications for the U.S. economy? To answer this question, one needs to understand how the United States is connected to the rest of the world economically.

Business enterprises in the United States sell goods and services to individuals, corporations, and governments all around the world, just as our foreign counterparts purchase goods and services from U.S. providers. For example, we buy BMWs from Germany, shoes from China, and wine from France; and we sell Cray computers to

Japan, Boeing jet aircraft to Singapore, and wheat to Russia. Both U.S. corporations and individuals invest in the stocks and bonds of foreign companies, just as foreigners invest in U.S. companies. Some corporations may even gain financial control of foreign enterprises, or secure outright ownership of them (such as Sony's purchase of Columbia Pictures). Foreign governments buy U.S. Treasury securities, and the U.S. Department of the Treasury buys foreign currencies on the open market.

International economic relationships are clearest when we look at U.S. companies selling products made in the United States to buyers in foreign lands, or when U.S. consumers buy goods made overseas. They get far more complex, for example, when a U.S. company produces a product on foreign soil using materials imported from one or more other nations, and then transports that product back to the United States for sale. Of course, these relationships can exist in reverse, that is, when foreign-owned companies produce products in the United States for sale here or in other countries. Illustrations are easy to find: Toyota automobiles assembled in Kentucky by American workers, using a combination of American- and Japanese-manufactured components; jet aircraft manufactured by Boeing but employing parts and technological devices made by Mitsubishi and Fuji; and McDonalds hamburgers and french fries prepared by foreign workers in countries on nearly every contintent, using both domestic ingredients and those imported from the United States.

Just take a simple economic transaction and notice the complicated economic relationships inherent in it. Buy a new Subaru Legacy Outback automobile, assembled in Indiana, and create the following effects. Assuming that the purchase is made in the United States, the American-owned dealership profits from the sale; the salesman earns a commission; the sale contributes to a sales volume sufficient to keep demand at a level that justifies the retention or addition of workers in the assembly plant, as it does for top Japanese management in the plant. Similar benefits accrue to component suppliers in both Japan and in the United States. In addition, the money paid for the car ends up in a Japanese-owned bank account in the United States and becomes available to be loaned to American borrowers. Stockholders, both foreign and domestic, also benefit to the extent that this sale parallels enough others to keep the company acceptably profitable. The sale value of the automobile adds to the U.S. gross domestic product (GDP), even though it is the product of a foreign-owned corporation.

Nations are caught in a web of international economic relations. In a real sense, a foreign economy may rely on both domestic and international investors for its capital, on other nations for needed raw materials, and on the citizens of still other nations for consumer demand. Some national economies are more interdependent than others.

Table 4.1 compares the relative dependence of selected national economies on international trade. The U.S. economy is far less dependent on international trade than are the economies of most other nations. Consider the case of Taiwan, which is three times more dependent on international trade than is the United States. Japan's position toward the bottom of the list probably surprises most readers. Although Japan enjoys a healthy favorable trade balance, led by a large surplus in manufacturers, its economy is far more self-sufficient than is generally appreciated. Other than importing needed raw materials and agricultural foodstuffs, Japanese

TABLE 4.1   International Trade as a Component of National
Economies: Selected Countries, 1997

Country	International Trade as a Percentage of GDP	Exports as a Percentage of GDP	Imports as a Percentage of GDP
Taiwan	82.3	42.9	39.4
Canada	66.1	35.1	31.0
Korea	60.3	29.4	30.9
United Kingdom	52.2	25.1	27.1
Germany	44.7	24.1	20.6
China	36.2	20.3	15.9
Singapore	26.3	12.8	13.5
United States	24.9	11.9	13.0
Indonesia	22.3	12.1	10.2
Japan	16.0	8.7	7.3
Russia	4.7	3.1	1.6

SOURCE: U.S. Department of State: *Country Reports on Economic Policy and Trade Practice*, 1997.

firms tend not to import anything that they can make domestically. Russia's economy, in comparison, is even more self-sufficient of those listed, with imports comprising less than 2 percent of its GDP.

The U.S. economy has steadily become more reliant on international trade over the past three decades (see Table 4.2). Until 1969, U.S. exports and imports combined rarely amounted to more than one-tenth of the GDP. Since that time, the real volume of trade has grown at more than twice the national rate of output, so that by 1997 the combined value of exports and imports constituted nearly a

TABLE 4.2   International Trade as a Component of the U.S.
Economy: Selected Years, 1961–1998

GDP	Exports of Goods and Services ($ billions)	Exports as a Percentage of GDP	Imports of Goods and Services ($ billions)	Imports as a Percentage of GDP
1961	26	4.8	22.7	4.1
1965	35.4	4.9	31.5	4.4
1969	49.3	5	50.5	5.1
1973	91.8	6.6	91.2	6.6
1977	158.8	7.8	182.4	9
1981	302.8	9.7	317.8	10.2
1985	303	7.2	417.2	10
1989	509.3	9.3	589.7	10.8
1993	658.6	10	719.3	11
1998	931.4	11.0	1100.6	13.0

SOURCE: *Economic Report of the President*, February 1999, 326; *Survey of Current Business*, April 1999, Table 1.

quarter of the GDP. That level is far from trivial. The volume of both exports and imports was larger than consumer spending for durable goods, nonresidential investment, or housing investment, to put its size in perspective.[4] Within overall international trade, imports hold a decided edge over exports—the implications of which are discussed below.

THE U.S. TRADE BALANCE

The United States' relative position in international trade is popularly measured by its trade balance, or the difference between exports and imports of goods and services. Americans typically look to the trade balance as an indicator of how well the United States is doing vis-à-vis the rest of the world. They do so, however, in the sense of whether the United States is "winning" or "losing" in the international economic arena. For most Americans, a decidedly favorable trade balance indicates winning, whereas a negative balance points to losing. This simplistic view merits critical discussion, which follows later in this chapter.

Fewer Americans realize that international economic transactions include more than trade in goods and services. In reality, they also include flows of income on foreign investments and unilateral transfers abroad. Together, they comprise the current account of the U.S. balance of payments.

Foreign investment can take two forms: *direct* investment and *portfolio* investment. Foreign direct investment can be defined as the ownership or control by individuals or corporations in one country of 10 percent or more of the voting securities of a corporation in another country, or the equivalent interest in an unincorporated enterprise. Foreign portfolio investment is the ownership or control of less than 10 percent of a company's voting securities, plus foreign party holdings of company or government bonds. Thus investment income equates to the profits from direct investment, dividends on stocks, and interest.[5] In the 1990s, growth in foreign investment exceeded even the rapid growth of trade.

Unilateral transfers include such transactions as government aid to other nations, private cross-national humanitarian aid, and personal income transfers from workers on foreign soils to family members back home. Net unilateral transfers involving the United States have been negative for most of this century, reflecting the disproportionately heavy flow of U.S. foreign assistance, including military aid, from the United States to foreign nations.

Table 4.3 shows the U.S. current account balance for 1998. The account was $233.4 billion in deficit. The trade deficit alone totaled $169 billion, reflecting a deficit in goods that outstripped a surplus in services. Deficits in investment income and net unilateral transfers added to the overall deficit. The 1998 deficit continued a trend that began in the 1980s. Before then, the current account was seldom far from balance. Figure 4.1 illustrates the changes that have occurred over time. Clearly, large negative balances in goods during the 1980s and 1990s have been the major factor contributing to the deficit condition.

In addition to the current account component, the U.S. balance of payments keeps track of the international flows of capital that pay for the foreign trade, finan-

TABLE 4.3   U.S. Current Account Balance, 1998 (Billions of Dollars)

	Goods	Services	Investment Income	Net Unilateral Transfers	Balance on Current Account
Exports	671.1	260.4	242.6		
Imports	919.0	181.5	265.1		
Balance	-247.9	78.9	-22.5	-41.9	-233.4

SOURCE: *Survey of Current Business*, April 1999, Table 1.

cial investments, and unilateral transfers. Both theoretically and from an accounting standpoint, the sum of foreign trade, income on foreign investments, and net unilateral transfers must equal the capital flows that finance these transactions. They fail to do so in practice because of statistical discrepancies in the data.

The U.S. trade deficit in goods is widespread geographically, as Figure 4.2 illustrates. By area, the largest deficit in goods exists with Asia. U.S. goods trade with

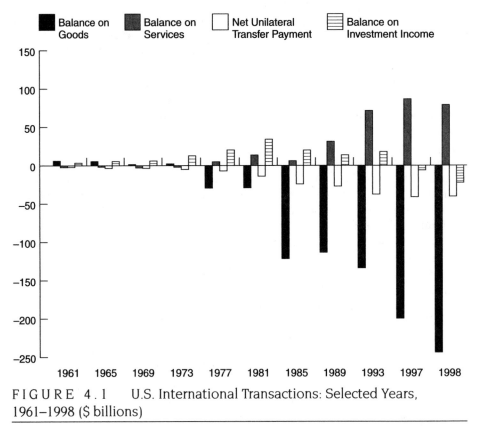

FIGURE 4.1   U.S. International Transactions: Selected Years, 1961–1998 ($ billions)

SOURCE: *Economic Report of the President*, February 1998, *Survey of Current Business*, April 1999, Table 1.

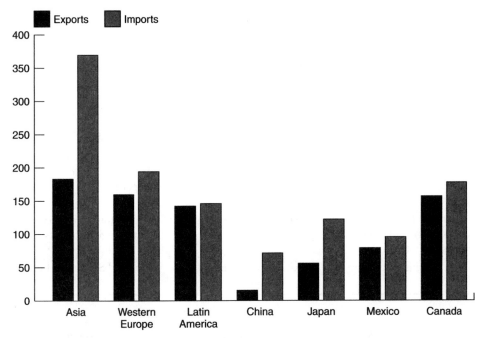

FIGURE 4.2   U.S. Trade in Goods for Selected Areas and Countries, 1998 ($ billions)

SOURCE: *Survey of Current Business*, April 1999, Table 2.

Japan and China accounts for about two-thirds of that deficit. More moderate deficits in goods exist for trade with Western Europe and Latin America, as well as with Canada and Mexico, the United States' partners in the North American Free Trade Agreement (NAFTA).

The above description provides a geographical portrait of U.S. trade relations during 1998, the most recent year for which data were available. It will surely change.

Factors Affecting the U.S. Trade Balance

Several factors affect the U.S. trade balance with other nations. They are highlighted in Table 4.4. All exert some effect, but some factors appear to be more consequential than others. Among them, the *condition of the U.S. economy and that of America's major trading partners* appears to be of greatest significance. When our trading partners' economies experience strong growth, the increased personal income generated by that growth provides the financial resources for individuals and businesses to buy more U.S. exports. Strong growth also fosters a consumer-minded psychology. As foreign consumers feel more inclined to spend, and act on that inclination, U.S. exports benefit along with other goods produced and sold in those lands. Of course, the relative proportion of benefit is a product of the other factors

T A B L E   4 . 4   Factors Affecting U.S. Exports and Imports

Factor	Export	Import
Economic growth of trading partners	Higher growth, higher U.S. exports	Not applicable
Economic growth of U.S. economy	Not applicable	Higher growth, higher imports
Value of the U.S. dollar	Higher dollar, lower exports	Higher dollar, higher imports
U.S. prices relative to foreign prices for similar goods	Higher U.S. prices, lower exports	Higher U.S. prices, higher imports
Quality and status of U.S. goods relative to foreign goods	Higher U.S. quality/status, higher exports	Higher foreign quality/status, higher imports
Trade policies, including barriers to trade	Higher foreign barriers, lower exports	Lower U.S. barriers, higher imports

listed in Table 4.4. Conversely, when foreign economies sag, the associated lower demand depresses U.S. export sales along with other sales.

When the U.S. economy grows healthily, American consumers and businesses are more inclined to increase their spending, benefiting imports along with domestically produced goods. Again, the other factors come into play in influencing the benefit distribution between imports and goods produced in the United States, as we shall soon see.

But before we get into that, this is probably a good time to complicate matters a bit, harkening back to an earlier discussion. Since we are considering forces that affect exports and imports, we should clarify how the U.S. government counts exports and imports. It is clear that a General Motors car produced in the United States and sold in Costa Rica is treated as a U.S. export and a Costa Rican import. But what about a General Motors car made in Mexico and sold there? It is counted neither as a U.S. export nor import. The sale, instead, becomes part of Mexico's GDP—not part of the United States', even though the car was produced by a U.S. corporation. Now, what if that General Motors car assembled in Mexico is brought across the border and sold in the United States? It then is treated as a U.S. import and a Mexican export. From an accounting perspective, it reduces U.S. GDP, since the GDP, in national income accounting terms, is the sum of consumption, investment, government spending, and exports *minus* imports. Does it make any difference if that Mexican-produced auto incorporates components and parts made in the United States? The auto itself counts as a U.S. import, but the components and parts manufactured in the United States are treated as U.S. exports.

The globalization of production obscures how economic growth can affect a country's trade balance. Take again the example of the General Motors car produced in Mexico but sold in the United States. To the extent that the production of General Motors cars sold in the United States increasingly moves to Mexico, a rapidly growing U.S. economy that heightens demand for General Motors cars would, in that case, contribute to rising U.S. imports, not exports. And indeed this is happening. Nonetheless, such nuances still remain exceptions to the direction of the effects highlighted in Table 4.3 and discussed above, but their incidence is increasing.

The *value of the U.S. dollar* can affect U.S. exports and imports. In theory, a higher dollar contributes to lower exports and higher imports. A rising dollar makes U.S. exports more expensive in foreign nations. Concomitantly, it makes U.S. imports cheaper. A falling dollar has the reverse effect, making exports cheaper and imports more expensive. The rise of the dollar on foreign exchange markets in the late 1990s reflected not only the sustained growth and fundamental strength of the U.S. economy but also the financial crisis taking place throughout much of Southeast Asia, with its economic ripples felt in the north of Asia, as well. The sinking value of Southeast Asian currencies against the dollar contributed to a quickened decline of the Japanese yen, a downturn that began almost two years before the onset of Southeast Asia's financial crisis and that has also been accelerated by falling Japanese interest rates. The U.S. dollar also rose against the Canadian dollar and the Mexico peso, the currencies of the United States' two biggest trading partners, but at a more moderate pace. In contrast, the Chinese yuan managed to maintain its fixed value against the dollar, but pressures to devalue are mounting in China at the time of this writing (see Table 4.5).

The stronger dollar appears to have been related to a further deterioration in the U.S. trade balance (a decline shown in Figure 4.1), although it is difficult to disentangle its effects from the extent to which economic growth in the United States has fostered imports. A continuing strong dollar will make Asian imports attractive to U.S. consumers, and will keep U.S. exports comparatively expensive overseas. Should the dollar strengthen and all other factors remain about the same, the U.S. trade balance can be expected to worsen. To mitigate that outcome, the U.S. government in the summer of 1998 intervened aggressively in world currency markets

T A B L E   4 . 5   Nominal Exchange Rates: Composite 1996 and 1998

Country	Current Units per U.S. Dollars		Percentage Decline in Foreign Currency Value
	June 4, 1996	June 3, 1998	
Indonesia	2,333.00	11,650.00	80.0
Thailand	25.40	42.00	39.5
Malaysia	2.50	3.92	36.2
Philippines	26.20	38.90	32.6
Japan	109.00	138.00	21.0
Taiwan	27.80	34.20	18.7
Mexico	7.46	8.81	15.3
Canada	1.37	1.45	5.5
China	8.32	8.28	no decline

SOURCE: Federal Reserve Bank of New York.

by buying yen and selling dollars. Such a strategy can prove effective in the short run, but in the long run it cannot stem currency flight that is prompted by continued weak economic fundamentals.

A separate but related factor to the exchange rate is the *price of similar goods from one country to another*. If a drought in France, for example, greatly drives up the price of French wines relative to comparable premium California Napa Valley wines, American consumers will be more inclined to purchase the relatively cheaper California wines. Yet this tendency will be modified a bit if at the same time the value of the dollar rises against the franc. However, it would have to rise enough to sufficiently offset the basic price difference. If, as a twist to this example, France and most of Europe experienced general inflationary pressures (not shared by the United States) that significantly increased the price of its goods across the board, including the price of wine, then that inflation could contribute to a softening of the franc's value in relation to the dollar, thereby countervening somewhat the inflationary price increase. As this example suggests, prices and exchange rates can interact with each other in complex ways.

The relative perceived *quality of goods* and the *status* that they confer on their owners are other factors that can affect exports and imports. If Americans perceive Toyotas to be better built than Fords, they will gravitate toward Toyotas, all other considerations being equal. On price, they may even be willing to pay more for a comparably equipped Toyota if they believe that it provides greater value over its useful life. If "yuppie" tastes in the United States dictate that one be seen driving an Acura, Audi, or Honda, in contrast to a Lincoln, Pontiac, or Plymouth, then peer status considerations will tend to prompt them to purchase the more desirable foreign model, even if it is priced higher than a comparably equipped domestic model. Similarly, the desire of a Mexican youth to wear American-brand clothing in preference to domestic brands can exert the same kind of effect on consumer choice. The former predisposition operates in favor of U.S. imports, while the latter supports U.S. exports. One way to help improve the U.S. trade balance is to change tastes, so that both U.S. and foreign consumers prefer American products. Advertising can work toward that end, but advertising in the United States in support of American goods is counteracted by the advertising here of foreign-controlled multinational corporations who milk foreign-product status preferences for all they are worth. But, as has been discussed above, lines get blurred when we consider American-brand Nike shoes made in Malaysia, or Hondas assembled in Ohio. Still, the brand-name country association and the perceived quality and status of the product seem to exert the most compelling enticements.

Finally, national *trade policies* can affect a country's trade balance. A country can erect both legal and nonlegal barriers to trade that discourage the import of selected goods in order to protect domestic goods from foreign competition. Specific legal barriers include tariffs, quotas, and domestic content requirements. Each merits discussion. *Tariffs* are taxes on imported goods, which raise the effective price of those goods to consumers, making them less price competitive and thereby biasing the options of consumers away from imported goods. *Quotas* limit the amount of imported goods allowed into a country. *Domestic content requirements* mandate that a certain percentage of a final product be manufactured or assembled in the home country.

Short of these legal barriers, nations may negotiate *voluntary trade restrictions*, by which one country agrees to limit its exports of certain goods to another country. These agreements are not motivated by the unilateral magnanimity of the country doing the limiting. Rather, they are typically the product of intense negotiations between two nations, often prompted by threats of legal restrictions if exports are not curbed "voluntarily."

Long-standing relationships between suppliers and distributors can constitute still another significant nonlegal barrier to free trade, by rendering it difficult for outsiders to break into these entrenched networks. This can be the case even when outside enterprises are able to offer a comparable or better product at a cheaper price. Intranetwork loyalty weighs heavily in the business equation. Japan provides a case in point, as is discussed at greater length later in this chapter. Its interlocking structure of ownership reinforces this exclusivity. Yet Japan is not alone in this regard. Observers of the Southeast Asian economic crisis point to network cronyism as a central element of the overextended financial dealings that have led to bank closings, investor panic, and corporate failures.

Free Trade and U.S. Trade Relationships

The United States is one of the world's leading proponents of free trade. America's attachment to free trade is tied normatively to its classical liberal inheritance that values individual liberty, governmental restraint, and the market as the fairest allocator of resources in society.[6] Classical liberalism holds that the individual is best positioned to decide what is in his or her best interest and to act on it. Restraints on trade constrain economic free choice. They put the interests of a limited number of producers (those who benefit from trade restraint) above a vastly larger body of consumers. In doing so, barriers to free trade not only constrain economic choice; they also restrict the size of the economic pie. Free trade, conversely, expands economic output well beyond what a domestic economy could produce for its nation's citizens. Nations trading freely enjoy mutual benefit. Consumers benefit because they have a greater variety of goods from which to choose, and producers benefit because they can specialize in those areas in which they are favorably positioned to secure a profitable share of the international market, whether abundant natural resources, low costs of production, or a pool of skilled workers underlie that favorable positioning.

The benefits of specialization in international economic commerce were first recognized in the early nineteenth century by classical economist David Ricardo, who wrote about the virtues of what he labeled *the law of comparative advantage.*[7] Simply put, countries produce goods that people in other countries want and for which the exporting nation holds an advantage over other nations in producing those goods. Countries trade with nations enjoying a comparative advantage because they see it in their residents' best interest to do so. Assuming that a number of countries share a comparative advantage in exporting a natural resource or producing a given product, then competition among them holds down prices and keeps countries from being held captive by a single supplier or producer. A nation that turns to imports from countries that hold a comparative advantage in particular goods can marshal its resources to export to others goods for which it has a distinct advantage. In doing so, it can reap the advantages of economy of scale. World economic efficiency is enhanced, as nations are free from having to incur the investment and operating costs of producing all of what they need domestically, and of suffering the many inefficiencies inherent in economic dependency.

The law of comparative advantage seems straightforward when we consider such goods as Colombian coffee, Saudi Arabian oil, Turkish hand-knotted rugs, and Swiss watches. None of these nations, however, has a corner on the market. But they still have elected to specialize in producing those goods in sizable numbers for sale in international markets. They have taken advantage of abundant natural resources or built on historical legacy. Yet other nations have elected to specialize in producing products for which they have no natural resource advantage or long-standing affinity. China's greatly expanded production of shoes and clothing, or Japan's dominant position in electronic goods and automobiles, serve as examples.

What accounts for this emphasis? In China's case it is differential costs in factors of production. The labor-intensive nature of production gives low-cost Chinese labor a comparative advantage in the manufacture of shoes and apparel. Worldwide demand justifies market entry; the Chinese have no intrinsic attachment to shoe or clothing production. Rather, Chinese entrepreneurs know that they can use their cost-of-labor advantage to compete effectively in those markets. In the case of Japan, its industries held no comparative advantage in electronic goods in the decades immediately following World War II. Moreover, its automobiles were highly suspect in international markets. They were hardly known for quality in the 1950s and 1960s. Yet Japanese industrialists saw a fertile market opportunity and, with government assistance, invested heavily in modern plants and the technology necessary to produce quality automobiles that were price competitive. The same is true for electronic goods such as radios, stereos, and televisions. Both industrial entrepreneurs and government planners set out to acquire a sizable slice of the world market, and they did it.[8]

The United States has become the largest market for Japanese exports. Japan, in turn, is the United States' third largest export market, behind Canada and Mexico. The United States exports less to Japan than it imports from Japan. The U.S. deficit in goods with Japan stood at $65.3 billion in 1998, comprising 26 percent of the total U.S. goods deficit for that year. That can be compared to goods deficits of $34.4 billion with all of Western Europe, $3.7 billion with Latin America, and $121.5 billion with the rest of Asia, excluding Japan. China, alone, accounted for about $57 billion of that last amount—a level approaching the U.S. goods deficit with Japan.

The growing gap with Japan is the product of continued increases in Japanese automobile and capital goods exports to the United States, enlarged by the dampening effect that slow economic growth in Japan has had on demand for U.S. exports. The rising deficit with China, which doubled between 1994 and 1998, largely reflects greatly expanded U.S. imports of labor-intensive, low-cost consumer goods from China.[9]

Americans tend to view these trade deficits as evidence that the United States is losing in international economic competition, drawing on their fondness for the sports metaphor alluded to earlier. To the extent that Americans spend more on

Japanese and Chinese goods than Japanese and Chinese spend on American goods, money, in net, moves from U.S. hands to Japanese and Chinese hands. Those funds become available to be saved or spent by their new owners. Large trade surpluses give nations the financial wherewithal to pay for needed imports. In a real sense, Japanese automobiles sold in the United States pay for Arab oil imported by Japan. Some of the money, however, finds its way back into U.S. hands, either spent on U.S. exports or invested in U.S. securities, thus cushioning the net outflow of U.S. dollars. Nonetheless, the general public typically overlooks this reality as they sort out the winners and the losers.

The public also tends to identify trade deficits with job loss. After all, a trade deficit translates into net demand that is satisfied by foreign enterprises. Had an equivalent demand been met by domestic producers, greater employment opportunity would have existed at home. The popular temptation, then, is to ascribe job loss to mounting bilateral trade deficits. If only U.S. firms had produced the dollar amount of goods in deficit, fewer Americans would be out of work, or so the reasoning goes. This line of thinking assumes several things: that the U.S. economy has the capacity to absorb the displaced production; that a match exists between unemployed U.S. workers and the jobs that have been "taken away" producing foreign imports; and that U.S. policymakers and the public would accept the higher inflation that would surely accompany such increased economic activity.

As bilateral trade deficits mount, so do calls to reassess the fairness of U.S. trade relationships. And U.S. trade with Japan receives the greatest attention, even though it is likely that China will soon replace Japan as the single, largest national contributor to the U.S. trade deficit. Japan's place under the microscope is not surprising. For one thing, the American media has devoted the most attention to the U.S. trade deficit with Japan. Coverage of U.S. trade with China tends to be far more benign than that devoted to the U.S. trade relationship with Japan. Coverage of the former often builds on the theme of the opportunities that expanded economic intercourse with China holds for the United States. At the same time, the media highlights the political tension that exists over the United States expanding its economic relationships with a regime that shows little regard for human rights, at least as judged by American standards. In balance, though, the lure of expanded U.S. access to vast potential Chinese markets appears to carry the day.

With Japan, the focus too is on access, but the tone is far less hopeful. Editorial comment frequently questions whether the United States and Japan are playing on a level field in their economic dealings, whether Japan is playing by a different set of rules. According to Paul Krugman, the answer to this query depends in good part on how the focus is sharpened. If the focus is on the legal terms of trade, then Japan's trade policies do not appear to be all that atypical. Although Japan is openly protectionist when it comes to agricultural goods, Japan's tariff rates on manufactured goods are not out of line with those of other industrial nations.[10] And the Clinton administration has made progress in reducing restraints on U.S. exports to Japan. As noted in the 1998 *Annual Report of the Council of Economic Advisers*, the United States and Japan negotiated 33 trade agreements since the beginning of the Clinton presidency, building on the U.S.-Japan Framework for a New Economic Partnership

Agreement, reached in 1993. Negotiated agreements cover lowered Japanese barriers to U.S. exports in such sectors as automobiles and auto parts, insurance, financial services, telecommunications, and medical technology. Although the Clinton administration notes improvements that meet expectations in some areas, it acknowledges that progress has fallen short of expectations in others. The greatest market inroads have been made in automobile and auto parts. By 1997, U.S. automobile and auto parts exports to Japan exceeded those to Western Europe.[11]

Despite progress in lowering barriers to increased U.S. exports to Japan, the Japanese economy operates in an environment that protects established companies and selectively restricts the free flow of foreign goods into its markets. Long-standing loyalties in distribution systems, interlocking ownership, discriminatory standards in bidding procedures, and time-consuming and costly equipment testing and certification procedures conspire in favor of domestic enterprises.[12] Perhaps Japan's protracted economic malaise will foster greater internal efforts to root out economic inefficiencies that both hamper domestic productivity and limit U.S. access, but strong norms mitigate the prospect of significant change.

China also presents significant barriers to U.S. exports. In fact, its legal barriers are more onerous than Japan's. Notable barriers include an average tariff rate of 23 percent, quotas that restrict the types of goods that domestic Chinese firms can purchase, and licensing requirements that often have mandatory product inspections tied to them. In addition, Chinese law requires that U.S. firms operating in China sell their goods through a Chinese trading company.[13]

Despite these obstacles, the United States has made headway in cutting into the huge Chinese market, as U.S. exports to China grew at an average annual rate of 14 percent between 1991 and 1998, compared to U.S. export growth to the rest of the world of about 6 percent.[14] Sales of aircraft, industrial machinery, and telecommunications equipment led the way. Nevertheless, Chinese imports to the United States in 1998 still topped U.S. exports to China by a 4:1 margin. To put this in perspective, the equivalent ratio for U.S. trade with Japan stood at slightly over 2:1 for that same year.[15]

Regionalization and the North American Free Trade Agreement

The logic of increased economic efficiency and mutual benefit through free trade should prompt nations to reduce remaining barriers to trade, and that is just what has happened around the world since World War II. Still, nations have gone about the task differently. Some, including the United States, have pursued bilateral agreements aimed at breaking down trade barriers between trading partners. As discussed earlier, highly publicized United States negotiations with Japan and China provide contemporary examples of the pursuit of that approach. Another approach, in which the United States has been a leading force, has involved a large number of nations coming together to agree on broad reductions in tariffs and ways to reduce nontariff barriers to trade. The General Agreement on Tariffs and Trade (GATT) represents the embodiment of this approach. The United States and twenty-one other nations created the agreement in 1947. Since its beginning, 124 nations of the world have joined, and there have been eight rounds of negotiations, including the most recent Uruguay Round, which produced an agreement in December of

1993. It called for a one-third reduction in tariffs worldwide, a 36 percent reduction in agricultural subsidies (the first time that agriculture was included in the GATT), and a phaseout of quotas on textile imports worldwide. Congress approved implementing legislation in 1994.

Still another approach involves expanding free trade within a geographic region, with the goal of strengthening the economies of the nations within that region, as well as advancing the economic interests of the region as a whole. The North American Free Trade Agreement (NAFTA) among the United States, Canada, and Mexico took effect on January 1, 1994, and is to be fully implemented by 2008. Table 4.6 summarizes its major provisions pertaining to tariffs, quotas and import licenses, investments, rules of origin and domestic content requirements, and health and the environment.[16] NAFTA's provisions advance free trade among member nations; yet they also give preferential treatment to members over nonmembers. Members share the benefits of multilateral reductions in tariffs and quota restrictions—benefits not shared by nonmembers. Moreover, rules of origin and domestic content requirements also advantage members over nonmembers. For example, while motor vehicles and parts that contain at least 60 percent local content can move from one member nation to another without tariffs being imposed, those that do not are subject to existing tariff rates. The rationale behind this provision is to ensure that members benefit economically from foreign trade within North America, by limiting the extent to which they can incorporate into the final product components and parts made outside NAFTA countries. If this provision were not imposed, firms of member nations might succumb to the temptation to rely on cheaper foreign components and parts, thus reducing their costs and increasing their profits while escaping tariffs—a reward intended for member nations who share the economic pie. Still, there should be no doubt that domestic content provisions are anti–free trade. Although they fence in a certain amount of industrial

TABLE 4.6   Major Provisions of NAFTA

Area	Provision (When fully implemented)
Tariffs	Eliminates all tariffs on roughly 9,000 categories of goods produced and sold in member nations
Quotas and import licenses	Eliminates all quotas and import licenses applied at the border
Investments	Prescribes the imposition of special requirements on investments made by businesses or individuals of one member nation in another member nation
Rules of origin/domestic content requirement	Prevents goods produced either completely or in large part outside member nations from being exported duty-free among member nations. Requires that goods contain at least 50 percent North American content to move duty-free across borders
Health and the environment	Guarantees that no member nation would be forced to reduce its health and environmental standards

production and its associated economic benefits, they depress worldwide economic efficiency and invite other nations to adopt similar barriers to free trade.

Congress approved U.S. participation in NAFTA partly in response to policies of the European Union (EU), an association of European nations formed in part to lower trade barriers among its members and to make them more competitive internationally. Just as the EU sought to realize the benefits of freer trade among its members, so did NAFTA. This was a rational economic strategy for the members of both associations because, after all, their leading trading partners could be found among their respective association's membership. Thus securing the benefits of intra-associational trade could be expected to pay immediate dividends to member nations.

Despite their protective elements, associational agreements such as NAFTA and EU can be seen as steps toward broadened free trade, as nations begin by liberalizing trade within their respective regions. Once successful, the lure of expanded cross-regional trade may well prompt participants to remove protective barriers. And to the extent that the international community, through instruments such as GATT, can agree to further trade liberalization, the perceived need for either protection or retaliation should break down somewhat. Broadly lowered barriers themselves narrow protective differences between associated members and outsiders. However, there are those who view regional arrangements far less sanguinely, seeing them as stumbling blocks, rather than building blocks, to widened international trade.[17]

FOREIGN DIRECT INVESTMENT

In addition to the trade that takes place between nations, U.S. citizens and U.S.-owned companies invest in foreign securities and businesses, just as their foreign counterparts make similar investments in the United States. Investors secure assets that generate income. Investment income, in turn, shows up as a component of the U.S. current account. Depending on the form of investment, income can include interest on bonds and other securities, dividends on stocks, and profits from direct investment. Profits from direct investment are counted as income whether they are distributed or reinvested. The U.S. balance on investment income has been positive for every year since World War II, except for 1997 and 1998. (See Figure 4.1 for the period since 1960.) Given the international economic climate in 1997 and 1998, it should not have been surprising that the downturn could be attributed to a large increase in foreign holdings of U.S. Treasury securities, in response to America's economic strength and the economic insecurities confronting most of Asia at that time. Nor should it be surprising, for the same reason, for that relationship to continue up to the end of the twentieth century.

Of all the forms of foreign investment, foreign direct investment receives the greatest popular attention. Recall that foreign direct investment is defined as individual or corporate ownership or control of 10 percent or more of the voting securities of a corporation in another country, or the equivalent interest in an unincorporated enterprise in that country. Images of Japanese ownership of Pebble Beach Golf Club or New York's Rockefeller Center, or of Columbia Pictures or Firestone, are more alarming to Americans than the knowledge that Japanese and other foreigners invest in Treasury bills or corporate bonds. Even their investment in U.S. stocks causes little alarm, as long as foreign investors stay far from management control. In a real sense, these so-called portfolio investments pay a compliment to the United States and its economy. Foreign purchase of U.S. Treasury securities keeps their interest rates lower than they would be without that foreign investment, thus reducing the federal government's interest costs; and foreign purchase of U.S. company stocks supports their price in equity markets. Outright foreign ownership or control of U.S. companies and landmarks is another matter.

Another form of foreign direct investment appears to be less troublesome to Americans, and that is the foreign ownership of production plants and branch offices in the United States. Just as large U.S. multinational corporations expanded production plants and branch offices around the world, building on their early foundations in Western Europe, so have foreign nations increasingly located them in the United States. Consider Mercedes Benz's automobile assembly plant in Alabama, Honda's in Ohio, or the many big-city locations for branches of Germany's Commerzbank or Japan's Sumimoto bank.

During the 1990s, growth in foreign direct investment outpaced even the rapid growth in foreign trade. Although direct investment in both directions grew at a pace unrivaled in American history, U.S. direct investment abroad regained its historic edge for most of the decade, reversing a late-1980s pattern of higher foreign investment in the United States.[18] Yet, as an exception to the trend, 1998 found the United States attracting greater foreign investment than its citizens and businesses invested abroad. For 1998, net private capital outflows for direct investment totaled $132 billion, while net inflows to the United States amounted to $196 billion,[19] likely reflecting the comparative strength of the U.S. economy and its status as a relative safe-haven for foreign investment.

Furthermore, the composition of U.S. foreign direct investment has shifted significantly over the past two decades. Whereas U.S. investment in manufacturing exceeded that in services for most of the 1980s, that relationship reversed itself in the 1990s, led by sharp increases in the financial, insurance, and real estate sectors.

The United States continues to lead all nations in both originating foreign direct investment and hosting it. The United Kingdom and Canada receive the greatest share of U.S. direct investment abroad, and the United Kingdom, Japan, and the Netherlands, in that order, make the greatest direct investment in the United States.[20] About three-fourths of U.S. direct investment abroad remains in developed, industrial countries, despite recent increases in U.S. direct investment in emerging markets. For instance, although China is the second largest host to worldwide foreign direct investment, China attracts less than 1 percent from the United States. Yet during the 1990s the U.S. position in China increased over threefold.

Direct investment and trade are related. The Toyota Corporation, for example, could decide to expand its assembly plants in Japan in an effort to meet rising U.S. demand for Toyota automobiles, or it could elect to open assembly plants in the United States. Its choice represents both a business and a political decision. On the business side, Toyota could reduce both its transportation and labor costs by establishing new plants in the United States. As an economic offset, however, a U.S. location makes Toyota more dependent on American-made components and parts. But that increased dependence serves as a political asset, as do the American jobs created by the plants. An additional political consideration is that Toyotas made and sold in the

United States do not count as Japanese exports, and they contribute to the U.S. GDP. If they were made in Japan and transported to the United States for sale, they would add to America's trade deficit with Japan—a touchy matter politically.

The benefits of foreign direct investment seem less clear than the benefits of trade that result from comparative advantage. Still, they can accrue to both the host and the investing country. The host country benefits not only from the jobs created in foreign-owned plants and offices but also from the demand that these new enterprises create for machinery, parts, supplies, and services—most of which are provided domestically. In fact, one study found that foreign companies operating in the United States purchased from U.S. suppliers 80 percent of the materials and services used in production.[21] Other benefits can come in the form of technology transfer and management improvement, both of which can increase productivity in the host country.

The investing country also stands to benefit. Direct investment in foreign nations increases their personal income, all other things being equal, enabling their residents to increase their consumption of imports, including those from the investing country. Direct investment can also create trade opportunities, improving a nation's trade balance. As is the case of the United States, its multinational corporations export more to their overseas affiliates than they import from them.[22]

INTERNATIONAL TRADE, INVESTMENT, AND EMPLOYMENT

The debate over whether the United States should participate in NAFTA highlighted the relationship between trade policy and employment. In voicing his opposition to NAFTA, Ross Perot, a third-party candidate for the presidency in both 1992 and 1996, warned Americans of the "giant sucking sound" of jobs being pulled south of the border that would follow congressional approval of NAFTA. He predicted the loss of up to 6 million U.S. jobs to Mexico, compared to the legislation's supporters who forecast the creation of over a million new jobs in the United States resulting from the added Mexican demand for U.S. goods that could be expected to flow from greater economic activity in Mexico. Organized labor in the United States echoed Perot's fears, creating the anomaly of a Democratic president championing NAFTA's approval and facing the strong opposition of a traditionally loyal political ally. President Clinton's position prevailed in Congress, but it took overwhelming Republican support in the House to bring about victory. Republicans voted 132–43 in favor of NAFTA approval, while Democrats opposed it by a 102–156 margin.

The rationale that trade liberalization between the United States and Mexico would benefit both economies won out. Supporters argued that NAFTA would open up Mexico's market for U.S. goods, repairing a relationship in which it had been more difficult for U.S. goods to get into Mexico than for Mexican goods to make it into the United States. Supporters also pointed to the expected rise in Mexican demand for U.S. exports that could be expected to accompany the personal income gains of Mexican workers.

Although several years have passed since NAFTA went into effect, it is difficult to isolate its effects on the economies of member nations. Strong U.S. economic growth since NAFTA's creation—coupled with Mexico's balance-of-payments crisis, significant currency devaluation, and deep mid-decade recession—exacerbate the difficulty of separating NAFTA's effects from the larger macroeconomic factors affecting trade between the two countries. Studies by DRI/McGraw-Hill[23] and the Federal Reserve Bank of Dallas,[24] done after about three years of experience with NAFTA, conclude that NAFTA has independently made modest contributions to the growth of U.S. exports to Mexico, and to the U.S. employment gains associated with them—a conclusion consistent with the U.S. Department of Commerce's findings.[25]

A recent study conducted under the auspices of the Federal Reserve Bank of Chicago, employing macroeconomic modeling, forecasts that although Mexico will realize the greatest economic benefits, NAFTA will benefit the economies of all North American member nations as it proceeds toward full implementation in 2008. The study's author concludes that his "dynamic analysis suggests that NAFTA generates real output and trade flow increases that are roughly twice as large as those predicted by previous analyses."[26] Whether this forecast will prove overly optimistic, only time will tell.

No evidence supports the kind of massive migration of jobs from the United States to Mexico predicted by Ross Perot. Still, this is not to suggest that U.S. jobs have not been displaced to Mexico. During the first three years of NAFTA's existence, the U.S. Department of Labor certified 99,497 U.S. workers as eligible for benefits under the Transitional Adjustment Assistance (TAA) program, which was designed to assist workers who lost their jobs due to production shifts to Mexico or Canada. Of that total, only approximately 32,000 persons actually applied for benefits; many of the others presumably found jobs in the meantime.[27] U.S. net employment increased during the same period by nearly 8.6 million jobs, and Mexican employment experienced a strong recovery from its recessionary low. In fact, unemployment in both the United States and Mexico has continued to fall since, dropping in Mexico from 7.6 percent during the height of the 1995 recession to approximately 4.5 percent at the end of 1998.

It is true, as noted earlier in this chapter, that in the late 1990s the United States has run a trade deficit with Mexico, but that trade deficit is clearly not the product of displaced jobs. It reflects the economic health of the United States and the strength of the dollar in relation to the devalued Mexican peso. As the U.S. demand for imports has risen, so has Mexico's demand for U.S. exports—facilitated by Mexico's own strong economic recovery. Both have increased markedly since the mid-1990s; it is just that U.S. imports have grown faster.

A rising percentage of U.S. imports from Mexico represents components or finished goods produced by U.S. multinational corporations or joint U.S.-Mexican ventures, with lower-cost Mexican employees performing the more labor-intensive work. However, as skill levels have risen in the Mexican workforce, so have jobs in automobile and consumer electronics industries, on top of the traditional export-oriented employment in goods such as textiles and toys.

U.S. multinational corporate employment growth in Mexico has not been limited to export-oriented activities. Firms such as Wal-Mart and Sears have increasingly turned to the Mexican market itself for sales, selling American-labeled clothing to brand-conscious Mexicans.[28] As noted earlier, these sales contribute to Mexico's GDP, and do not count as either U.S. exports or imports. They do, however, contribute to the profit of the U.S. firms involved, as they do to Mexican aggregate personal income—income available to purchase U.S. exports. The Mexican case furnishes further illustration that manufacturing has become a truly international affair, a reality that will be explored later as the discussion turns to foreign direct investment.

Beyond U.S. economic relationships in North America, the evidence suggests that trade is not a major contributor to job displacement in manufacturing. Analysis by the Council of Economic Advisers of data from the 1980s found that technological change accounted for a far greater percentage of job loss in manufacturing than did trade. Even in the worst year of that decade, trade contributed no more than 10 percent of the observed displacements from manufacturing; in most years it contributed significantly less.[29]

Despite the reality that some workers will lose jobs as a result of changing trade relationships, in the aggregate the trade deficit and the average rate of unemployment are pretty much unrelated over the long run.[30] Is the same true for foreign direct investment? In answering this question, we need to revisit the relationship between foreign direct investment and trade.

Foreign direct investment and trade are interrelated in a number of ways. Foreign direct investment can be a substitute for trade, but it can also be a vehicle for trade. In the former sense, U.S. firms may elect to invest in enterprises abroad in response to quotas or high tariffs that limit exports or significantly raise their price. Direct investment allows U.S. firms to obtain substantial equity interests in operations abroad that can sell in those markets unhindered by trade restrictions. In the latter sense, foreign direct investment can facilitate trade. That occurs, for example, when one unit of a multinational corporation acquires materials or parts from another located in a different country, or when that unit ships a finished product for sale by still another foreign unit of that company. Again, considerations of comparative advantage will tend to dictate the direction of these relationships, but the point is that much of the trade that exists between nations would not exist if it were not for foreign direct investment. In fact, the Council of Economic Advisers found that cross-border transactions between units within multinational corporations accounted for one-third of U.S. exports and two-fifths of U.S. imports in a recent year.[31]

What about the relationship between foreign direct investment and jobs? Don't U.S. corporations "export" jobs when they acquire productive facilities or expand their operations in other lands? Although they clearly do create employment opportunities abroad, that does not mean that those jobs would have otherwise been established in the United States. Yet there can be no doubting the fact that U.S. firms provide jobs for workers around the globe. By 1990, about one-fifth of the total output of U.S. firms was produced by foreign workers residing outside the United States.[32] One need only look at the experience of U.S. multinationals such as General Electric and Whirlpool. Whirlpool, America's largest supplier of domestic appliances, makes most of its products in Mexico and Europe, and General Electric is Singapore's largest single employer. Some of the goods produced return to be sold in the United States, counting as U.S. imports; the rest get sold outside the United States. Regardless, foreigners, not Americans, hold those jobs. This does not mean that foreigners have taken those jobs, one for one, away from Americans. For reasons related to supply, market proximity, and labor cost differentials, it cannot be assumed that those jobs would have otherwise been created in the United States. Some assuredly would have, but others are truly additive.

Why Worry About the Trade Deficit or Foreign Investment?

If the trade deficit cannot be found to cost jobs in the aggregate, and if foreign direct investment (U.S. investment abroad and foreign investment in the United States) is about a wash, why worry about them? Or, put differently, if a nation can have a strong economy—with good economic growth, low inflation, and low unemployment—and have its national budget balanced, why worry about any trade deficit that might exist at the same time? Both scenarios describe conditions in the United States in the late 1990s. So, why worry? Perhaps we should not worry all that much. After all, empirical evidence suggests that there is no long-run relationship between a country's economic performance and its trade balance.[33] Even a superficial glance at the contemporary short-run experience of the United States and Japan, or of the nations of Southeast Asia and Western Europe, should bring that point home. The United States in the late 1990s enjoyed a strong economy while its trade deficit remained high by historical standards. Japan continued to run a sizable trade surplus while its economy stagnated and then fell into recession. The economies of a number of Southeast Asian nations fared even worse than Japan's, but their trade balances showed a mixed pattern. Western European nations, in contrast, experienced strong economic growth along with positive trade balances.

If the trade balance is not correlated with national economic performance, does the picture change much if the focus is widened to include income on foreign investments and net unilateral transfers? No, the change is typically only marginal. The case of the United States is no exception. Nonetheless, these additions do provide a more complete accounting of international economic relationships. As noted earlier, the United States ran a $233.4 billion current account deficit in 1998, with $169 billion arising from international trade. In essence, that means that individuals and organizations worldwide invested more in the United States than their U.S. counterparts invested abroad. But why speak of investment so broadly here? The relationship to investment income seems straightforward. When individuals or organizations in one country buy foreign bonds, the purchasers acquire assets and receive a flow of interest payments from the sellers. By buying those bonds, the buyers invest in that foreign land and acquire claims against its sellers. Now how does foreign trade come in here? The relationship is similar. When Americans buy Japanese cars, for example, they transfer dollars ultimately into Japanese accounts in U.S. banks and acquire claims on those banks, thus investing in the United States. The deposits, in turn, become available for U.S. banks to lend to others. When the Japanese owners do transfer money out of that account to buy U.S. Treasury securities, American real estate, or the stock of U.S. corporations, they are transferring their investments from one vehicle to others, not making new investments per se. But as economist Robert Eisner reminds us, the Japanese essentially invested in the United States the moment they sold their automobiles to American buyers.[34] The same logic applies to the acquisition of services across national borders.

In the aggregate, then, a nation's current account balance theoretically equals its net foreign investment position, statistical discrepancy notwithstanding. A negative net foreign investment position represents a drain on U.S.-owned resources, as assets and the income streams they produce move from U.S. ownership to foreign ownership. At a negative net investment of $233 billion, these greater foreign claims on the United States amount to about 2 percent of U.S. GDP, not an insignificant level. If we assume a real rate of return (nominal rate minus rate of inflation) of, say, 4 percent on these claims (a level that appears reasonable given the experience of the late 1990s), the annual cost would be about $40 billion a year—less than half a percent of the GDP. To put that in perspective, economists have found that a reduction in the U.S. unemployment rate of just one-half of 1 percent would increase the GDP by approximately $80 billion a year, enough to cover the income outflow twice over.[35] The appropriate conclusion, then, is that although the negative net investment position of the United States is not insignificant, it must be considered in relation to the economy's overall performance.

In another sense, a net negative investment position results from the fact that the United States spends more than it earns. If consumption spending rises faster than national income, the only way that investment spending cannot fall is for foreign investment to rise; and that is what has happened in the United States, as the United States experienced rising deficits in its current account. In other words, foreign capital filled the gap between domestic saving and domestic investment. That allowed U.S. citizens and businesses to live beyond their means, so to speak—consumers satisfying their tastes for foreign goods, and businesses taking advantage of foreign capital. Add to this mix the recognition that the inflow of foreign capital acted to keep U.S. interest rates lower than they otherwise would have been, and the trade deficit, broadly conceived, does not appear all that bad.

National Saving and the Trade Deficit

If the United States were to increase its rate of national saving, its current account deficit would decline. Saving would displace consumption, and increased domestic saving would narrow or eliminate the gap between domestic saving and investment. Thus it is not surprising that economists, such as Paul Krugman,[36] regard America's low saving rate as a key economic problem. Yet to reduce America's trade deficit in goods, it is not enough to decrease consumption in relation to personal income alone; consumption expenditures must be switched, as well. That involves changing U.S. consumers' appetite for foreign goods.

Government can act to increase national saving by cutting any national budget deficit that might exist. That becomes easier, as recent U.S. experience suggests, when strong economic growth swells government revenues. When economies sag and government revenues fall short of estimates, deficit reduction requires tax increases or expenditure reductions. However, both tax increases and expenditure reductions act to dampen demand and make economic matters worse. Should the economy go into recession, people and businesses would get hurt. Rising unemployment and falling personal income leads to reduced consumption. Consumption of both domestic and foreign goods falls, even though the rate of decline might be higher for one category over the other. As consumption of foreign goods falls, so does the trade deficit. Thus, as Robert Eisner reminds us, recessions can cure trade deficits, but the "cure" inflicts far more economic pain than the malady created. Remember that strong economic growth at home fosters consumer confidence and demand that ripples through the economy as businesses increase production to meet that demand. To the extent that imports to meet some of that demand rise faster than do exports to the rest of the world, the trade deficit will rise. Would it make good policy sense to choke off prosperity in order to reduce the trade deficit? Of course not. So most American policymakers stand ready to tolerate a trade deficit in a sound economy, particularly when a balanced budget or budget surplus contributes to increased national saving.

The Contribution of Fairer Trade

Isn't it possible, though, to reduce the U.S. trade deficit by getting other nations to engage in "fairer" trade, by opening access to their markets in the same way that the United States gives them access to its markets? Unbridled free trade would accomplish this, of course; but the reality is that countries engage in protection to different degrees. Critics of America's foreign trade policy, such as Robert Kuttner, William Greider, and Lester Thurow, see countries such as Japan and China dealing with the United States largely on their own terms.[37] They expand their export industries, and the United States provides the demand for their goods, which translates into increased foreign reserves for them. Proponents of fairer trade want the federal government to threaten unfair traders with import restrictions—and follow through, if necessary—unless they provide U.S. industries with greater unrestricted access to their markets. Corporations whose access is thwarted lobby the administration and Congress to take a tougher stand.

President Clinton's state visits to Japan and China have included an element of cajoling aimed at winning lower restrictions on U.S. exports, and some limited successes have been achieved. Although it is reasonable to expect continued progress toward barrier reduction, a major turnaround appears unlikely. It is not ultimately in America's interest for Congress to impose sanctions on Japan and China, for any restrictions on imports will likely cost the United States as much or more in lost exports.

AMERICAN ASCENDANCY AND THE FADING ASIAN PARADIGM

Just as Japan's economic ascendancy appeared unstoppable in the 1980s and the very early 1990s, so did the export-oriented economic growth enjoyed by the other Pacific Rim nations during most of the 1990s, that is, until the so-called Asian flu hit several East Asian economies. Even as Japan's economy cooled, Asia's remarkable economic growth prompted observers to extol the virtues of the Asian miracle and the Asian formula for economic success. That formula has included high saving and investment rates, government industrial policy supporting exports, selective import barriers, interlocking ownership, and entrenched networks of suppliers and distributors. With the notable exceptions of Singapore and Hong Kong, East Asian governments have had a strong presence in the economy, which has been used to pursue a form of mercantilism aimed at strengthening the nation while building the economy. Beyond regulation, governments in East Asia have not been adverse to pressuring banks to lend to favored firms positioned to advance their economic agenda or financially benefit friends or family members of top government officials, leading popular journalists to brand these relationships as forms of "crony capitalism."

With the benefit of retrospection, analysts have been quick to attribute the Asian crisis of the late 1990s to the dysfunctional side of several of these formulaic elements. The themes of overextended investment, excessive risk taking, and political intervention in support of risky loans have permeated their critiques, as analysts suggest how these elements contributed to the spreading financial panic that gripped Indonesia, Thailand, Malaysia, and Korea, and that spilled over into other Asian nations. Several East Asian currencies lost substantial portions of their value, stock markets plummeted, and banks failed.

Faced with growing withdrawals of money by foreign creditors and large short-term debt to foreign banks, Indonesia, Thailand, and Korea turned to the International Monetary Fund (IMF) for help. The IMF—an international agency, which has the United States as its top financial supporter—imposed a different formula for economic success as a condition for its loans to enable Asian banks to pay back foreign creditors. That formula centered on increased foreign access to Asian markets, deregulation (outside of heightened government scrutiny of financial institutions), the closure of weak domestic banks, and easier opportunities for foreign financial institutions to operate on Asian soil. The "IMF way" looked a lot like the "American way," prompting Harvard economist Jeffrey Sachs to accuse the IMF of doing the United States' bidding in securing greater U.S. access to markets that would not have opened wider without the IMF's intervention.[38]

There is no question that the lure of the "American way" has increased its attractiveness in the recent past. It is, however, much too early to judge whether the "American way" is overlaying, much less supplanting, the "Asian way." Donald Emmerson, a political economist specializing in Southeast Asia, does not see an "Americanization" of Asia in the offing, although he does recognize that Asian nations are facing mounting pressures, both economic and political, to pursue greater economic and political freedom—an effort that Emmerson suggests will produce some change toward those ends, but with a continued distinctive Asian twist consistent with "Asian values" and tradition.[39]

FOREIGN TRADE POLICY IN AN ERA OF AMERICAN ASCENDANCY

The international trade policy of the Clinton administration has centered on expanding free trade and opening markets abroad for U.S. goods, services, and investments. It has pursued that agenda on several fronts, including an internationally coordinated effort to reduce barriers on a broad multilateral and reciprocal basis, as represented by U.S. leadership in GATT; a cooperative regional effort, as embodied in NAFTA; and bilateral negotiations.

Although the U.S. Constitution gives the legislative branch the ultimate authority to regulate international trade, Congress has delegated a great deal of operational authority to the executive branch, to which Congress looks for policy leadership. Typically, Congress allows the president to negotiate trade agreements, which since 1974 have been subject to final approval by Congress. The president has several advisors who assist him in leading international economic policy. The most important include the secretaries of the Departments of Treasury and Commerce, the Federal Reserve Board chair, and the U.S. trade representative, a special post created in 1963. It is the trade advisor who, under the president's general direction, negotiates trade agreements and resolves trade disputes with foreign nations.[40]

The Clinton administration has been active in its campaign to secure greater U.S. access to foreign markets. Following its first-term legislative victories in Congress over NAFTA and GATT, the Clinton administration turned its attention to further liberalizing trade in the Americas, and to bilateral trade liberalization with Japan and China, as discussed earlier in this chapter.

The United States is well positioned in the international economic community to lever considerable resources in support of its international economic position. In addition to its clout within the IMF, the United States is also a key player within the World Trade Organization (WTO); and it has not been shy about using its influence in these organizations as a resource in its bilateral negotiations. As a case in point, the Clinton administration has tied its willingness to support China's membership in the WTO to progress in bilateral negotiations with China.[41]

There is no doubt that the soundness of the U.S. economy has aided the Clinton administration in pursuing its international economic policy. In contrast to Asia's economic instability and the unanswered questions surrounding Europe's monetary union, the United States looks to be a relative economic safe-haven at the turn of the century. Its economic strength magnifies the world's reliance on the United States and enhances its political influence in international affairs. Yet as Alan Greenspan acknowledged, no country "can remain an oasis of prosperity unaffected by a world that is experiencing greatly increased stress,"[42] even one as well positioned as the United States.

NOTES

1. Alan Greenspan, *Testimony before the Subcommittee on Domestic and International Monetary Policy of the House Committee on Banking and Financial Services*, July 22, 1997.

2. Mortimer B. Zuckerman, "A Second American Century," *Foreign Affairs* 77, no. 3 (May/June 1998), 18–31.

3. Paul Krugman, "America the Boastful," *Foreign Affairs* 77, no. 3 (May/June 1998), 32–45.

4. Norman Frumkin, *Tracking America's Economy*, 3d ed. (Armonk, NY: M. E. Sharpe, Inc., 1998), 151.

5. Ibid., 148.

6. Robert E. Lane, "Market Justice, Political Justice," *American Political Science Review* 80 (June 1986), 383–402.

7. David Ricardo, *On the Principles of Political Economy and Taxation*, in *The Works and Correspondence of David Ricardo*, ed. Piero Straffa (Cambridge MA: Cambridge University Press, 1966).

8. For a comprehensive illustration of this point see Chalmers Johnson, *MITI and the Japanese Miracle* (Stanford, CA: Stanford University Press, 1982).

9. Christopher L. Bach, "U.S. International Transactions, Fourth Quarter and Year 1997," *Survey of Current Business*, April 1998; Thomas Klitgaard and Karen Schiele, "The Growing U.S. Trade Imbalance with China," *Current Issues in Economics and Finance* 3, no. 7 (May 1997); *Survey of Current Business*, April 1999, Table 2.

10. Paul Krugman, *The Age of Diminished Expectations* (Cambridge, MA: The MIT Press, 1994), 138–143.

11. *1998 Annual Report of the Council of Economic Advisers*, 235–236; Michael Gerlach, "Keiretsu Organization in the Japanese Economy: Analysis and Trade Implications," in *Politics and Productivity: How Japan's Development Strategy Works*, ed. Chalmers Johnson, et al. (Cambridge, MA: Ballinger Publishers, 1989), 141–174.

12. *1997 Country Reports on Economic Policy and Trade Practices* (Washington, DC: U.S. Department of State, 1998), Japan, 3–4.

13. Klitgaard and Schiele, 1–2.

14. Ibid., 1–2; *Survey of Current Business*, April 1999, Table 2.

15. *Survey of Current Business*, April 1999, Table 2.

16. The provisions highlighted in this table are drawn from discussions found in Linda M. Aguilar, "NAFTA: A Review of the Issues," *Economic Perspectives* 17, no. 1 (July/February 1993), 12–20.

17. Robert Lawrence, "Emerging Regional Arrangements: Building Blocks or Stumbling Blocks," in *Finance and the International Economy*, ed. Richard O' Brien (New York: Oxford University Press, 1991), 22–35.

18. *1998 Annual Report of the Council of Economic Advisers*, 249–250.

19. *Survey of Current Business*, April 1999, 47.

20. *1998 Annual Report of the Council of Economic Advisers*, 253.

21. William L. Zeile, "Merchandise Trade of U.S. Affiliates of Foreign Companies," *Survey of Current Business*, (October 1993), 63.

22. *1998 Annual Report of the Council of Economic Advisers*, 257.

23. The results of DRI's contracted study are summarized in the U.S. Department of Commerce's *Study on the Operation and Effect of the North American Free Trade Agreement*, submitted to Congress in April 1997, as required by the NAFTA Implementation Act.

24. David M. Gould, "Distinguishing NAFTA from the Peso Crisis," *Federal Reserve Bank of Dallas*, September/October 1996, 6–10.

25. U.S. Department of Commerce, *Study on the Operation and Effect of the North American Free Trade Agreement*, April 1997.

26. Michael A. Kouparitas, "A Dynamic Macroeconomic Analysis of NAFTA," *Economic Perspectives*, 21, no. 1 (January/February 1997), 14–35.

27. *Study on the Operation and Effect of the North American Free Trade Agreement*, 21–22.

28. *The Economist* 347, no. 8073, 13–14 (special section on manufacturing).

29. *1998 Annual Report of the Council of Economic Advisers*, 244–245.

30. Krugman, *The Age of Diminished Expectations*, 48.

31. *1998 Annual Report of the Council of Economic Advisers*, 250.

32. *The Economist*, 347, no. 8073, 3–4.

33. David M. Gould and Roy J. Ruffin, "Trade Deficits: Causes and Consequences," *Economic Review* (Fourth Quarter 1996), 10–20.

34. The logic of these relationships is drawn from Robert Eisner's discussion of net foreign investment and the current account in his book *The Misunderstood Economy* (Boston: Harvard Business School Press, 1994), 69–71.

35. This line of argument is again drawn from Robert Eisner. See Ibid., 79.

36. See Krugman, *The Age of Diminished Expectations*, 50–58.

37. Robert Kuttner, "Globalism Bites Back," *The American Prospect*, no. 37 (March-April 1998), 6–9; William Greider, *One World, Ready or Not: The Manic Logic of Global Capitalism* (New York: Simon & Schuster, 1997); Lester Thurow, *Head to Head* (New York: Murrow, 1992.)

38. Jeffrey Sachs, "The IMF and the Asian Flu," *The American Prospect*, no. 37 (March-April 1998), 16–21.

39. Donald K. Emmerson, "Americanizing Asia?", *Foreign Affairs* 77, no. 3 (May/June 1998), 46–56.

40. See Stephen Cohen, et al., *The Fundamentals of U.S. Foreign Trade Policy* (Boulder, CO: Westview Press, 1996).

41. *1998 Annual Report of the Council of Economic Advisers*, 233–234.

42. Alan Greenspan, *Remarks Before the Committee on the Budget*, U.S. Senate, September 23, 1998.

CHAPTER 5

Government Regulation

Although America's political culture values individual freedom highly, public policymakers and citizens alike recognize that the unbridled pursuit of private interest can harm the broader public interest, and that government has an obligation to intervene selectively and limit individual freedom for the common good. Yet America's classical liberal inheritance puts the onus on government to justify its intervention in private spheres of activity. The issue of when, and to what extent, government should control individual or group activity is an inherently political question that lies at the heart of public policymaking. Policymakers, both elected and appointed, make those choices on the public's behalf, and they typically justify them as being in the public interest. But what constitutes the public interest is itself a political question, one that gets resolved through authoritative governmental action, whether that be legislation, court decisions and rulings, or regulation.

This chapter focuses on regulation that has economic implications, broadly conceived, in which government requires individuals or organizations to behave in certain ways under the credible threat of sanctions for noncompliance. In the United States, federal government agencies exercise regulatory authority that is vested in them by acts of Congress or, under certain restrictions, by executive action of the president. Congressional acts provide the legal framework for regulation, empowering government agencies to issue the very regulations that command individuals or organizations to behave in certain ways, but those regulations must be consistent with the enabling legislation. That enabling legislation may be drawn quite narrowly, specifying not only the intent of the law but also the conditions, standards, and procedures pertaining to it; or it may attach only general statutory guidelines to its statement of legislative intent. In the latter case, Congress gives government agencies considerable discretion in implementing the law. In exercising delegated administrative discretion, government agencies engage in rule making, a process that results in their issuance of regulations that have the force of law. A similar process operates in the states.

Government regulation tends to evoke strong feelings—in the abstract, and in application. Concerns in the abstract center on views of the appropriate role of government, particularly whether government is going too far in intervening in private affairs. Those who prefer self-interested action and limited government put the heaviest burden on government to justify its intervention. Others who see a constructive role for government to play in the economy and in society are more welcoming of government intervention as a check on the negative spillovers of self-interested behavior. The former view individuals as the best judges of their own interests, and they see the economy and society benefiting from this aggregate pursuit of self-interest. The latter worry that unrestrained pursuit of self-interest will come at the expense of collective goods.

In the contemporary rhetoric of politics, regulation has taken on a pejorative association with big government, bureaucratic red tape, and inefficiency. Those seeing it that way draw a reasonably rigid line between the private and public spheres; and within the private sphere, they consider the market to be the best and most efficient allocator of value. The market makes goods available that individuals and organizations want, as firms—motivated by profit—compete to satisfy those wants, using price as the information medium of voluntary exchange. For Milton Friedman, the wonder of the market is that an efficient economic order can emerge as the *unintended* consequence of the actions of many individuals or organizations, each acting in the pursuit of self-interest.[1] Friedman's presumption is to let the market work, that is, unless the conditions that allow markets to function effectively are threatened or fail to be met. Government, then, has an obligation to step in and correct the defect. Preservation of the market becomes the justification for intervention.

Certain conditions must be met for the market to work effectively. First, exchange must be voluntary. Second, prospective buyers must be able to choose from among available equivalent goods; and, other than price differences, the choice of doing business with one seller rather than another must be relatively costless. For instance, this dictum would be violated if transportation costs of doing business with a competitor were so high as to render it uneconomical, even after consideration of price competitiveness. Third, there must be freedom of entry and exit. Would-be competitors must be free to enter into competition in search of a share of the market, and enterprises must be free to pull up stakes when market conditions dictate. Fourth, all costs must be borne by the parties involved in a market transaction; uncompensated costs must not spill over to third parties. Finally, government must not define the substance of the economic product, the specific array of goods and services available, or their distribution.

The greatest threats to the free market come from *monopoly practices* and *negative externalities*. The effective working of the market is premised on free choice. Consumers must be free to take their business elsewhere if they find prices too high or quality lacking. However, consumers cannot exercise that freedom of choice if businesses are not free to enter the market and provide them with viable alternatives. Businesses will enter the market only when they see an opportunity to compete successfully and make a satisfactory profit. Unrestrained market economies offer incentives for firms to increase their market share. Firms can do that by raising the perceived value of their products, by improving product quality and offering competitively low prices, and through the effective use of advertising that stimulates consumer desire. Their success at expanding market share may prompt some of their less successful competitors to decide that it is in their self-interest to exit the market altogether rather than to pursue unsuccessful competition. Other firms may find it in their interest to be taken over by successful competitors who are seeking opportunities to expand their market presence.

As another means to expand market share, successful firms may elect to join forces and merge their enterprises. Mergers not only can broaden market penetration and increase the operating efficiency of the resulting enterprises; they also can improve their competitive position, squeezing out less well-positioned competitors. Extending this scenario, it is possible to end up with only one or a few firms dominating a market. When a single firm reaches a dominant position over ineffective competition, and is able to influence prices through independent action, economic theory suggests that consumers will be the losers, facing reduced choice and higher prices than would occur with competition. When only a couple of viable firms remain in a market, the danger exists that they may be tempted to collude rather than to compete, dividing the market between them and sharing the profits garnered from prices set higher than would exist if they were in competition.

Not only do consumers face the potential of restricted supply and high prices under these conditions, but the economy suffers as well, as firms no longer face the competitive pressures that prompt them to operate as efficiently as possible. Thus government has an incentive to intervene and restrict monopolistic practices. It does this by applying antitrust policy.

Externalities arise when the actions of private participants in the economy impose costs on others who fail to be compensated for them (negative externalities), or when the actions of private participants confer benefits on others who fail to pay for the benefits derived (positive externalities). Government regulators tend not to concern themselves with positive externalities, since no party is directly harmed or disadvantaged in the relationship, even though it becomes possible for some individuals to reap benefits while avoiding costs, raising the problem of inequity. A prominent example is the open union shop, in which workers need not be union members. Union members pay dues which, in part, pay the salaries of union officials who bargain with management for higher wages for workers. If their bargaining proves successful, union members benefit through higher earnings; but so do nonmembers, who bear none of the costs of union endeavors. Other than considerations of cross-worker inequity, no uncompensated costs are *imposed* by one party on another, although the very possibility of "free rider" benefits probably depresses would-be union membership. That is why many states have laws requiring all workers to join the required union, an option permitted by federal law.

The case of negative externalities is different. One party benefits by offloading costs, and another is harmed by absorbing the consequences of the first party's actions. Industrial point-source pollution (pollution that can be traced to a fixed point of discharge) provides a salient example. Polluters impose costs on others. Those who pollute a river or stream can impose costs on downstream users. The costs may be direct, for example, when downstream communities must pay to treat the water to standards of drinkable quality; or they can be indirect, when pollution levels prevent people from swimming or fishing in those waters, depriving them of valued recreation. Air pollution also imposes costs—the personal costs of respiratory illness on the most medically vulnerable, and the larger burden on society of paying for the health care costs of those requiring treatment for conditions exacerbated by air pollution. Although government can employ fines to exact payment from industrial plants that exceed allowable emission levels, those directly affected go uncompensated, unless they successfully sue polluters as compensation for the effects they have suffered. The use of fines serves as surrogate compensation for the costs borne by society, and they also serve as a policy tool to bias the options of industry, which must weigh the costs of fines against the costs necessary to reduce pollutants to acceptable levels.

An industry operating purely in its corporate self-interest, focusing on the financial bottom line, has an incentive to pass costs outside the corporation. Reducing pollution emissions entails increased expenditures. Therefore, industries have to balance the costs of investing in devices that reduce emissions with the consequences of not doing so, including fines and negative public opinion that might cost them sales in the marketplace. If there were no government-imposed counterbalance, firms might be more willing to push the limits of negative public opinion in order to maximize profits.

What about pollution that cannot be readily attributed to specific sources? It is one thing to be able to trace chemical pollution in a waterway to an industrial source and allocate costs back to it, and it is quite another thing to be able to trace auto emission air pollution back to the respective vehicle operators. It is much easier for government to place requirements on automobile manufacturers to design their products in ways that reduce emissions. Beyond that, the external costs that automobile users impose on society through air pollution essentially go uncompensated. Sure, gasoline taxes impose costs on users, but the revenues from those user charges go toward highway and road improvement—improvements that often facilitate more automobile use, which produces even greater pollution. Although government can enact pollution taxes of various sorts, such as a tax imposed on the annual mileage use of registered motor vehicles, with the revenues directed toward environmental cleanup, such an initiative would likely fail the test of political feasibility. As an alternative, government could increase existing motor fuel taxes in an effort to raise revenue while discouraging use, perhaps allocating some of the newly found revenue to subsidize mass transit as part of an effort to entice motorists to abandon their automobiles in favor of public transportation. To the extent that motorists make the shift in large numbers, vehicle emissions could be significantly reduced. However, policymakers in the United States have been far less inclined than their European counterparts, for example, to bias individual options to that extent. On behalf of individual freedom, U.S. policymakers, for the most part, have left to individuals the largely unhindered vehicle-use choices that collectively impose environmental costs on the rest of us—a policy stance that contrasts with the regulation of point-source pollution.

In addition to protecting against market failure and addressing externalities, government regulation also seeks to *control or reduce the risk* faced by individuals in the marketplace.[2] Government does this by developing standards for products, production processes, and the information that manufacturers are required to disclose to consumers. Common illustrations include the control of financial institutions, insurance, prescription drugs, food safety, television and radio broadcast standards, and workplace safety, as well as ingredient and nutritional labeling on consumable products. In addition, government licenses providers of certain services, such as physicians, nurses, attorneys, stockbrokers, and even cosmetologists.

Government also intervenes in the marketplace to *ensure equity of service provision and fair price* in those markets in which self-interest might lead monopolies or near-monopolies to allocate service and price in ways that maximize user revenues and corporate profits. The areas of public utility and transportation regulation serve as prominent examples. The former covers such services as telephone, natural gas, electricity, and water. The latter applies to rail, airline, and trucking transportation. With public utilities, government regulation might mandate universal service and control the prices charged to residential users, which, based on cost allocation, would be higher in the absence of governmental control. Government regulators fill the revenue gap by allowing utilities to charge business users more than cost allocation justifies, creating, in effect, a cross-subsidy. A similar relationship pertains to urban residential and rural residential users, in which urban users subsidize rural users.

With the regulation of transportation, government has acted to require providers to serve unprofitable geographic areas in exchange for the right to serve highly profitable ones. In both public utilities and transportation, government has granted providers a reasonable operating profit and, in return for their cooperation, has restricted competition. Yet as is discussed later in greater detail, legislative action at both the federal and state levels has selectively removed government from the business of directing service provision, setting rates, and controlling the entry of competitors in commercial transportation.

States play a significant regulatory role in the U.S. federal system. For instance, they license practitioners in certain professions and occupations serving the public; have the primary responsibility for regulating public building safety, insurance, and electrical power; and have secondary responsibility in regulating banking and environmental pollution. At the same time, federal law has greatly limited or reshaped the states' regulatory power in such areas as trucking, natural gas, and telephone service.

Government regulatory policy has taken different turns over time, and those turns have largely been a response to changing perceptions of what constitute public problems. The following section traces the currents of regulatory policy in the United States and the tools that regulatory policymakers have chosen to use over time in several important sectors of the American economy.

PROBLEM PERCEPTION AND REGULATORY POLICY

The roots of modern government regulation lie in the late nineteenth century, a time of rapid industrialization and transition from competing regional economies to a truly national economy.[3] Railroad expansion, added to established steam-powered waterway transportation, provided a national transportation infrastructure that fostered the growth of a national economy and greatly expanded interstate commerce. Nationally chartered banks and growing stock exchanges provided the capital in support of the industrial consolidations that led to a swiftly expanding corporate-based national economy. A growing number of state-chartered banks capitalized more limited regional economic operations.

The late nineteenth century was a period of steep economic growth punctuated by wide swings of the business cycle. It was also a period of increasing tension between the emerging corporate-based economy and family-owned businesses, on the one hand, and between industrially led urbanization and increasingly radicalized agrarian interests, on the other. This tension was exacerbated by foreign immigration, the swelling of central cities, changes in the organization of production, and rising labor militancy—changes that foreshadowed even more intensified social pressures in the early twentieth century. Corporations engaged in takeovers and mergers, and formed trusts (in which the trust held stock in a number of related industries and exercised management authority over them). The largest and most prominent trust was the Standard Oil Trust that in 1879 controlled 40 different oil companies. Mergers combined 4,227 businesses into 257 corporations in the years between 1897 and 1904 alone, giving birth to industrial giants such as U.S. Steel and International Harvester.[4]

The rise of third-party political movements in the 1890s reflected growing social dislocations and discontent with change. Feeling squeezed by urban industrial interests, radical agrarians threw their support behind the newly formed People's Party, commonly referred to as the Populists. The Populists called for the institution of an income tax and government-induced economic stimulation through unlimited coinage of silver. They also advanced a platform of nationalization of railroads and telegraph companies.

As rails came to crisscross the nation, the railroad became the predominant commercial transportation mode in America. It provided shippers with the most flexible, efficient, and timely mode of transportation available. Yet despite the railroad's national geographic reach, made possible by both federal and state land grants, the states, not the federal government, played the major role in regulating railroads for most of the nineteenth century. Shippers soon came to argue that the different and often conflicting regulations undermined the very efficiency that the railroad offered. Moreover, shippers in the Midwest and the West raised their voices against the growing monopolistic practices of the few railroads serving their regions, some of which were sanctioned by state regulation. Agricultural interests were successful in forcing new state railroad regulations and antitrust laws in seventeen states.[5]

The Rise of Economic Regulation

Faced with rising complaints from both agricultural and other commercial interests over rates, and reacting to an important 1886 U.S. Supreme Court decision that struck down state regulation on the basis that the "right of continuous transportation" was necessary for commerce, both the House and Senate quickly took up legislation that would substitute national regulation for state regulation.[6] Their efforts resulted in passage of the Interstate Commerce Act of 1887, which created the Interstate Commerce Commission (ICC). Congress granted the ICC power to set "just and reasonable" rates in the public interest, and delegated to the regulators the authority to implement that criterion. These actions marked the federal government's entry into national economic regulation.

For the remainder of the nineteenth century and through the first five decades of the twentieth, the federal government pretty much confined its regulatory intervention to economic matters. A shift to social regulation, also referred to as protective regulation, would largely wait until the 1960s.

The Sherman Antitrust Act of 1890, following closely on the heels of the Interstate Commerce Act, was the first in a series of congressional initiatives designed to constrain the ability of companies to merge, form trusts, or conspire to fix fares, rates, and prices. However, it created no enforcement mechanism. It was not until 1903, during Theodore Roosevelt's first term as president, that Congress created the Antitrust Division of the Justice Department to lead antitrust enforcement. Yet the legislation's ambiguous intent and questions about the extent of the division's authority rendered it less than an aggressive enforcer, leading its administrators to demure to the courts for guidance. Reacting to the courts' ready willingness to intervene, Congress, with President Woodrow Wilson's blessing, created the independent Federal Trade Commission (FTC) in 1914 and gave it the powers to promulgate rules, initiate complaints based on its investigatory analysis, and take enforcement actions against violators. In that same year, Congress strengthened the federal government's regulatory hand by enacting the Clayton Act, which extended antitrust controls, principally by prohibiting price discrimination if its effects were to lessen competition significantly or to create a monopoly. It was not long, however, before the courts jealously reined in the FTC's enforcement power. With the exception of Congress's creation in 1920 of the Federal Power Commission to regulate the interstate sale of electric energy on the wholesale market and the interstate transportation and sale of natural gas, the next wave of national economic regulation would come in the 1930s from a Democrat-controlled Congress sympathetic with Franklin Delano Roosevelt's New Deal.

Under the pressure of economic dislocations caused by the Great Depression, New Deal regulations were aimed at reducing risks to participants in the market economy, as well as restoring their confidence in America's financial institutions. Toward that end, new regulatory initiatives included the Federal Deposit Insurance Corporation (FDIC) in 1933 and the Securities and Exchange Commission (SEC) a year later. The former was instituted to insure bank deposits against loss resulting from bank failure, a growing occurrence during the Great Depression's early years. The latter was established to regulate the selling and buying of stocks and securities, to provide consumers with information about transactions, and to prohibit transactions based on insider information, that is, information about corporations' business intentions not available to the public.[7]

New Deal legislation also authorized the federal government to regulate telephone and radio communications, in addition to interstate trucking and interstate commercial airline transportation. Congress created the Federal Communications Commission (FCC) in 1934. Not only would the FCC regulate what could be transmitted by telephone line or radio signal (later by broadcast or cable television); it also controlled service entry through its authority to grant licenses. Congress, the following year, extended the government's regulatory authority by charging the ICC to regulate interstate trucking. Prior to Congress's passage of the Federal Motor Carrier Act of 1935, motor carrier regulation fell to the states, creating a national patchwork of inconsistent intrastate regulatory practices. No regulation of interstate trucking existed at all. Under the 1935 legislation, federal regulation of interstate trucking extended to entry, routes, rates, service abandonment, and mergers. The federal act became a model for subsequent amendments of state regulation of intrastate trucking, fostering greater uniformity of state regulation than existed prior to federal regulation.[8] Three years later, in 1938, Congress created the Civil Aeronautics Authority (renamed the Civil Aeronautics Board in 1940) to regulate the commercial airline industry, and gave it the authority to control entry and approve routes, flight schedules, and service abandonment.

All of these regulatory initiatives functioned to restrain competition, instead of promoting it as was the goal of much nineteenth- and early twentieth-century regulation. They had as their goal to ensure reliable service provision without destabilizing competition. To do so, competition would have to be controlled, with regulated providers guaranteed a "just and reasonable" return on their investment. In all three instances noted above, the regulated industries actively supported federal regulation. In turning to protection over competition, the federal government set itself up for what would be increasing criticism that the regulated industries had come to capture the government's regulatory authority and advance their own economic interests rather than the public interest.

The United States' entry into World War II turned national policymakers' attention toward mobilizing the economy for war. New Deal regulations remained in place, but America's industrial output significantly shifted to the manufacture of military goods, although corporations moved with less than alacrity in leaving their domestic markets early in the war. The War Production Board, created by President Roosevelt under the authority granted to him by the War Powers Act of 1941, hastened the process of conversion by restricting industry's ability to use raw materials for the production of consumer goods. The Board came to exercise central control over the allocation of raw materials and production.

With war's end, central planning and control gave way to a transition back to a consumer-oriented domestic economy, initially involving canceling defense contracts and compensating firms for foregone income. In addition, the federal government faced the daunting task of disposing of the large surplus of raw materials and equipment that had accumulated toward the end of the U.S. military campaign. With these challenges met, and with the regulatory inheritance of the Progressive Era and the New Deal firmly in place, policymakers and organized interests turned their attention to providing the infrastructure and services necessary to accommodate the population explosion that took place following the war. Waves of "baby-boomers" filled schools, triggered a construction boom, and increasingly placed demands on America's transportation systems. Regulation took a respite as Americans focused on education, jobs, and family life, that is, until rising social activism in the 1960s reenergized regulatory fervor—regulation that took a new direction.

The New Social Regulation

While the so-called old regulation tends to focus on economic relationships, particularly those pertaining to markets, rates, and the obligation to serve, the new social regulation shifts the focus to the *conditions* under which goods and services are produced and the physical characteristics of the products and the byproducts produced.[9] Whereas economic regulation typically affects one industry at a time, such as communications or commercial transportation, social regulation spreads its effects broadly across the economy and society. Social regulation, like economic regulation, responds to changes taking place in society and the extent to which policymakers see them as problematical and meriting public action.

The environmental movement, which gained strength in the 1960s, is a case in point. It raised the specter of growing environmental risks and mobilized citizen activism that found expression through the rise of environmental interest groups. The publication in 1962 of Rachel Carson's *Silent Spring* provided dramatic testimony of how agricultural pesticides find their way into the air, water, crops, animals, and humans. Beyond their effects, she argued that government and the scientific community did not seem to care much about the consequences of environmental pollution for public health. The resulting, highly publicized counterattack from the chemical industry sparked the beginnings of a national debate.

Other notable events focused the public's attention. The Cuyahoga River, running through Cleveland, Ohio, became so polluted with combustible wastes that it caught on fire in 1969, creating a spectacular image on prime-time national television and on the front pages of newspapers throughout the country. Accounts of polluted lakes and other waterways, hazardous dump sites, and worsening air pollution in metropolitan areas increasingly captured the attention of the media and the public at large. Americans apparently came to realize that the environment could not be taken for granted; benign neglect would not solve what had popularly come to be recognized as real and growing problems. The throngs who turned out across the country for the first "Earth Day," in April 1970, gave vivid testimony to the fact that environmental quality had taken its place on America's policy agenda.

Growing public attention to the risks of environmental pollution both sensitized and motivated fledgling consumer interests to explore and raise the risks of unsafe consumer products. Books such as *Unsafe at an Any Speed* became popular bestsellers, and Ralph Nader became the recognized leader of the consumer protection movement in America. Its activism followed a wide array of consumer interests, including automobile and consumer product safety, food and drug safety, deceptive advertising, and financial dealings.

About the same time, organized labor took an increasing interest in workplace safety, concentrating on measures to prevent job-related injury and illness. It used a 1968 mine disaster in West Virginia, which killed seventy-eight miners and received prime-time media attention, to symbolize the workers' plight. Public interest groups played a negligible role in the ensuing debate. In reality, fortuitous political events paved the way for legislative attention. President Richard Nixon took interest in identifying himself with a governmental response, seeing it as a way of wooing blue-collar workers and thereby broadening his political appeal.[10]

Of the three areas, the national public debate became most intense over environmental protection and consumer product safety. Workplace safety never received the same amount of media attention as that devoted to the other two areas. Its debate was largely confined within Washington circles—among the executive branch, Congress, and organized labor and business associations. Each, however, percolated during the late 1960s, leading to legislation enacted in the early 1970s during the Nixon administration. That legislation together created three new regulatory authorities: the Environmental Protection Agency (EPA) in 1970; the Occupational Safety and Health Administration (OSHA), also in 1970; and the Consumer Product Safety Commission (CPSC) in 1972. Congress established the EPA within the executive branch, giving the president the power to appoint its administrator, subject to Senate confirmation, and it created OSHA as an agency within the Department of Labor. In contrast, Congress established the CPSC as an independent regulatory agency, one of the few independent commissions created after the New Deal. Of the three, the EPA has engendered the greatest controversy and has had the widest impact, yet has been able to expand its regulatory reach while enjoying sustained public support, even as policymakers advanced deregulation in other policy areas. It merits closer scrutiny.

The Environmental Protection Agency and Environmental Protection: The Embodiment of Social Regulation

Prior to Congress's passage of the Environmental Protection Act in 1970, which created the EPA, and subsequent enabling legislation directed at air and water pollution control, the federal government played only a limited role in environmental protection. The scant authority that existed was spread among several executive branch agencies, including the Departments of Health, Education, and Welfare (HEW); Interior; and Agriculture. What little environmental regulation that existed fell to the states, selectively assisted by local governments. But that fact should not be interpreted to mean that the United States has been free of environmental problems.

In its formative years, the vast expanse of the western frontier held the promise of unbounded resources that settlers could put to their use. The sheer quantity of land and unspoiled natural resources accommodated the needs of the early pioneers, seemingly without adverse effects on those resources. At the same time, the industrial revolution of the late nineteenth and early twentieth centuries and rising urban populations in the Midwest and Northeast offered early evidence of a tension between economic growth and environmental quality. Extensive coal burning blackened the skies of many an industrial city by the early twentieth century. Outbreaks of contaminated drinking water prompted cities to regulate water systems. In rural areas, loggers cleared large tracks of virgin lands, spurring Congress to create national forests and a national park system for protection. State legislatures, urged on by Progressive or Populist governors, enacted parallel legislation that created state forests and wildlife preserves. Despite these actions, government's role, at all levels, remained limited.

Before Congress greatly strengthend the federal government's environmental regulatory hand in the early 1970s, its early role in water pollution control was restricted to providing grants and technical assistance to local governments for the construction of sewage treatment plants. And although Congress in the mid-1960s required states to establish their own water quality standards and draft plans to implement them, the states were slow in responding. Without minimum national standards, many states were hesitant to take any action that might give nonresponsive states a competitive advantage in keeping and attracting industrial development.

The federal government was somewhat more active in addressing air pollution. Following California's lead, Congress focused its attention on the automobile as a major source of air pollution in urban areas. It authorized HEW to set emission standards for all automobiles sold in the United States; and HEW, in turn, applied California's already-existing standards nationally. Beyond the control of emissions, President Johnson in 1967 urged the adoption of national air quality standards, a tougher position than he had taken on water quality. Congress approved only a study of the matter, and passed the legislative ball to the states, requiring them to adopt their own air quality standards, paralleling national legislative action on water quality. Not surprisingly, the vast majority of states once again put off compliance.[11]

The year 1970 marked a significant point of departure in federal environmental policymaking. Three reasons can be offered for the policy breakthrough. The first centers on the growing media attention given to environmental pollution and such happenings as the Cuyahoga River fire and the National Earth Day demonstrations, alluded to earlier. The second points to the heightened activity of environmental interest groups and their influence on the public debate. Two reports from Ralph Nader's group, entitled *Vanishing Air* and *Water Wasteland*, presented highly critical assessments of what he viewed as federal neglect of serious air and water pollution problems, adding fuel to the proverbial fire. The former publication pointed the finger of blame at Maine Senator Edmund Muskie, a prominent Democratic leader in the Senate, who refused to throw his support behind national air quality standards. The third reason touches on pure political advantage. President Nixon's 1970 State of the Union address devoted considerable attention to the environment, prompting observers to view his emphasis as a direct challenge to Muskie, who was then the front-runner for the Democratic presidential nomination in 1972. Nixon's stance levered Muskie to reverse his position on national standards.[12]

Congress's passage of the 1970 Environmental Protection Act created the regulatory infrastructure to place the federal government firmly in the lead on environmental protection nationally. Yet the newly created EPA still lacked the policy tools it needed to protect the quality of America's air and water. Without additional enabling legislation, the federal government's role would continue to be one of monitoring pollution; assisting the states in defining their own policies, priorities, and standards; and providing limited financial assistance to support state efforts.

Subsequent companion legislation gave the EPA the authority it needed to oversee the cleanup of the nation's air and water.[13] Congress first addressed air pollution. The Clean Air Act of 1970 served as the legal foundation for the national government's partial preemption of what had been a role essentially left to the states. It contained four major provisions. First, Congress charged the EPA with setting air quality standards that would apply nationwide. No longer would the states be allowed to determine what constitutes acceptable levels of air pollution within their borders. After all, polluted air can be blown across state lines, theoretically from states possessing lax standards to adjoining states having much tougher ones. In addition, given interstate competition over economic development, some states might elect to gain a competitive advantage over others by limiting their environmental regulations. Under the legislation, states could only elect to establish tougher standards for major pollutants and could not loosen the minimum federal standards. Second, the act required the states to prepare implementation plans for the EPA's approval, showing what efforts would be made to bring a state's air quality into compliance. Third, it required automobile manufacturers to reduce emissions by 90 percent for all 1975 models or face a $10,000 per vehicle fine, even though the technology to do so was not available at the time. Fourth, it charged the EPA with establishing emission standards for electric power plants. Procedurally, the act also importantly gave citizens the right to sue polluters (for not complying with the standards) and the EPA (for not enforcing them).

Under the federal government's oversight, this landmark legislation delegated to the states the responsibility to monitor compliance and enforce it. The states, in turn, could carry out those functions directly or delegate the day-to-day tasks to local government agencies. In the latter case, that responsibility frequently resides at the county level or with metropolitan air quality districts that cut across county lines. But if states or local governments failed to carry out their delegated responsibilities properly, EPA personnel could step in and take over the job of monitoring and enforcing compliance.

In 1977, Congress amended the Clean Air Act, ironically both to expand the EPA's authority and to extend compliance deadlines. Under the 1977 amendments, states were required to submit plans for controlling industrial pollution, including illustrations of how emissions from new industrial sources in noncomplying areas would be offset by corresponding reductions from existing sources. The legislation also required states to use permits to control the addition of new fixed-pollution sources, and it mandated that smokestack scrubbers be installed on all coal-burning power plants. The amendments also required states to establish vehicle emission testing programs in counties whose air failed to meet federal air quality standards. For states not in compliance, the federal law authorized the EPA to withhold federal grants-in-aid for highways and sewage treatment (an example of the use of sanctions that cross over to other policy areas), as well as to prohibit states from issuing permits that would increase aggregate air pollution from industrial sources. At the same time, the amendments extended the heretofore unmet deadline for automakers to comply with the strict federally prescribed auto emission standards, in recognition that significant progress had been made, although the mandated 90 percent reduction had not been fully attained on schedule.

Government's strengthened regulatory role over air pollution during the 1970s made a difference in improving America's air quality. Despite economic growth and an expanding population, the President's Council on Environmental Quality found that the five major air pollution emissions (particulates, sulfur oxides, nitrogen oxides, hydrocarbons, and carbon monoxide) declined by 21 percent between 1970 and 1980.[14] Days in which the air was determined to be unhealthy declined by about one-third in forty metropolitan areas between 1974 and 1980. Nonetheless, air pollution remained a serious national problem: seven major cites still averaged over 100 unhealthy days a year from 1978 to 1980.[15]

Water pollution regulation followed a similar path. Again following President Nixon's lead, Congress passed enabling legislation that greatly increased the EPA's regulatory authority over water quality. The Water Pollution Control Act of 1972, commonly referred to as the Clean Water Act, set minimum national standards, industry by industry, for the release of point-source pollution. It also addressed the problem of non–point-source pollution, such as that caused by fertilizer or agricultural waste runoff into groundwater, rivers, lakes, and other waterways, although

Congress stopped short of setting national standards. Instead, it authorized funds for state and local planning bodies to analyze the extent of non–point-source pollution and develop plans to address the identified problems. Without any accompanying federal mandate, little came of the effort.

Subsequent national water quality legislation extended the federal government's reach. The Safe Drinking Water Act of 1974 directed the EPA to promulgate maximum allowable levels of different chemicals and bacteriological pollutants in local water systems. Subsequently, the 1977 amendments to the Clean Water Act authorized additional federal aid for sewage treatment plant construction and, as we have seen with air quality policy, extended deadlines for industries to comply with the point-source standards set in 1972.

Compared with the documented improvement found in air quality, the picture appears to be less clear for water quality. The over $30 billion in federal sewage grants helped to give communities the resources necessary to treat raw sewage before it is discharged into public waterways, but most U.S. cities still did not have adequate secondary sewage treatment facilities by 1980.[16]

Adequate data do not exist to allow any definitive conclusion about whether America's rivers, streams, and lakes were cleaner in 1980 than in 1970, although Lakes Erie and Ontario showed well-publicized signs of rejuvenation. Conventional wisdom is that water quality at least did not deteriorate during the 1970s, despite population and industrial growth, and that it probably improved somewhat.[17]

President Jimmy Carter, toward the end of his administration, and prior to his defeat in November 1980, vowed to continue to move forward in protecting the environment, extending the progress that had already been made—progress, he noted, "for which we are being repaid many times over."[18] His successor, Ronald Reagan, failed to share these sentiments. Instead, he questioned whether America's investment in environmental regulation and pollution control could meet the scrutiny of cost-benefit analysis. He also challenged the EPA's record on ideological grounds, seeing it as an example of overextended big government. Holding up the ideals of private enterprise and the free market, Reagan focused on the costs to the private sector of complying with what he viewed as the burgeoning environmental regulation of the 1970s. He promised to reverse what he saw as overregulation.[19]

Symbolizing the administrations's altered policy course, President Reagan appointed Anne Gorsuch (later Burford) as administrator of the EPA. Gorsuch, a corporate attorney whose clients included many industries hostile to the EPA's expanded environmental role, came into office clearly sympathetic to industry's perspective on regulation. Several other top appointees came from the very industries that the EPA regulates. Kathleen Bennett, a lobbyist for the American Paper Institute, became assistant administrator for air, noise, and radiation; Robert Perry, a ranking attorney with the Exxon Corporation, became general counsel; and Rita Lavelle, a public relations officer for Aerojet-General, became assistant administrator for hazardous and toxic wastes.[20]

Gorsuch kept many agency positions vacant, and used Reagan-initiated budget cuts to eliminate still others. Total employment at the EPA dropped from 14,269 at the beginning of 1981 to 11,474 by November 1982. The headquarter's staff in Washington dropped from 4,700 to 2,500.[21] These reductions took a significant bite out of the agency's ability to monitor and enforce compliance with environmental protection legislation. In Gorsuch's first year in office, the number of lawsuits filed by the EPA against the biggest polluters fell from 250 to 78.[22]

Mounting congressional opposition, particularly among Democrats, spurred on by highly mobilized environmental interest groups, forced Gorsuch to resign in 1984, but not until Congress took the extraordinary step of citing her for contempt. The resignations of other initial Reagan appointees soon followed. Gorsuch's replacement, the highly regarded William Ruckelshaus, who had previously served as EPA administrator and who enjoyed bipartisan support in Congress, ushered in a period of restored stability to the EPA, along with renewed enforcement activity.

In the aftermath of rocky relations with Congress during his first term, and faced with rising popular support for environmental protection, Reagan and his Office of Management and Budget (OMB) eased their hostile forays against environmental regulation. Yet that softened stance did not keep President Reagan in 1986 from vetoing a congressionally approved revision of the Clean Water Act. In response, Congress overrode his veto, drawing on the sizable support of Republicans in both chambers. Importantly, the 1987 amendments added the requirement that the states develop EPA-approved plans for controlling pollution from nonpoint sources. Toward that end, Congress required municipalities to regulate stormwater runoff in the same way they regulate the discharge of polluted water from industrial plants.

George Bush, Reagan's presidential successor, campaigned in support of the environment. Once elected, he proclaimed himself to be the "environmental president," separating himself and his administration from the policy stance of his predecessor. As a gesture of his commitment, Bush appointed William Reilly, a former president of a major environmental interest group, the Conservation Foundation, to head the EPA. The real test of Bush's commitment to the environment would come over deliberations with Congress over amending the Clean Air Act, which had last been modified in 1977—a task put off during the Reagan years.

The product of presidential-congressional negotiations, the Clean Air Act of 1990 attempted to create a balanced approach aimed at making continued progress in cleaning up the air. Nonattainment areas and mobile-source pollution were singled out for attention. The amendments gave states time limits within which to bring the areas into compliance with federal standards, ranging from three to twenty years for ozone and from five to ten years for carbon monoxide. They also placed controls on a wider range of emission sources than ever before, including gasoline stations, body shops, paint manufacturers, industrial-sized bakeries, and many other enterprises. Enhanced controls on mobile sources of pollution required conversion to oxygenated fuels in areas not complying with carbon monoxide standards, affecting areas in which one-third of the nation's population resides.

The 1990 amendments also toughened the automobile inspection and maintenance requirements included in the 1977 amendments, requiring more sophisticated testing methods for those metropolitan areas most out of compliance with federal standards for ozone emissions. The enhanced test measures auto emissions during both acceleration and deceleration, and tests the effectiveness of the governing electronic sensors and controls found in newer cars.

Reflecting the Bush administration's initiative and its influence at the apex of Bush's popularity, the 1990 legislation is notable for departing, in part, from the traditional approach to environmental regulation. Previous legislation relied on a "command and control" approach, built on the concepts of standards and enforcement. Congress established the goals, the EPA developed standards, and the states developed plans to apply and enforce them. Threatened sanctions or legal action by the EPA often won compliance, but they also kicked off what was commonly a protracted series of negotiations and moves and countermoves that resulted in compromise, frequently culminating in the EPA's conditional approval of state plans. Attention then moved to the steps that state and local governments, as their agents, might take to remove the conditions, commonly precipitating another wave of negotiations.[23]

The traditional regulatory approach relied on technology-forcing standards tied to permit granting, which led industries to install smokestack scrubbers, filters, and other equipment to reduce emissions. A new approach introduced *market-based incentives* into air pollution regulation, aimed at reducing components of urban smog and sulfur dioxide emissions that create acid rain. Although the EPA continued to set overall emission caps, it permitted states to develop plans that allowed regulated industries to buy and sell emission credits. The system works like this: as long as the aggregate emission ceiling for an area is not penetrated, a firm could increase its emissions beyond what it would be allowed if other industries in a nonattainment area reduced their emissions below target levels, in effect leaving room for the first firm to pollute more than it would otherwise be allowed. But what incentives exist for firms to reduce their emissions even more than required by the EPA?

Based on the market principle of self-interested behavior, the 1990 act provided an incentive for firms to do more than required, and that incentive is economic return. By adopting technology that reduces pollutants more than required, firms produce "excess pollution credits" that can be sold to other industries faced with reducing their own emissions. Rather than incurring the capital expense required to come into compliance, these other industries can elect to buy some or all of the excess credits—a proposition that might appear to be a good short-run business deal for the company doing the buying. Thus, as the rationale goes, the overall ceiling on emissions is not broken, and the individual firms doing the trading are acting in what they believe to be their corporate self-interest. Experience already suggests that electric utilities, which emit about 70 percent of the sulfur dioxide pollution in the United States, will be the major players in emission credit trading. Across the nation, trading in emission credits has been most active in California and in the Northeast.

As President Clinton began his second term in office, the EPA further toughened its air-quality standards. The 1990 Clean Air Act requires the EPA to review air-quality standards every five years to ensure that they adequately protect the public health. In November 1996, the EPA proposed new, more restrictive standards for ozone and particulate matter. After a series of hearings, the EPA announced the final version of the new standards on July 16, 1997, amid opponents' efforts to get Congress to pass a bill blocking their implementation. Industry officials, aligned with the National League of Cities and the National Association of Counties, led the opposition. Facing a certain presidential veto, Congress demurred.

Under the new regulations, the ozone standard changed from .12 parts per million measured over one hour to .08 parts per million measured over eight hours. For particulate matter, particles as small as 2.5 microns in diameter would be regulated, compared to the previous 10-micron standard. Opponents have questioned whether the incremental health benefits justify enterprises' costs of compliance, and both opponents and supporters of the toughened standards have debated not only the assumptions underlying projections of costs and benefits but the quality of the supporting science as well.

The new regulations give metropolitan areas time to meet the new standards. The EPA will not cite areas for noncompliance until 2004 for ozone and 2005 for particulate matter; however, the local governments in each area, working with their state environmental protection department, must develop plans that indicate how compliance will be attained. As a concession to congressional interests concerned about the justification for the tightened standards, the EPA committed to complete another full scientific review of the health effects of fine particles before it would designate any area out of compliance and impose controls. Nevertheless, communities and businesses in targeted areas are expected to take steps toward compliance with both the toughened ozone and particulate standards.[24]

Environmental protection has proved to be an area of enduring popular public support. Public support has been the counterbalance against efforts to reverse the expansionary course of environmental regulation. It mitigated attempts by the Reagan administration to weaken the EPA's rule-making and enforcement roles, and it served as a trump card in Bill Clinton's struggles with Congress over national policy and budgetary priorities. The expansion of environmental regulation stands in contrast to the wave of deregulation that swept through some areas of government regulation in the late 1970s and continued to the turn of the century.

DEREGULATION

Well before presidential candidate Ronald Reagan campaigned successfully on an agenda that called for lower taxes, reduced domestic spending, and a retrenchment in government regulation, progress had already been made in reducing economic regulation. Deregulation of commercial transportation that occurred during the late years of the Carter administration set the stage for a host of deregulatory initiatives that followed in the 1980s and 1990s.[25]

Airline deregulation started the deregulatory ball rolling. Prior to deregulation, the Civil Aeronautics Board (CAB) regulated five central aspects of interstate commercial airline operations: entry; routes; exit, or route abandonment; fares; and airline mergers. The CAB's guiding principle seemed to be ensuring the stability of the airline industry and the service it provides. Regulation insulated airlines from competition with each other, as well as from would-be new entrants. It also protected the jobs of airline employees and set up a structure that permitted wage demands from organized labor to be readily built into the approved rates. It should not be surprising, therefore, that both the established airline industry and its employee unions opposed deregulation.

The impetus for deregulation came from within the regulatory agency itself, although increasing pressure from consumer groups for expanded and cheaper airline service encouraged the CAB's inclinations. Both the CAB regulators and consumer advocates were influenced by entrepreneurial experiments taking place in Texas and California in *intrastate* commercial air transportation. CAB's authority was limited to interstate operations; it did not apply to intrastate air transportation. Thus absent state regulation, new entrants could enter and compete for service between a state's major metropolitan areas. And that is what the new maverick airline, Southwest Airlines, did in Texas. Operating smaller, more economical aircraft, and offering no-frills service, Southwest charged lower fares than could the regulated carriers. It also frequently flew into smaller, secondary airports located closer to city centers, making itself highly accessible to intrastate commuters. Another carrier, Pacific Southwest Airlines, followed suit in California. Although the state of California regulated fares for intrastate flights, they were based on the lowest-cost carrier, not the average cost followed by the CAB; so Pacific Southwest enjoyed a price advantage over the interstate carriers. Both airlines quickly proved popular with the public and expanded their passenger loads. They became exemplars for consumer groups of what greater competition could mean for the airline passenger.

In 1975, after John Robson became chairman, the CAB allowed limited experimentation with discount fares, and commissioned a thorough study of regulation and its effects. Although the study recognized the element of service equity that regulation ensured, in balance its tone was critical, reflecting the resulting operational inefficiencies and high costs to consumers. The new chairman, Alfred Kahn, became a champion of deregulation within the Carter administration, and he had little difficulty winning the support of the efficiency-oriented, engineering-educated president. With the administration's active support, Congress passed the Airline Deregulation Act of 1978 (the same year Congress also partly deregulated interstate wholesale sales of natural gas). The act allowed the CAB to give up all control of routes and fares, leaving fare-setting to competition in the marketplace, and to grant entry to any "fit, willing, and able" applicant. Concerning route abandonment, the legislation established a subsidy program to make it financially worthwhile during a transition period for a certified carrier to continue to provide service to those smaller communities previously served under regulation. Thereafter, the market would determine whether airlines would choose to continue service. Left with nothing significant to regulate, the CAB ceased to exist after 1984.

Following airline deregulation, the Carter administration and Congress turned their attention to interstate commercial rail and trucking transportation. American industry and agriculture relies heavily on railroads and trucks to carry their goods and products across the nation. Railroads offer shippers less flexibility than do trucks, but they also charge much lower rates for service. They carry approximately three-fourths of intercity freight ton miles but account for only about one-fourth of the costs of domestic freight transportation.[26] Railroads are best suited to shipments over long hauls and to points that have convenient access to the fixed rails. Heavy and bulky goods, such as agricultural machinery and construction materials, are most efficiently transported by rail. So are agricultural commodities and natural resources, such as coal and iron ore, that must travel long distances to market. Trucks tend to carry shipments over shorter distances than do the railroads; and their inherent flexibility and timeliness make them the mode of choice for most shippers, that is, unless shipping destinations, the types of goods carried, and delivery timelines are satisfactory enough to prompt shippers to take advantage of sizable cost-savings that rail transportation affords.

As discussed earlier, rail transportation has been subject to government regulation far longer than has trucking. The ICC regulated rates, the abandonment of service, freight car utilization, and mergers. Compared to trucking, the entry of new competitors has not been a prominent focus of railroad regulation. The high fixed costs of operation and the railroad industry's declining share of interstate freight miles have combined to discourage prospective new entrants into the industry. In approving rates, the ICC used value-of-service pricing, pricing based on the value of goods being shipped rather than the costs of providing the service. High-value shipments of manufactured goods subsidized shipments of low-value goods, such as grain and other agricultural produce. In response, shippers of manufactured products turned to trucking as a better value. As railroads lost revenues to trucking, they petitioned the ICC to permit them to abandon service on unprofitable route segments—a practice to which the ICC was typically unsympathetic. Yet, at the same time, the pricing system continued to give the railroads a decided government-approved advantage over trucking for the transport of low-value goods.

The ICC also regulated freight car utilization. The nation's network of fixed track created inter-railroad dependence, since freight often moves from an origin served by one railroad, through areas served by another, and out to a destination served by a third. Because it would be highly inefficient to transfer goods from one railroad's cars to another's, railroads rent the other's cars and hitch them to their own locomotives for their portion of the haul. The ICC regulated the interline rental rates that railroads can charge one another, and set the rates low, creating another cross-subsidy of sorts. In effect, the larger railroads with the greatest geographic coverage and number of cars subsidized the smaller railroads having fewer cars. As would be expected, the subsidizers argued for a fairer, market rate of return on their loaned capital.

Drawing on the experience of airline deregulation, President Carter threw his support behind railroad deregulation. In October 1980, Congress passed the Staggers Rail Act, which opened the way for greater market pricing of service and allowed for the abandonment of unprofitable routes. In passing the legislation, Congress also addressed the market disadvantage that regulation had placed the railroads in vis-à-vis trucking. The act provided that where sufficient intermodal competition exists, the ICC could exempt a number of commodities from rate regulation altogether, allowing the market to set prices. Under the partial deregulation that occurred, the ICC allowed double-stack containers, which increased the railroads' operating efficiency and rendered them even more price-competitive with trucking for the transport of manufactured goods.

Trucking deregulation followed a similar timeline to that of railroad deregulation. Compared to rail deregulation, the movement to trucking deregulation turned even more to rooting out the inefficiencies of the regulated system and reducing costs to shippers. In fact, the debate over trucking deregulation more closely resembled the debate over commercial airline deregulation than that over railroad deregulation. As noted earlier, the ICC exercised many of the same regulatory functions as did the CAB, including entry, routes, exit, rates, and mergers. Its regulation of entry included controls not only on the ability of existing licensed carriers to compete in the industry itself, but on their ability to transport goods other than those they were expressly authorized to carry. Once a motor carrier obtained the authority to transport a particular type of commodity, agricultural products, for example, it then had to secure the authority for specific routes. This combination of commodity and route authorization created a highly segmented system, often causing truckers to make empty backhauls because they either lacked the route authority to carry goods of whatever type back to their point of origin, or they possessed the route authority but lacked the authority to carry a type of commodity that was otherwise available for transport. Thus entry and routes became central foci of the case to improve efficiency.

Based on the experience of airline deregulation, which included increased flight availability and price reduction for most consumers,[27] advocates of trucking deregulation assumed that freer entry and greater trucker flexibility in serving routes would improve the entire system's efficiency and result in lower costs to shippers. ICC regulators come to share this perspective toward the end of the decade. Unlike rail, with its high fixed costs and rigid route structure which mitigated competition from within the industry (with the railroads worried much more about their ability to compete with another transportation mode, namely trucking), trucking offered few intrinsic obstacles to competition from within. In the absence of regulation, an enterprising entrepreneur need only acquire a truck and licensed drivers to begin competing on the basis of price and service quality. Compare that to the start-up costs in the railroad business of purchasing locomotives, rail cars, and track rights. It was this relative ease of entry that, in the first place, prompted the trucking industry in the early twentieth century to seek ICC regulation in an effort to restrain competition and ensure profitability.

Unlike the path to railroad deregulation, trucking deregulation got a boost from the courts. Under a 1977 decision that supported the complaint of an applicant denied entry by the ICC, the court ruled that the ICC could no longer consider whether existing carriers could provide the service sought by a new entrant. It could base its decision only on whether entry would serve a useful purpose and whether existing carriers would be harmed. Congress's enactment of the Motor Carrier Act of 1980 followed the judiciary's lead and opened up entry widely. Under the act, new entrants only had to show that the proposed service was useful and that they were fit, willing, and able service providers. The statutory basis of presumption shifted in favor of ICC approving the application. Competition ballooned as a result, and the rates charged shippers fell accordingly. The increased competition brought with it improved service. Where carriers used their newly found freedom to readily abandon unprofitable routes, greater freedom of entry brought in new carriers in many instances to serve abandoned routes.[28]

With deregulation, the ICC did not go out of business, as had the CAB. Yet its workforce declined by over two-thirds in the ten years following enactment of the Motor Carrier Act of 1980.[29] Congress replaced it with the Surface Transportation Board in 1995.

The deregulation of commercial transportation embodied an idea whose time had come. The ingredients for policy change were present and reinforcing. Martha Derthick and Paul Quirk offer five reasons why deregulation of commercial airline and trucking became such a compelling force in commercial transportation policymaking. They argue that (1) elite opinion converged in support of reform, cutting across political parties, ideological predispositions, and academic disciplines; (2) officeholders in positions of leadership advocated reform and took supportive initiatives; (3) the early procompetitive initiatives of the regulatory commissions set the deregulatory agenda and precipitated the opposition of the regulated industries, which turned to Congress for protection—inviting Congress to take an institutional stand on the issue; (4) the combined weight of factors 1 to 3 influenced Congress to pass legislation in support of deregulation; and (5) the affected industries found themselves at a disadvantage in their efforts to poke holes in the widely supported idea of deregulation and to mobilize the support of opinion leaders and policymakers.[30]

The cases of commercial airline, railroad, and trucking deregulation also appear to fit John Kingdon's theoretical framework created to help us understand agenda setting and policy change.[31] These cases seem to be instances in which the independent streams of problem recognition, policy development, and political support came together to set the deregulatory agenda and coalesce political support for a preferred policy option that appeared to solve the problem as defined. Policymakers and policy entrepreneurs came together in defining the problem in airline and trucking regulation as one of economic inefficiency, whereas they viewed the problem in railroad regulation as primarily one of rate and service inequity, even though deregulation did allow the railroads to operate more efficiently through more flexible freight car utilization and expanded cooperative ventures with the trucking industry. The regulators themselves pursued a policy course that had been shaped by expert policy entrepreneurs who drew on the findings of empirical studies of the effects of regulation. That policy course found the support of presidents and congressional leaders who used the same standards of judgment as had the regulators and policy entrepreneurs in defining the problem and evaluating alternative courses of action to solve it as defined.

The deregulation of commercial transportation also illustrates the phenomenon of policy learning at work. The debate over trucking and railroad deregulation was greatly influenced by the earlier debate over airline deregulation. It established the "givens"[32] of problem definition and the choice of policy instruments, facilitating their transfer from one related policy area to another. It also influenced the terms of future debates over deregulation, although an important new ingredient—technological change—came to affect problem definition and alternative possibilities in contemporary debates. Its effects were felt most in telecommunications deregulation and, to a lesser but still significant degree, in electric energy deregulation.

Telecommunications Deregulation

Congress's passage of the Telecommunications Act of 1996 represented the first major overhaul of federal telecommunications policy since the Communications Act of 1934, which created the Federal Communications Commission and gave it the power to regulate long-distance telephone services and prices. The original act also waived federal antitrust laws, essentially sanctioning AT&T's hegemony in a highly noncompetitive market. The telecommunications giant enjoyed an unchallenged monopoly position in long-distance service, was the exclusive provider of telephone equipment nationally, and provided over two-thirds of local telephone service.[33] The burden fell on would-be competitors to demonstrate that their entry was both "necessary and desirable in the public interest," a criterion similar to that applied earlier to commercial transportation.[34] The company promised in return to run a widely accessible, technically advanced and reliable interconnected system. Non-AT&T local providers connected for a price to the Bell network for access to AT&T long-distance lines. This pattern held into the 1970s.

While AT&T controlled the line-based national telephone network, changes in technology enabled entrepreneurs to position themselves as prospective competitors. The development of microwave technology in the 1950s offered the potential to send high-quality voice transmission along microwave relay points. A new company, Microwave Communications, Inc. (MCI), petitioned the FCC in 1963 for the right to establish a microwave link between Chicago and St. Louis to service business users, arguing that the experiment would not harm the existing telephone network and users' ability to connect to it. The FCC granted its approval by a narrow 4 to 3 vote. The majority recognized that the relatively new technology held promise for expanded future use, and they saw the immediate limited application as a miniscule threat to AT&T's revenues.

After a successful but highly limited beginning, MCI wanted to expand its operations and connect its private-line business users to AT&T's local telephone switches. The FCC denied its 1978 request. MCI then successfully appealed the FCC's ruling to a federal appellate court, which ruled that the FCC had no compelling reason to deny connection.[35] The concept of competition was gaining a foothold in telecommunications decision making, which should not be surprising, given the times. Recall that 1978 was also the year in which Congress deregulated both commercial air service and interstate wholesale sales of natural gas.

Four years earlier, the increasingly competition-oriented Antitrust Division of the Justice Department filed suit in federal district court alleging that AT&T used its monopoly power to prevent manufacturers other than its wholly owned subsidiary, Western Electric, from competing to connect customer equipment to the AT&T-controlled network, and that AT&T's entrenched position in long-distance service thwarted competition. But before the court could decide the case, the FCC decided to begin certifying competitors' equipment for use on the AT&T network. That decision, coupled with MCI's victory, prefaced the greater deregulation that was to come.[36] Neither case, however, derailed the suit, which picked up steam after the 1980 general election.

In 1980, AT&T asked to have the suit dismissed. The presiding judge, Harold Greene, refused the petition in a strongly worded statement that signaled his pro-competitive sympathies. With the handwriting on the wall, AT&T and the Justice Department settled the suit in January 1982. AT&T agreed to divest itself of its seven regional operating companies that provided networked local telephone service, but it would retain its long-distance services, Western Electric, and its Yellow Pages directory services. The divestiture decree also required that competing long-distance companies get the same connections to local networks as those afforded to AT&T.[37] Despite the agreement, telecommunications regulation changed little at the state level. States continued to regulate local telephone companies, including entry and rate-setting.

At the federal level, the deregulation bandwagon continued to roll. In 1984, Congress deregulated the cable television industry, an action that would later be reversed in 1992, following steep increases in subscription fees charged to consumers. The Cable Communications Policy Act of 1984 expressly proscribed local telephone companies from offering cable television services, a market they were eager to enter. Local companies also chafed to get into the long-distance business, and cable companies wanted to offer local telephone service. The long-distance companies also wanted to provide local telephone service but worried that their entry into the local-service market would enable local companies to justify their desire to offer long-distance. The growing appetite for interservice competition and the business prospects it offered loomed large in the public debate into the 1990s, but not much changed regulatorily or legislatively. It was not until 1995 that the FCC removed AT&T's dominant provider status and allowed it to compete freely in pricing its long-distance services.[38]

Technology continued to change, however. By the early to mid-1990s, advances in digital technologies, along with a greatly expanded fiber-optic communications highway that crisscrossed the nation, removed the remaining technical barriers to interservice competition. They permitted competitors to bypass local companies' connections; and they opened up the possibility of bundling services, including regular and cellular telephones, Internet access, and cable television.[39] The new digital-compression technology, developed in 1990 by researchers at General Instrument Corporation, provided the capability to transmit high-quality television pictures in digital form. In doing so, it also created the ability for the binary information flowing over cable television, telephones, and computers to be interchangeable. As Dick Oluffs puts it,

> Once a transmission is digitized, there is no principal difference, aside from volume of information, between a telephone call and a televised baseball game. If the conduit for the information is big enough, and the machines at both ends are capable of sending and receiving the information, the distinctions between cable, broadcast, and telephone companies disappear.[40]

Both regulators and the regulated interests appreciated full well that these technological developments brought down the technical walls that had divided telecommunications service providers and, with them, a justification for separate regulation of the different telecommunications services. Technically, cable operators could offer local telephone service, and local telephone companies could offer video programming and long-distance telephone services. Local telephone companies could provide communications and information services through Internet connections, and long-distance telephone companies could provide local telephone service. Broadcast television could sell its signals and programs over land-based cable and fiberoptic lines, in addition to over the airwaves. Without regulatory impediments, a single provider, such as a local phone company, could provide local and long-distance telephone service, cable television programming, and Internet connection.

Since these possibilities exist technically, the key issue then becomes the extent to which government will permit unbridled competition in a giant communications market. That question was answered preliminarily through the Telecommunications Act of 1996, which passed both chambers of Congress by lopsided margins (414–16 in the House, and 91–5 in the Senate).

Congress set in motion a process that, when followed, would lead to significant deregulation of telecommunications. The act granted the regional Bells the right to offer long-distance services once the FCC determined that they had opened their markets to viable competition over local telephone service. It required local telephone companies to allow competitors to connect with their networks at any technically feasible point in order to complete calls, and it required that the connection be equal in quality to that which the local company provides itself. The act also set a course toward deregulation of cable television, eliminating price controls in April 1999 for more than basic service packages, or earlier if local telephone companies entered the market and provided video programming to a comparable number of households. Price controls on basic service packages would remain in place until the competition requirement is met, even if that were to occur after March 31, 1999. To allow cable television competition by local phone companies, the law eliminated a ban on telephone companies offering video services.[41]

The act gave the FCC power to preempt state or local regulatory efforts to inhibit competition. Yet it also charged the states with taking steps to ensure universal service at a reasonable cost. Congress's juxtaposition of market-based competition and universal access to service at a reasonable cost represents a compromise between those wanting full deregulation (the Republican leadership in Congress) and those committed to the principle of universal service (President Clinton and Democratic congressional leaders). The resulting partial preemption put a premium on interservice provider competition within a more integrated telecommunications system while guarding the public's right to local telephone service at a fair price.

In signing the Telecommunications Act of 1996, President Clinton praised it as a tool for advancing a telecommunications revolution led by technological innovation that chafed under "outdated laws, designed for a time when there was one phone company, three TV networks, and no such thing as a personal computer." Continuing, he remarked that "today, with the stroke of a pen, our laws will catch up with our future. We will help to create an open marketplace where competition and innovation can move as quick as light."[42]

The experience of the first three years following deregulation has shown that, contrary to President Clinton's optimism, competition in the telecommunications industry has not moved as fast as light. In fact, the record is at best mixed. The regional Bell companies have been slow to provide new competitors with interconnections for local telephone service, prompting critics to conclude that the regional Bells prize holding on to their monopoly position more than they do the opportunity to compete in the already highly competitive long-distance market.[43] In fact, by the spring of 1999, other carriers had gained only 2.7 percent of the local telephone service market.[44] However, there are signs that telecommunications companies are positioning themselves for interservice competition when the time is right.[45] For instance, AT&T purchased Tele-Communications, Inc. (TCI), the United States' second largest cable provider, and Media One, another large cable company. AT&T also contracted with Time Warner, the nation's largest cable company, to get access to its network and to provide service over it.[45] In another move, US West acquired Continental Cablevision for $5.3 billion.[46]

Electricity Deregulation

Just as technological advances provided the means for expanded competition in telecommunications, they also opened the door to competition in the electric power industry. Advances in the generation and distribution of electric power have led the way. They enabled policymakers to question tenets underlying the traditional belief that electric power provision best took the form of a natural monopoly—given the need for large, high-cost plants, particularly coal-fired plants—that could produce power on an efficient and cost-effective economy of scale and maintain large reserves of emergency capacity. However, the introduction of advanced natural gas-turbine technology has allowed power producers to reach the same economies of scale in much smaller, lower-cost plants. In fact, a new innovation allows gas–turbine technology to reach even higher levels of efficiency than the traditional coal-fired plants made possible. It involves combining two turbines so that the waste heat from the primary turbine is used in a second turbine.[47] Gas–turbine technologies have also been able to generate and store competitively priced energy in small quantities that can be used to complement other energy sources during peak demands. Yet it should be recognized that the efficiencies realized by these new technological innovations are dependent on the price of natural gas remaining roughly in its present position relative to other energy-generating sources.

Another restraint on competition that changing technology has diminished deals with optimum loading of the electricity grid. Service reliability is enhanced when the grid contains only as much power as will be used. Because of the technical nature of loading the grid, supporters of monopoly have argued that a single enterprise is best suited to manage grid loading, and that additional players would only increase the chances of grid failure, leading to power outages. Technological advances have allowed for greater control of the electrons on the grid, and thereby reduced failure rates. That technology is called Flexible AC Transmission System (FACTS), and it allows for electronic rather than mechanical switching on the electricity grid, greatly increasing control of electrons and making single-enterprise management of demand placed on the grid far less significant in ensuring grid reliability.[48]

Although technological barriers to competition have been coming down, government regulation still limits competition over electric power provision. Change, however, is in the air. The proponents of deregulation have won significant victories at the state level, and the debate over federal deregulation is building nationally. In the current environment, the states, through public service commissions, are responsible for regulating investor-owned utilities, including universal-service requirements, retail rates, safety standards, and relations with customers. For municipal-owned utilities, local government councils establish service parameters and set retail rates. At the national level, the Federal Energy Regulatory Commission regulates the wholesale sale of electric power and its interstate transmission. Its powers extend to rate-setting, as well as to service and safety standards.

Federal regulation dates back to 1935, when Congress passed two major pieces of legislation: the Federal Power Act, which created the Federal Power Commission (later renamed the Federal Energy Regulatory Commission) to regulate interstate electricity transmissions, and the Public Utility Holding Act, which split up the handful of large holding companies operating across state lines that controlled most of America's electric-power generation. The act also restricted the activities of the resulting enterprises to defined geographic areas. It was that latter action that solidified the vertical integration of the industry, by which those companies came to own the generating facilities, transmission lines, and distribution systems within their own exclusive service areas. State regulation, which preceded federal regulation and had its roots in the Progressive Era, regulated providers' virtual monopoly status and guaranteed them a cost-plus rate of return on their investment.

In addition to its regulatory role, the federal government became a direct provider of electricity in the 1930s. In 1933, Congress created the Tennessee Valley Authority (TVA) to provide electricity to much of Appalachia. Three years later, Congress took another step to electrify rural America by establishing the Rural Electrification Administration (now known as the Rural Utilities Service) and charging it with providing subsidized loans and grants to rural electric cooperatives. Congress took both initiatives to help develop rural areas economically and widen access to electric power where investor-owned utilities were least likely to provide it. Those programs continue today, even though the rationale for their creation no longer seems to apply, given rural America's transformation since the New Deal.[49]

The patterns of regulation established in the 1930s remained largely intact until the 1990s, when two federal initiatives, influenced by technological change and the growing debate over telecommunications deregulation, spurred competition in the interstate wholesale electricity business. The first saw Congress take action, when in 1992 it passed the Energy Policy Act, which permitted electricity generating facilities not sharing cost accounts with a parent utility to compete with one another and sell electricity in the wholesale market. The act also required utilities owning transmission lines to carry that power to electricity wholesalers and end-use retail customers (the latter as part of a state-mandated direct-access program) at nondiscriminatory, cost-based rates. The second action came four years later from the Federal Energy Regulatory Commission itself, when it mandated that transmission-owning utilities charge themselves for transmission service at the same rates they charge other parties under the 1992 act's terms.[50]

Following those inroads, the contemporary debate, both in the nation's capital and in the states, focused on whether competition among electricity providers should be broadened so that deregulated "free wheeling" of electricity over transmission lines could be extended to all utility customers. That could happen as a result of either state-by-state deregulation or federal statutory preemption. Regardless of the route, such deregulation would allow retail customers to choose their energy provider in much the same way they choose who provides their long-distance telephone service. Most observers expect that the resulting competition should lower the market price of electric power. Yet deregulation of retail utility service raises a number of thorny issues, including those of universal access to service at a fair price; potential cost and rate shifts from large industrial customers to small businesses and residential customers; reliability of service; and the recovery of "stranded costs," that is, those costs tied to previous investments in power generation that do not contribute to competitive pricing.[51] Examples of stranded costs include investments in old-technology power plants, long-term fuel and power contracts, and the costs associated with decommissioning nuclear power plants. Whereas regulation allows utilities to build cost-recovery into the rates they charge customers, competition puts utilities with high stranded costs at a decided disadvantage.

Since the Federal Energy Regulatory Commission's 1996 order, subsequent deregulatory initiatives have come from the states, not the federal government. Deregulation has been variously accomplished through legislation, public service commission rule making, or a combination of the two. As of June 1, 1999, legislatures in twenty-two states,[52] typically responding to gubernatorial initiatives, have approved legislation to deregulate or restructure the electric utility industry and pave the way for competition in retail sales. California, an early leader in deregulation, along with Massachusetts, opted for full customer choice of electricity providers. Yet as of October 1998, only about 1 percent of customers in both states opted to switch electric providers.[53] Other states—including Montana, New Hampshire, Pennsylvania, and Rhode Island—have begun to phase in choice or operate limited pilot projects. The remaining states have adopted framework legislation that committed their states to move toward retail competition and consumer choice, pending agreement on how best to achieve it, or have adopted administrative rules to initiate deregulation.[54]

This flurry of state activity has divided congressional leaders over the desirability of federal deregulation of electric power. For those supporting federal legislative action, giving states the option to deregulate is not sufficient. Supporters argue that the federal government has an obligation to require all states to let their residents decide who will provide them with electricity and enjoy the savings that they expect competition to bring. Opponents worry that national deregulation would redistribute costs by drawing power away from states with low-cost electricity to more financially attractive markets in other states, thus raising the price of electricity for those who had previously benefited from lower prices. Opponents also worry that national deregulation would primarily benefit the largest electricity users, whose business competitors would covet most, and leave residential users with little rate relief or even rate increases. They see residential users in rural areas most in jeopardy. Yet supporters counter that competitors have doggedly gone after households' business after deregulation of long-distance telephone service. They also argue that competition should benefit all users, even though the extent of that benefit may vary. In any event, supporters point to the expected aggregate cost savings nationally. The Clinton administration, for one, has projected that national utility deregulation could save consumers up to $20 billion a year.[55]

Before advancing federal deregulation, it appears that Congress is willing to wait to see how many states elect to deregulate electric power on their own. Those states that have initiated deregulation by the time of this writing have, for the most part, been states with relatively high energy costs. Legislators in states where con-sumers are already enjoying low costs tend to be less than enthusiastic about deregu-lation. Although deregulation could lower costs further, it also is likely to draw power away from low-cost areas to higher-cost areas. The task of putting together a coalition in Congress large enough to pass federal electricity deregulation will not be as easy as finding majority support for deregulation in a high-cost state.

The politics of electricity deregulation are also complicated by government's in-volvement in power production. Greater competition poses a threat to the small and less-efficient municipal power providers. If municipal power users switch to competitor-supplied power, the affected municipalities will suffer revenue losses. Those high-cost municipal providers that use comparatively high electric rates as a form of taxation will be most vulnerable. Congressional representatives whose dis-tricts include a high number of municipally owned power plants will feel the cross-pressures of their constituents' interests in the potentially lower electricity rates that competition can bring and the likely loss of business and tax revenues that competition can pose for their political colleagues who lead municipalities in their districts.

RISING PROCESS CONSTRAINTS ON REGULATION

This chapter has looked at regulation and deregulation along distinct substantive policy lines, exploring the rationale for government action; the political forces ar-rayed in support of, and in opposition to, government action; and the economic im-plications of government's authoritative choices. As has been apparent, govern-ment regulatory and deregulatory policy has taken different turns over time, and those turns have largely been a response to changing perceptions of what constitute pressing public problems. But in addition to using regulation or deregulation to ad-dress problems along sectoral lines, policymakers have altered their perceptions over time about the desirability of regulation and deregulation as desirable tools of state-craft. Regulation won out for most of the twentieth century; both presidents and members of Congress viewed it, in balance, as promoting the public interest. Yet, as Jeffrey Cohen argues, until the 1970s policymakers rendered that judgment more on what they believed to be perceived problems and economic and political forces at work in the substantive policy areas under scrutiny than on normative grounds or any real sense of the macroeconomic implications of regulation.[56] That came to change in the 1970s, as regulations grew and extended further into areas of social policy, and as the economy went into recession in mid-decade and suffered from stagflation (both high unemployment and high inflation) toward the decade's end.

Both Presidents Ford and Carter connected expanded regulation to America's economic ills and lent their support to deregulation as an appropriate policy re-sponse. President Reagan gave regulatory restraint an ideological wrapping, consis-tent with his call for reduced government penetration in society and the economy, striking a chord that resonated with America's liberal normative inheritance. For candidate and then President Reagan, the federal government needed to tax and regulate less—leaving more income in the hands of individuals to decide how to spend it, and more room for the market to determine economic outcomes. That sentiment, and the public's response to it, made a strong impression on Reagan's presidential successors and the Congresses with which they dealt. Not only did it release a second wave of deregulation; it also engendered a string of presidential controls on new regulation. The presumption had shifted. Presidential controls placed the onus on government to justify its regulatory interventions, and forced regulators to maneuver their proposals through executive screens and tests.

President Reagan set up the most formidable controls. In addition to creating the Task Force on Regulatory Relief and appointing Vice President George Bush as its chairman, Reagan issued two important executive orders that erected regulatory hurdles. The first, issued in 1981, required that a cost-benefit analysis accompany all proposed major regulations. It also changed the Office of Information and Regulatory Affairs (OIRA), which had been created in the OMB as a provision of the 1980 Paperwork Reduction Act, to review agency analysis, perform independent cost-benefit analysis when deemed needed, and screen out proposed regulations that failed to meet the standard of efficiency.

Early in his second term, Reagan raised the bar again, requiring that regulatory agencies disclose regulations being planned, not just those in the process of being advanced. The new order forced regulatory agencies to evaluate how consistent the planned regulations are with the president's policy agenda. On the basis of that review, the OIRA could prevent executive-branch agencies from promulgating regulations inconsistent with the president's program. President Bush continued these practices.[57]

When President Clinton took office in 1993, he rescinded Reagan's order requiring cost-benefit analysis, and replaced it with one of his own, Executive Order 12866. In doing so, Clinton took away the OMB's authority to detain proposed regulations that fail to meet the cost-benefit test. In its place, the new order requires agencies to identify and evaluate alternative regulatory options, including comparing their costs and benefits, before advancing a regulatory proposal. However, a study of the OIRA's review of proposed regulations found that agencies widely ignored the requirement, either focusing only on the preferred alternative, or failing to compare benefits to costs.[58] To date, the Clinton administration has chosen not to enforce the requirements stringently, giving agencies greater freedom to shape their case in support of regulation when it is consistent with the president's agenda. In response, Republican congressional leaders have threatened to make every effort to pass legislation that imposes a rigid cost-benefit test on the OMB, reining in the administration's freedom to apply that standard as it sees fit.[59] The question remains whether such a mandate would escape a presidential veto, for President Clinton appreciates, just as did his predecessors, that rule making is a political process through which participants seek to advance their policy and political objectives.

NOTES

1. Milton Friedman, *Free to Choose* (Chicago: University of Chicago Press, 1980), 5.

2. This insight comes from John G. Francis, in his *The Politics of Regulation: A Comparative Perspective* (Cambridge, MA: Blackwell Publishers, 1993), 11–17.

3. This discussion draws on Marc Allan Eisner's historical analysis in *The State in the American Political Economy* (Englewood Cliffs, NJ: Prentice-Hall, 1995).

4. Eisner, *The State in the American Political Economy*, 99.

5. Marc Allan Eisner, *Regulatory Politics in Transition* (Baltimore: Johns Hopkins University Press, 1993), 47–72.

6. *Wabash, St. Louis & Pacific Railway Co. v. Illinois*, 118 U.S. 557 (1986), cited in Eisner, *The State in the American Political Economy*, 113.

7. Jeffrey E. Cohen, *Politics and Economic Policy in the United States* (Boston: Houghton Mifflin Co., 1997), 264.

8. Donald V. Harper, *Transportation in America: Users, Carriers, Government*, 2d ed. (Englewood Cliffs, NJ: Prentice-Hall, 1982), 468.

9. William Lilley III and James Miller III, "The New Social Regulation," *The Public Interest*, 47 (Spring 1977), 52–53.

10. Steven Kelman, "Occupational Safety and Health Administration," in *The Politics of Regulation*, ed. James Q. Wilson (New York: Basic Books, 1980), 236–266.

11. Kenneth J. Meier, *Regulation: Politics, Bureaucracy, and Economics* (New York: St. Martin's Press, 1985), 141–143.

12. This analysis largely comes from Kenneth Meier in his *Regulation: Politics, Bureaucracy, and Economics*, 143–144, although it is supplemented by the insights of Alfred Marcus in his chapter "Environmental Protection Agency," appearing in *The Politics of Regulation*, ed. James Q. Wilson, 267–303, and those of Charles O. Jones in his *Clean Air* (Pittsburgh: Pittsburgh University Press, 1975), 191–193.

13. The following discussion incorporates and selectively revises material written by the author and included in Dennis L. Dresang and James J. Gosling, *Politics and Policy in American States and Communities*, 2d ed. (Boston: Allyn & Bacon, 1999), 415–418. It appears with permission of the publisher.

14. Norman J. Vig and Michael E. Kraft, "Environmental Policy from the Seventies to the Eighties," in *Environmental Policy in the 1980s: Reagan's New Agenda*, eds. Norman J. Vig and Michael E. Kraft (Washington, DC: Congressional Quarterly Press, 1984), 17.

15. The Council on Environmental Quality, *Environmental Quality, 1981* (Washington, DC: Government Printing Office, 1981), 33, 243, 246.

16. Helen M. Ingram and Dean E. Mann, "Preserving the Clean Water Act: The Appearance of Environmental Victory," in *Environmental Policy in the 1980s: Reagan's New Agenda*, 255–256.

17. Ibid.

18. *Environmental Quality, 1980* (Washington, DC: The Council on Environmental Quality, 1980), iv.

19. Michael E. Kraft, "A New Environmental Policy Agenda: The 1980 Presidential Campaign and Its Aftermath," in *Environmental Policy in the 1980s: Reagan's New Agenda*, 29–50.

20. Norman J. Vig, "The President and the Environment: Revolution or Retreat," in *Environmental Policy in the 1980s: Reagan's New Agenda*, 87.

21. Ibid.

22. Susan Welch, et al., *American Government*, 4th ed. (St. Paul, MN: West Publishing, 1992), 578.

23. R. Shep Melnick, "Pollution Deadlines and the Coalition for Failure," in *Environmental Politics*, eds. Michael S. Greve and Fred L. Smith (New York: Praeger, 1993) 89–104.

24. *Oral Testimony of Fred Hanson, Deputy Administrator, Environmental Protection Agency, Before the Subcommittee on Commercial and Administrative Law, Committee on the Judiciary, U.S.*

House of Representatives, July 20, 1997; Jackie Cummins Radcliffe and Jeff Dale, "Defining Dirty Air," *State Legislatures* 23, no. 5 (May 1997), 20–25.

25. This discussion of the deregulation of commercial transportation relies on the work of Charles F. Bonser, et al., *Policy Choice and Public Action* (Upper Saddle River, NJ: Prentice-Hall, 1996), 217–240; and Martha Derthick and Paul Quirk, *The Politics of Deregulation* (Washington, DC: The Brookings Institution, 1985), especially Chapters 1, 2, and 7.

26. Bonser, et al., *Policy Choice and Public Action*, 235.

27. John E. Robson, "Airline Deregulation: Twenty Years of Success and Counting," *Regulation* 21 (1988), 17–22; Adam D. Thierer, "Twentieth Year of Airline Deregulation: Cause for Celebration, Not Re-regulation," *The Heritage Foundation Backgrounder* (October 28, 1997); Steven A. Morrison and Clifford Winston, *The Evolution of the Airline Industry* (Washington, DC: The Brookings Institution, 1995), 6–19.

28. Paul Teske, et al., *Deregulating Freight Transportation: Delivering the Goods* (Washington, DC: The AEI Press, 1995); Clifford Winston, et al., *The Economic Effects of Surface Freight Regulation* (Washington, DC: The Brookings Institution, 1990).

29. Cohen, *Politics and Economic Policy in the United States*, 274.

30. Derthick and Quirk, *The Politics of Deregulation*, 238–245.

31. John W. Kingdon, *Agendas, Alternatives, and Public Policies*, 2d ed. (New York: Harper-Collins, 1995).

32. A concept contributed by Herbert Simon which gets at the way decision makers simplify choice by screening out cues that are inconsistent with a restricted set of options in harmony with ingrained predispositions, or "givens." See his *Administrative Behavior* (New York: Macmillan, 1958).

33. Jon Healey, "Information Network: Congress Tries to Merge Public Goals with Industry Interests," *The Information Arena: Making Communications Policy for the Next Generation, Congressional Quarterly Special Report*, 52, Supplement to no. 19 (May 14, 1994), 11.

34. Dick W. Oluffs III, *The Making of Telecommunications Policy* (Boulder, CO: Lynne Rienner Publishers, 1999), 35.

35. The FCC's *Execunet* decision (*MCI Telecommunications Corporation v. FCC*), 1979.

36. Oluffs III, *The Making of Telecommunications Policy*, 53.

37. Ibid., 55; Elizabeth E. Bailey, "The Evolving Politics of Telecommunications Regulation," in *A Communications Cornucopia*, ed. Roger G. Noll and Monroe E. Price (Washington, DC: The Brookings Institution, 1968), 390–392.

38. Bailey, "The Evolving Politics of Telecommunications Regulation," 392.

39. Oluffs III, *The Making of Telecommunications Policy*, 102.

40. Ibid., 102–103.

41. Dan Carney, "Congress Fires Its First Shot in Information Revolution," *Congressional Quarterly Weekly Report* 54, no. 5 (February 3, 1996), 289–294; Jon Healey, "Telecommunications Highlights," *Congressional Quarterly Weekly Report* 54, no. 7 (February 17, 1996), 406–420.

42. *Remarks by the President in Signing Ceremony for the Telecommunications Act Conference Report*, February 8, 1996.

43. Robert D. Boerner, "Reach Out, But Not Too Far," *State Legislatures* 24, no. 5 (May 1998), 32–33; Lisa Moskowitz, "Telecom Update: Baby Bells Fight Improved Net Service, *PCWorld online*, July 22, 1997, www.idg.net/idg_frames/english/content.cgi?vc=docid_0–73009.html.

44. David Masci, "Telecoms's Unfinished Business," *Congressional Quarterly Special Report*, 57, Supplement to no.19.

45. Kirk Victor, "Sleeping Watchdogs?," *National Journal* 31 (June 26, 1999), 1880–1884.

46. Boerner, "Reach Out, But Not Too Far," 32.

47. Richard E. Balzhiser, "Technology to Play Hand in Future Power Market," *Forum for Applied Research and Public Policy* 12, no. 3 (Fall 1997), 24.

48. Ibid., 25. Thanks go to Brigham Daniels for helping me to appreciate technology's contributions to electric-power deregulation.

49. Adam D. Thierer, "Energizing America: A Blueprint for Deregulating the Electricity Market," *Backgrounder*, no. 1100 (The Heritage Foundation, January 23, 1997c), 5–7.

50. "Electric Industry Restructuring: Issues and Opportunities for the States," *NGA Issue Brief* (February 2, 1997), 1; Eric Hurst, "21st Century Will Transform Power Industry," *Forum for Applied Research and Public Policy* 12, no. 3 (Fall 1997), 7–8.

51. Pamela S. Easter, "A Spotlight on Electric Deregulation," *Public Management* (February 1997), 11.

52. Charles Pope, "Barton Calls for Action on Electricity Derugulation Despite Daunting Problems," *CQ Weekly* 57 (June 19, 1999), 1469.

53. Wallace Roberts, "Power Play," *The American Prospect*, no. 42 (January-February 1999), 75.

54. "Actions to Restructure the Electric Industry: October 1998 Update," *NGA online*, www.nga.org.Pubs/Issue Briefs/1998/981013Electricity.asp.

55. Alan K. Ota, "Electric Power Competition: Slow Burner, Lots of Heat," *Congressional Quarterly Weekly Report* 55, no. 46 (November 22, 1997), 2901.

56. Jeffrey E. Cohen, *Politics and Economic Policy in the United States*, 275–277.

57. Ibid., 278–280.

58. Susan E. Dudley and Angela Antonelli, "Congress and the Clinton OMB: Unwilling Partners in Regulatory Oversight?," *Regulation* 20, no. 4, (Fall 1997) 17–18.

59. Alan Freedman, "GOP's Secret Weapon Against Regulations: Finesse," *Congressional Quarterly Weekly Report* 56, no. 35 (September 5, 1998), 2314–2320.

CHAPTER 6

Falling Through Capitalism's Cracks: The Needy and Government's Obligation to Them

W riting in the late nineteenth century, at a time when waves of European immigrants swept across the United States seeking better lives, Horatio Alger extolled the opportunity offered by America. For Alger, the United States presented few barriers to upward mobility, in contrast to Europe's much more rigid social divisions. His popular accounts of boys from poor families who rose to social and financial heights widely captivated American readers. For Alger and his millions of readers, the United States offered unbridled opportunity, if only individuals worked hard to succeed and had a little luck along the way. Escaping feudalism, Americans grew up cherishing the ethos of individualism and equality. They embraced what Louis Hartz labeled America's liberal tradition[1]—a tradition whose roots were deeply planted in the philosophical soil of classical liberalism, as discussed in Chapter 1.

That liberal tradition continues to shape Americans' attitudes and behavior. Individualism is deeply imprinted in America's political culture. Americans continue to prize personal responsibility and share an optimism about their ability to succeed. Their optimism, however, is based on personal initiative, not on active government intervention. The results of numerous public opinion polls taken in the mid to late 1990s provide consistent evidence in support of this conclusion.

Responding to a 1997 poll conducted by Opinion Research Corporation International for *USA Weekend*, nearly four-fifths of the respondents agreed with the proposition that people who work hard in this nation are likely to succeed.[2] In that same year, 85 percent of the respondents to a Gallup poll expressed satisfaction with their standard of living, and 84 percent felt satisfied with their future prospects.[3] In fact, polls since World War II have consistently shown that Americans see opportunity present if one makes the effort.[4]

Although expressing satisfaction with their economic lot, Americans take less comfort in the social directions they view the United States taking. In a 1997 survey conducted by the *Los Angeles Times*, half of those who responded that America is on the wrong track pointed to social problems as the culprit; only 19 percent pointed to the economy.[5] In a similar vein, 57 percent of those responding to a 1997 Wirthlin Worldwide survey identified social problems as the single most important problem facing the United States; only 13 percent identified pocketbook/economic problems.[6] The public debate over problems such as crime, illegitimacy, and poor educational performance has centered on the appropriate balance between personal responsibility, community involvement, and government action that should be reached in addressing them.

Although Americans value personal responsibility and initiative, and express optimism about making the most of opportunity through hard work, they are circumspect about government involvement in the economy and in society. In fact, compared to citizens in other industrial democracies, Americans accord government the narrowest role (see Table 6.1). According to the results of an International Social Service Project survey, Americans are most inclined to see government as having too much power, and least inclined to believe that government should redistribute wealth. Of those surveyed, only a higher percentage of Canadians oppose government providing jobs to all who need them. Moreover, a majority of Americans even take issue with the proposition that government should provide a decent standard of living for the unemployed—the only nation in which most respondents took that position. Worry that too generous benefit levels might undermine personal responsibility and provide a disincentive to seek work appears to underlie American reservations.

What about those who find themselves not just temporarily unemployed after steady attachment to the workforce, but who are without a job and needy over the long term—those who have fallen through the cracks of capitalism, so to speak? Here the situation becomes less clear, as the values of personal responsibility and altruism collide. Poll data reflect that ambiguity. When asked in 1997 by Princeton Survey Research Associates whether those on welfare have it easy because they get government benefits without having to do anything in return, or whether poor people have hard lives because government benefits do not go far enough for them to live decently, respondents were about equally divided in their appraisals, although previous surveys found respondents leaning more heavily toward the perception that recipients have it easy rather than hard.[7] Questions about whether poverty is the product of a lack of individual effort or circumstances beyond the individual's control have produced contradictory results.[8] About half of the respondents to a *New York Times* poll attributed poverty to circumstances outside of people's control. A later survey by Hart and Teeter Research Companies, which posed an almost identical question, elicited a much different response: almost two-thirds put the

TABLE 6.1   Comparative Public Opinion About the Role of Government

	Percentage of Those Responding										
	US	CA	FR	GER	IRE	ISR	JP	NZ	NOR	SP	SWE
What about government's power?											
Too much	66	46	44	34	38	37	21	54	43	56	27
About right	30	44	41	41	39	35	13	41	52	25	52
Too little	4	6	16	11	10	20	47	6	5	7	21
Should government redistribute wealth?											
Yes	33	42	71	53	64	70	44	37	57	74	59
Mixed feelings	24	15	13	17	14	18	23	18	19	10	20
No	43	41	16	21	20	12	26	42	25	12	21
Should government provide jobs for all who need them?											
Yes	39	35	73	76	69	74	49	54	80	88	65
No	61	39	27	19	30	24	29	44	20	9	35
Should government provide a decent standard of living for the unemployed											
Yes	48	65	82	78	90	62	58	61	93	90	91
No	52	31	18	14	8	37	22	35	7	6	9

Country Codes

US:	United States	IRE:	Ireland	NOR:	Norway
CA:	Canada	ISR:	Israel	SP:	Spain
FR:	France	JP:	Japan	SWE:	Spain
GER:	Germany	NZ:	New Zealand		

SOURCE: *Public Perspective* 9, no. 2 (February/March 1998), 32. Reprinted in revised form with permission of the Roper Center for Public Opinion Research, University of Connecticut, Storrs.

blame on people not doing enough to help themselves. When asked in 1997 by Princeton Survey Research Associates whether with welfare reform government would give up its proper role of helping poor people, or whether government would end a system that has kept people in poverty, 53 percent sided with the latter position. Yet a year earlier, two-thirds of those responding to another question from the Princeton group judged that the federal government is not doing enough to serve the needs of poor people.

This ambivalence reflects the tension that exists between two competing views of poverty and welfare in the United States: one shaped by America's ingrained classical liberal tradition, as discussed above, and the other a product of the Great Depression and the New Deal that followed. The public debate occasioned by the Great Society initiatives of the 1960s built on this latter perspective. But as policymakers and the general public became disaffected with the costs and outcomes of Great Society initiatives, their sympathies seemed once again to align more closely with traditional views.

TWO COMPETING VIEWS OF POVERTY AND WELFARE[9]

The first view prizes individualism and personal responsibility, and looks to the market as the fairest allocator of value in society. The market provides the mechanism through which people can better themselves by hard work, and wide access to public education and training programs offers the opportunity for individuals to position themselves to take advantage of opportunities that the market offers. To a significant extent, work and personal success are the benchmarks on which people judge each other. Beyond that, work itself is bound up with human dignity.

This perspective, commonly associated with modern-day conservatives, views poverty as an aberration, as a failure. Not only have the poor proved unable to succeed in an environment that fosters almost unlimited individual potential but they have often become financially dependent on others for their livelihood. Within a philosophical and cultural inheritance that values self-help, those who become dependent on public assistance are perceived as somehow not measuring up. If that dependence is prolonged, the poor then become subject to the criticism that they have become comfortable relying on the support of others. Critics worry, in turn, that that very dependence breaks the psychological link between effort and reward. Here the system of public welfare itself shares criticism. Critics see welfare as rewarding dependency. Benefits typically rise as family size grows, creating an incentive for welfare mothers to have additional children who become dependent on public assistance.

Critics also see the system as creating disincentives to work, as opposed to offering incentives that support work. Disincentives include benefit reductions that accompany part-time work. Although welfare reform in several states has lessened or removed these disincentives, and has promoted work over welfare, opposition to "the system" continues. When the financial return of work lifts the worker out of poverty but yields only a marginal increase in income over the combined value of cash assistance and allied in-kind benefits, the incentive to work for some becomes weak. In that case, governments resort to coercion, requiring welfare recipients to work, or at least to actively seek work, in return for publicly provided benefits that augment the dollar value of their work.

This view of poverty and welfare also distinguishes between the deserving and the not-so-deserving poor, making allowances for the former. Those who become poor because of something that has happened to them beyond their control, such as becoming blind or otherwise disabled, tend to be viewed differently from welfare recipients—as dependent against their will. The needy elderly receive similar public sympathy, even though they may not have worked enough to qualify for sufficient Social Security benefits to bring them out of poverty in their advanced years. The public nevertheless sees them as old, needy, and now unable to work. Conversely, the public often views welfare mothers as young and able-bodied, capable of providing for themselves and their families if only they had the drive.

The second perspective on poverty and welfare, often associated with modern-day liberals (as opposed to classical liberals, discussed above), focuses on the impediments to work faced by the poor who are left with no option but to resort to public welfare. This view sees welfare as meeting a real need. Its premise is that people do not choose to be poor and on welfare; they would rather be gainfully employed and have the ability to support themselves and their children. Their children certainly do not elect to be born into poverty and dependence. Some welfare recipients become unemployed and without income (after the expiration of any unemployment compensation benefits due them) through no fault of their own. Others face barriers to work, such as limited or inadequate education, lack of skills, and behavioral dysfunctions. They are the ones who have difficulty finding a job even during periods of low unemployment. They appear to be caught in a cycle of poverty and dependence, possessing few of the resources necessary to escape. In this sense, they can be seen as victims, and racial discrimination may make matters worse.

Liberals are quick to debunk what they believe are myths about welfare recipients. In response to the commonly held stereotype of large welfare families, they point out that families receiving AFDC benefits (the former Aid to Families with Dependent Children program, which Congress terminated in August 1996) had about the same number of children as the average American family—1.9 for AFDC families, compared to a national average of 1.8. They also note that only a tenth of AFDC families included more than three children, and fewer than 1 percent had more than five.[10] Liberals also challenge the notion of welfare dependency, drawing on longitudinal data developed at the University of Michigan which shows that slightly less than half of all women who began a stint on AFDC remained on the rolls for two years or less.[11]

Liberals also argue that the welfare system has worked, that it has kept needy people, mostly children, out of poverty. At the same time, liberals fault the welfare system for failing to provide uniform, or even minimal, benefit levels for recipients across the states. Under the former AFDC program, states were free to set benefit levels based on what their legislatures determined to be appropriate standards of need, creating substantial disparity among the states. That disparity, and the related cries of inequity, continues under the recent federal welfare reform, a subject to be discussed in greater detail later in this chapter. But before we examine government programs to assist the poor, we need to understand who is poor in America.

THE POOR IN AMERICA

Approximately one in seven Americans lives in poverty, as measured by the U.S. Bureau of the Census. Looking at children alone, the proportion rises to about one in five. Children are twice as likely to be poor than adults 60 years of age or older. In addition to age, race and ethnicity correlate with poverty. Although more whites are poor than either African Americans or Hispanics, African Americans and Hispanics are almost three times more likely to be poor than whites. Yet regardless of race or ethnicity, female-headed households with children are over six times more likely to be poor than married-couple families; still families headed by African American and Hispanic women are almost twice again more likely to be poor than those headed by white women.[12] Moreover, recent immigrants are twice as likely to be poor than native-born Americans. However, that difference erodes over time. In fact, after immigrants have been in the United States for twenty-five years or more, their average income parallels that of the native born.[13]

In 1997, there were 35.6 million poor people in the United States, about 2 million fewer than existed in 1959. During that same period, the poverty rate (the percentage of persons in poverty) dropped by about 40 percent.[14] As Figure 6.1 illustrates, the elderly realized the biggest gains. While the poverty rate for whites declined a bit over those years, it remained about the same for African Americans, but increased for Hispanics. Irrespective of race or ethnic origin, the poverty rate rose most dramatically for individuals living in female-headed households, just about doubling. It should not be surprising, then, that the poverty rate for married-couple families fell significantly.[15]

It is one thing to get a sense of who is poor and how poverty rates have changed over time, and quite another to put poverty into personal perspective. Perhaps the most immediate way to do that is to equate poverty with money. We all know how much income we earn annually, and we know how far it goes in meeting our needs. Using guidelines developed by the Department of Health and Human Services to establish a base for determining the financial eligibility of needy individuals for federal assistance, a single person was considered poor in 1998 if his or her income fell below $8,310—that's a little over $690 a month. A family of four with an income of $16,655, or about $1,388 a month, before taxes, was also considered poor. Given the cost of housing, food, and transportation alone, that income does not stretch very far.

The poor fall within the lowest 20 percent of income earners in the United States. Using the federal government's official definition of income, which does not include in-kind assistance (such as food stamps) or federal tax credits for the working poor, this bottom quintile received 3.6 percent of U.S. aggregate income in 1997. Adding these additional sources of income increases the bottom quintile's income share to 4.8 percent. That can be compared to the top quintile's nearly ten-

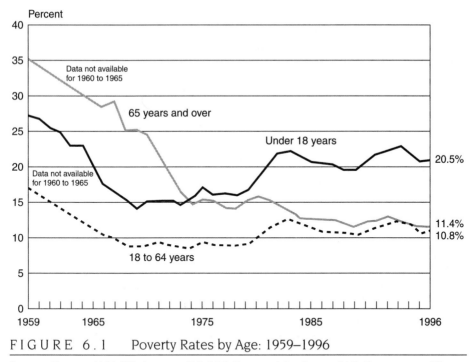

FIGURE 6.1   Poverty Rates by Age: 1959–1996

Source: *Poverty, 1996* (Washington, DC: U.S. Bureau of the Census, U.S. Department of Commerce, September 1997), www.censusgov/hhes/poverty96/povage96.html.

fold higher share of 45 percent, using this expanded definition of income. The point here is not to explore income inequality in the United States, for that was discussed in Chapter 1. It is to show the meager share of income that the poor have even after government assistance.[16]

GOVERNMENT ASSISTANCE

A distinction must be made in discussing government assistance. We typically associate government assistance with the redistribution of taxpayer revenues. Welfare payments come most readily to mind. General tax revenues support payments that go only to those individuals who meet a legally established means test. Almost everyone pays taxes to provide income assistance to a subset of the population that government officially determines to be needy. Welfare, therefore, constitutes public assistance. Yet not all programs that provide financial assistance to Americans take the form of public assistance, for which taxpayers foot the bill. Others are organized as social insurance programs, in which the recipients of financial support, and/or their employers pay into a fund from which monies are drawn to cover the cost of benefits. General taxpayer support is not involved. Only individuals who have paid into the fund, or on whose behalf employers have paid, are eligible for benefits. Contributions support benefits.

Social insurance benefits go to workers (or to dependents in some cases after the worker's death) who have retired or become injured, disabled, or temporarily unemployed—*regardless of financial need*. Major social insurance programs include Social Security and its companion health care program, Medicare; Unemployment Compensation; and Workers' Compensation. Social Security and Medicare are exclusively federal programs that rely on taxes paid by both workers and their employers to cover the cost of benefits on retirement. Unemployment Compensation is a joint federal-state program funded by taxes paid by employers, which provides cash benefits to workers during periods of temporary unemployment. Workers' Compensation is an exclusively state program providing income support and medical care to workers who have been injured or disabled on the job.

The distinctions between public assistance and social insurance programs are deeper than just the differences in their sources of funding and accounting. They affect how the public regards them. Whereas people equate public assistance with welfare, with a handout, they view social insurance programs as draws on prepaid accounts—accounts that were established and paid for through work. The popular perception is that benefits rightly belong to their recipients. These differences in public perception carry with them important social connotations that influence program content, conditions, and levels of financial and political support.

Public Assistance   .

Public assistance programs, generally labeled as welfare, are aimed at the needy in society, who must meet a means test to receive benefits. They consist of cash and in-kind assistance. Cash-assistance programs have taken two forms in the United States: assistance directed to families with dependent children, and to the so-called categorically dependent—the needy elderly, blind, and disabled. Unlike Social Security, categorical aid to the elderly is funded by general taxpayer revenue and is intended for those who have not worked enough to be eligible for Social Security. Major in-kind programs include health care, food stamps, and housing assistance.

Cash Assistance for Families with Dependent Children

Cash assistance for needy families with dependent children has been synonymous with public welfare in the United States. Before the 1996 reform, the program bore the title, Aid to Families with Dependent Children. Yet people most commonly referred to it by its acronym, AFDC. Its roots trace back to the New Deal, although Congress expanded the program in response to President Johnson's Great Society initiatives. With the 1996 reform, Congress changed its name to Temporary Assistance for Needy Families (TANF), symbolic of the program's reorientation from long-term dependency to temporary assistance leading to work.

The TANF program is the most recent and the most comprehensive of a series of efforts to reform public welfare in the United States. The new law gives states almost complete discretion to determine eligibility requirements and benefits levels. It places welfare-to-work performance requirements on the states, and allows states to place more restrictive work requirements on recipients than the federal government minimally requires. The federal legislation lets states decide how best to design programs that meet the federally imposed performance standards.

Most states had a head start in experimenting with welfare reform well before the new law took effect. The Family Support Act of 1988 allowed states to experiment with welfare reform, but required them first to get approval of the federal Department of Health and Human Services. By the act's demise in August 1996, 43 states had secured waivers from regulatory requirements.[17] Widespread state experimentation shifted substantial policymaking discretion from the federal government to the states, and advocates of even greater state administrative and programmatic discretion pointed to the large reduction of welfare caseloads that seemed to accompany state experimentation in support of their position. Caseloads indeed fell; that is not in question. Between 1993 and 1997, the number of persons receiving welfare fell by 28 percent, totaling almost 4 million recipients nationally (see Figure 6.2). What was disputed is the extent to which welfare experimentation resulted in caseload decline. A report by the president's Council of Economic Advisers attributed about one-third of the decease to state-initiated policy changes. The Council attributed another 40 percent to national economic growth, which created 12 million new jobs over the period.[18] Nevertheless,

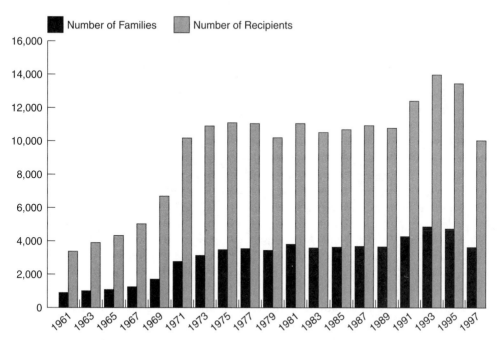

FIGURE 6.2   Changing Welfare Caseloads: Selected Years, 1961–1997

SOURCE: Administration for Children and Families, U.S. Department of Health and Human Services.

buoyed by what they saw as the fruits of state experimentation, reformers pressed for giving states broad flexibility in using welfare funds, without the necessity of seeking waivers.

Republican congressional leaders led the campaign for devolution. Having gained control of both chambers of Congress in the 1994 election, and drawing on the support of Republican governors whose states led the way in experimenting with welfare reform, Republican leaders successfully ushered a series of reform bills through Congress. President Clinton vetoed the first two, objecting to the first because it would have eliminated Medicaid as an entitlement program, and to the second because it would have forced states to deny cash assistance to additional children born to welfare recipients and would have reduced benefits to some disabled children who receive Supplemental Security Income (SSI), a federal program providing benefits to the needy disabled, blind, or elderly who fail to qualify for Social Security benefits. But, with those provisions removed in the GOP's third attempt, and with the 1996 election shortly approaching, President Clinton, who promised as early as the 1992 presidential campaign to end welfare as we know it, finally signed the reform legislation. Clinton called the occasion a historic opportunity to make welfare what it is meant to be: a second chance, not a way of life.[19]

In abolishing the AFDC program, Congress eliminated public assistance as a federal entitlement, ending its 61-year-old guarantee of providing whatever amount of funding is necessary to pay benefits to all who meet eligibility requirements. In its place, Congress created a fixed-appropriation block grant to the states. The federal government's financial contribution became effectively capped. The states could elect to spend more if they wished, but the legislation allowed them to spend less than they had in the past. This is the case because, unlike the former AFDC program, TANF requires no state match of federal funding, requiring only that states spend at least 75 percent of what they spent on AFDC and related programs. In return, they still receive from the federal government about what they got under the AFDC program.

The 1996 legislation provides for block grants to the states totalling $16.4 billion annually through the 2001 fiscal year, with the aid to be distributed based on states' federal funding for AFDC and related programs in either the 1994 or 1995 fiscal year, or the average of the 1992–1994 fiscal years, whichever is higher. Other provisions of the act make additional funding available to states under certain conditions. The first provision aids states facing above-average population growth and below-average benefit levels, and the second helps those states experiencing relatively high unemployment, defined minimally as a state unemployment rate of 6.5 percent or higher. The act contains separate appropriations of $800 million for the former purpose, and $2 billion for the latter. It also contains an additional $1 billion for performance bonuses, to reward states that are most successful in meeting the legislation's goals, such as moving welfare recipients to jobs, and reducing out-of-wedlock births. Given the need to evaluate performance, that provision did not take effect until the 1999 fiscal year, and funds remain available through the 2003 fiscal year.

Welfare reform not only holds the promise of limiting the federal government's financial exposure; it also gives state officials the cautious hope that they may have the fiscal luxury of reallocating state funds once spent on welfare to other pressing needs. Yet that hope hangs on a continuing strong economy and stable or declining welfare rolls. State officials recognize that a downturn in the economy, and particularly a recession, could quickly exhaust their state's ability to meet the cash-assistance needs of the growing ranks of eligible recipients. Welfare's loss of entitlement status, and its new dependence on the annual appropriations of Congress and state legislatures, leaves it with no guarantee that these elected bodies will respond to unmet needs. More will be said about this later.

The Requirements of the Temporary Assistance for Needy Families Program Placed on the States and on Recipients[20]

As alluded to above, federal welfare reform follows from a central premise: states should be in the driver's seat to design the specifics of programs that meet the objectives of the reform legislation. The new legislation puts the focus on results, not on means. States must meet requirements in order to receive federal grants without penalty, but state policymakers have a great deal of freedom to determine how the requirements can best be met. Key requirements center on the states' ability to move welfare recipients off the rolls and into jobs. The act required states to have at least 25 percent of their welfare caseload working in fiscal year (FY) 1997, with that percentage increasing to 50 percent by 2002. For states to be in compliance, single parents must work a minimum of 20 hours per week through FY 1999, rising to 30 hours per week thereafter. The primary wage earner in a two-parent family must work at least 35 hours per week, and both parents must work at least that amount if the family receives federally funded child care. Adults receiving welfare benefits must begin working within two years of receiving aid. States can exempt parents who have a child under one year of age from this requirement, but the act limits this exemption to a total of 12 months cumulatively.

Although the reform legislation places work requirements on the states, the use of the term *work*, in its traditional sense, is a bit of a misnomer. States can satisfy the work requirement by placing recipients in educational, training, and work experience programs. Actual work can include both subsidized and unsubsidized private-sector and public-sector employment, on-the-job training, and community service. States face having their block grants reduced by 5 percent in the first year they fail to meet the law's work requirements. Escalating penalties can increase the amount reduced to 21 percent of the block grant's value by the fourth year of noncompliance.

Along with the states, recipients themselves face penalties for not meeting the law's work requirements. Individual recipients face grant reductions commensurate with the amount of work or equivalent activity missed. For example, a recipient who is absent 50 percent of the time in a given period receives a 50-percent reduction in aid for that period. The law ultimately gives states the right to terminate the benefits of those who refuse to work at all, although states cannot rescind Medicaid coverage for their children. It also requires states to reduce recipients' benefits by at least 25 percent if they fail to cooperate with authorities in establishing the paternity of dependent children covered under the act. States can choose to withdraw their benefits altogether. Finally, the law requires unmarried parents under the age of 18 to attend school or a training program and live with a parent or legal guardian in order to qualify for federal assistance.

The law also limits the time that recipients can receive benefits financed by federal funds. States are prohibited from using block-grant funds to assist recipients who have received welfare for more than *five* years. Previously, no such limit existed in federal law; however, nearly half of the states had already imposed time limits through the waiver route.[21] The new legislation provides some flexibility in applying time limits to individual recipients, giving state administrators the prerogative to exempt up to 20 percent of their caseload from the time limit. It also allows states to impose a shorter, more restrictive time limit.

For the congressional architects of the law, the time-limit feature lies at the heart of welfare reform. As the new program's title suggests, they view welfare as temporary assistance, available to see people through periods of need on their way to employment. They see the work requirements, discussed earlier, as the tools necessary to speed up that transition from dependence to independence.

Dependency and the Value of Work

Getting recipients off of welfare and into jobs is not a new emphasis of federal welfare policy. The former AFDC program required recipients to register with state employment service offices and to actively seek employment as a condition for receiving aid. AFDC's now-defunct Work Incentive Program (WIN), established by Congress in 1967, added support services, such as remedial education, job training, and child care, to improve the employability of young welfare mothers. Yet most reviews of the WIN program questioned its success in getting recipients off the rolls and into jobs.[22]

This facilitative approach gave way in the 1980s to a more coercive orientation. Shortly after assuming office in 1981, President Ronald Reagan called on Congress to adopt a national *workfare* program requiring all able-bodied AFDC recipients to work for their benefits. Under his proposal, those recipients who failed to find jobs would be required to work a specified number of hours a week in public-sector employment, performing such tasks as snow shoveling, trash cleanup, and routine clerical duties. In comparison to the WIN program, the emphasis shifted from improving employability to actual work itself. Critics labeled the proposed program as "slavefare."

Although Congress rejected the notion of a national mandatory workfare program, it passed legislation in 1981 that provided incentives for states to enact their own workfare programs. In response, more than half the states created programs, but many elected to impose forced public service work only after employability and job search efforts proved unsuccessful.

State experimentation under the Family Support Act of 1988, alluded to earlier, contained a mix of traditional and new approaches. Although states continued to require recipients to participate in training aimed at enhancing their employability, they also secured federal waivers limiting the time recipients could receive assistance without actually working, and they instituted a number of provisions designed to modify recipients' behavior. States selectively refused to increase the benefits of welfare mothers who gave birth to additional children while on public assistance, cut the benefits of teen mothers or recipients whose children failed to attend school regularly, and required teen mothers and their children to live at home with a parent or legal guardian in order to receive benefits.

The Personal Responsibility and Work Opportunity Reconciliation Act of 1996, which abolished the AFDC program and replaced it with TANF, gave states the opportunity to continue their use of incentives and disincentives to bias recipients' behavior, but it also went further than any prior act of Congress in establishing work requirements and cutting off financial assistance to those who do not work after a period of time. As noted earlier, both states and recipients face financial penalties if they fail to meet work requirements—states in failing to move a sufficient percentage of recipients from welfare to work, and the recipients themselves for failing to work enough hours per week. Those unable to find employment face time limits on the welfare payments they receive in lieu of work.

America's normative inheritance, shaped by classical liberalism and the Protestant work ethic, has long valued work. European immigrants, most of whom came to the United States with few material resources, improved their economic and social lot through work. They may have started out poor, but they were poor *despite* work. Even as recently as 1959, over two-thirds of the poor were employed—the so-called working poor. Today, most of the poor are in need for lack of work. As recently as 1989, less than half of poor families had any earnings at all. Yet between 1959 and 1989, the poor's share of the U.S. population declined from 22 percent to 13 percent. This contrast has led political scientist Lawrence Mead to conclude that "the working poor left poverty, and the poor became almost by definition nonworking."[23] Although poverty for most persons is transient, Mead focuses his concern on the long-term poor—the 6 to 7 percent who are poor for more than two years. These tend to be the nonworking poor, most of whom live in female-headed families receiving public assistance.[24] Mead recognizes that the expanded public assistance born of the Great Society's war on poverty did indeed reduce poverty statistically, but he, like Charles Murray,[25] argued that it failed to achieve the hoped-for self-sufficiency that was expected to follow government's helping hand. Mead sees grave social implications in this shift from the working poor to the dependent nonworking poor. Not only does it weaken the valued link between personal effort and reward; it also offers dysfunctional lessons to the children of dependent adults. For Mead, the answer lies in substituting work for dependence. Government's efforts must be put into getting the long-term dependent poor into jobs and off public assistance, whatever the nature of the work involved, and even if that work is coerced.

Mead's 1992 book, *The New Politics of Poverty*, which highlighted the shift, discussed its implications, and offered policy advice, caught the attention of welfare reformers. Its analysis and policy recommendations particularly struck a resonate chord with Republican congressional leaders, who found academic support for their predisposed preference for work-centered welfare reform. Its findings and normative arguments found a central spot in the congressional debate leading to the landmark 1996 reform legislation. The value placed on work, and the antipathy felt toward dependency, led policymakers to the position of denying benefits to those who fail to find sustained work and exhaust their eligibility for *temporary* assistance.

Taking Issue with the Direction of Welfare Reform

Critics of welfare reform, while recognizing the value of work, see the 1996 reform as potentially hurting the poor. One prominent critic has been Mary Jo Bane, former assistant secretary for children and families in the federal Department of Health and Human Services during the Clinton administration, who resigned in protest from her position shortly after President Clinton signed the welfare reform legislation. Her objections centered on four key features of the legislation: the elimination of welfare's entitlement status and the associated loss of guaranteed assistance to dependent children; the states' prerogative to reduce their spending commitments to public assistance, leading to what she refers to as a "race to the bottom"; the dangers of the legislation's work and time provisions, which offer the prospect that unemployable recipients will be left without the means to support even a meager existence; and the social consequences of "child abandonment" arising from mothers with young children being forced to take jobs outside the home.[26]

Bane worries about the assumed feasibility of long-term welfare recipients transitioning to self-sufficiency, even in a good economy. Clearly, a good economy increases the job prospects of the more employable recipients—those who have the basic skills and aptitude to find employment, if only demand in the economy is strong enough to create the jobs necessary to employ them. If the economy stagnates or declines, their employment prospects dim, along with those of competing job-seekers. But what about the fortunes of the long-term unemployed, who typically face major impediments to employment? Although states can exempt some of them from benefit termination after they reach the five-year lifetime limit on financial assistance, critics question what will happen to those still unemployed recipients and their dependent children who are not exempted. Will they join the ranks of the homeless, increasingly turning to community based, nonprofit social service agencies for assistance?

Another visible critic of welfare reform, Harvard professor Christopher Jencks, shares Bane's concerns. He too questions the feasibility of moving welfare recipients into jobs. Yet, at the same time, he ponders the fortunes of those able to find minimum-wage jobs in a good economy. Jencks notes that Congress, at President Clinton's behest, acted to improve the lot of those welfare recipients able to find even minimum-wage employment, by expanding the Earned Income Tax Credit (EITC) available to the working poor. The liberalized EITC effectively adds about $2 an hour to the pay of a minimum-wage job for a single mother with two children working 35 hours a week—just barely raising that family out of poverty. So, those recipients at least able to find a steady, minimum-wage job improve their income, on the average, over what they received from public assistance, although minimum-wage employment can be anything but steady, being highly responsive to economic conditions. Yet for those able to find steady minimum-wage employment, their food stamp allotment is typically cut, as is any housing assistance they may have received. With these offsets, Jencks questions the extent to which their material situation is really improved, and he calls upon government to do more to support the material well-being of working mothers and their children. Like the supporters of welfare reform, Jencks sees social value in work; however, he wants the rewards of work to yield more than the market alone is prepared to provide.[27]

Although most social analysts acknowledge the intrinsic value of work, even though they take issue with the feasibility of employing welfare recipients, or with the adequacy of rewards that low-level employment brings, some challenge that very value base. Social critics such as Frances Fox Piven and Richard Cloward place a higher value on government-provided income protection for the poor than they do on the poor competing in the marketplace for subsistence employment. In their view, "social provisioning" provides security for the poor, protecting them from the effects of the market. It also benefits those more regularly attached to the labor force, who do not have to compete for jobs with those to whom government provides income protection. Fox Piven and Cloward see social provisioning as strengthening the bargaining position of working people, as competition for jobs is reduced. For them, then, functional social policy must include an adequate social parachute for the structurally unemployed or those who, at best, occasionally drift into jobs but who largely remain jobless—a policy they see benefiting workers, as well.[28] Their voices fall far from the mainstream in the current era of work-oriented welfare reform.

Social Security

Both policymakers and the general public look at Social Security differently than they do welfare. The value of work and the principles of social insurance and just deserts undergird their view of Social Security. Only those who were sufficiently attached to the U.S. labor force can receive Social Security benefits, and benefit levels reflect both the duration of work and the amounts of income subject to the Social Security tax. Both employers and their employees pay Social Security taxes that finance benefits paid to covered retirees. No general purpose taxes support benefits. The popular view is that retirees drawing benefits are only getting back what they deserve, based on their employer's and their contributions. Nevertheless, there is no question that Social Security redistributes income in society. Recipients who earned less during their working years receive a higher proportional return on taxes paid than do those who earned more and worked about the same amount of time.

Social Security, or Old Age Survivors Disability Insurance (OASDI), is administered exclusively by the federal government, and covers over 90 percent of the working population. Most federal workers and some state employees covered by their own retirement systems constitute the 10 percent not participating. Like public welfare, Social Security reduces poverty. Monthly Social Security checks keep about 40 percent of beneficiaries age 65 and older out of poverty. Benefits constitute the major source of income for almost two-thirds of Social Security recipients aged 65 or older, and they contribute 90 percent or more of the income for about one-third.[29] Without Social Security, these elderly individuals would live in poverty. Yet Social Security is not restricted to the poor. Since Social Security has no means test, as does public welfare, all eligible recipients with sufficient covered employment receive benefits, regardless of need. About 40 percent of Social Security benefits go to recipients with incomes above the U.S. median.[30] At the high end, approximately $48.1 billion in Social Security benefits (slightly more than 13 percent) went to households with incomes between $50,000 and $100,000 in 1997. Another nearly $16 billion went to households with incomes over $100,000, about the same amount that Congress budgeted for the TANF program in that year.[31] Social Security benefits provide only about 20 percent of the income for the top 20 percent of elderly income earners.

Although the Social Security program puts a minimum income floor under all Americans who have attained eligibility, providing the average retiree benefits equal to about 44 percent of preretirement income,[32] it *redistributes* income from those with high lifetime earnings to those with low lifetime earnings. As Joseph Quinn and Olivia Mitchell point out, each dollar of average (indexed) monthly earnings up to $437 in 1996 produced 90 cents of monthly retirement benefit. In comparison, each dollar of average monthly earnings between $437 and $2,635 added only 32 cents, and each additional dollar yielded only 15 cents.[33] Thus Social Security is far from an individual retirement account, into which individuals make contributions and market conditions determine yields credited to the account. Social Security, in contrast, ties benefit increases to a cost-of-living adjustment, which has recently run about 2 percent annually.

The Trust Fund: Reality or Fiction?

Social Security taxes pay for Social Security benefits. Under current law, both employers and employees pay a tax equal to 7.65 percent of the employee's gross salary, up to a limit established by law. That limit was $68,400 a year in 1998. Self-employed individuals pay 15.3 percent on the same taxable base. Of the amounts raised from each, 5.35 percent goes toward retirement and survivors benefits; .85 percent toward disability benefits; and 1.45 percent toward hospitalization benefits under Medicare, Social Security's companion health care program. (Those who qualify for Social Security also qualify for Medicare.) The federal government credits Social Security taxes to two separate trust funds, the Old Age and Survivors Insurance (OASI) and the Disability Insurance (DI) trust funds. Tax revenues supporting Medicare's hospitalization benefits are credited to the Federal Hospitalization Insurance (HI) trust fund. The tax revenues themselves are deposited in accounts of Federal Reserve banks and affiliated financial institutions across the country, from which the Treasury can borrow to pay for other federal spending when the rest of the federal budget is in deficit. The trust funds receive an IOU in exchange for the borrowed money.

The U.S. Treasury accounts for each of these funds separately, paying benefits from available tax revenues and investing any revenues not needed to pay benefits in U.S. government securities, which pay the prevailing market-rate of interest. Interest is credited to the respective trust fund account. From an accounting standpoint, any principal and interest available beyond what is needed to pay benefits constitute fund reserves. The Office of Management and Budget estimates that Social Security taxes will exceed benefit payments by about $40 billion in the 1999 fiscal year, contributing to a combined OASI and DI fund balance of $835 billion—the value of U.S. bonds held by the funds, along with the interest attributed to them.[34]

Employing the unified-budget concept, discussed in Chapter 3, the large federal budget deficits accumulated in the late 1980s and the first half of the 1990s would have been larger still had positive year-end balances not been available in many trust fund accounts, including those for Social Security. For example, the unified-budget deficit amounted to $269.1 billion at the end of the 1991 fiscal year. The deficit would have been $381 billion if it were not for an operating surplus of $111.9 billion in all of the federal trust funds combined. The Social Security trust funds contributed almost $53.5 billion of that aggregate annual operating surplus, when interest and other interfund receipts are included.[35] More recently, if the annual operating surpluses in the Social Security trust funds were taken out of year-end unified-budget calculations, the surplus existing at the end of the 1998 fiscal year would drop from almost $70 billion to about $20 billion.

It should be clear by now that Social Security is financed on a pay-as-you go basis. Current revenues cover current costs, which means that current taxpayers pay the cost of retirees' benefits. Today, about 3.3 workers covered by Social Security contribute to pay the benefits of every retiree, sufficient not only to meet outlays but to build up a U.S. securities–based reserve. This reserve represents a promise that if needed to pay Social Security benefits, the federal government will come up with the funds necessary to redeem the securities. As the wave of "baby-boomers" starts to retire in large numbers in about 2010, the cost of retirement benefits will increase significantly. Retirements will increase faster than the number of workers paying Social Security taxes. By 2020, the number of covered workers per retiree will drop to about 2.5 to 1. By 2030, forecasts point to only two covered workers per retiree.[36] These changing demographics spell trouble for the solvency of the OASDI trust fund, a dilemma touched on in Chapter 3 and discussed further in the next section.

Trust Fund Financial Integrity and the Needy

National policymakers tend to put off tough political decisions on problems that have distant consequences. The financial problems facing Social Security fall into this category: the alternatives are tough politically, and the policy consequences are reasonably distant. Analysts argue about the extent of the problem and when the day of reckoning will come; the *OASDI Trustees Report* on the status of the Social Security trust funds serves as the focal point in that debate. In its 1998 report, the trustees[37] forecast that annual tax revenues coming into the combined OASI and DI trust funds will exceed annual expenditures from those funds through 2012. Tax revenues begin to fall short of expenditures in the following year. In 2021, eight years later, total annual income, including interest income on accumulated assets, begins to fall short of annual expenditures, requiring that trust fund assets be redeemed to cover the shortfall. That pattern of asset redemption continues until 2032, when all assets are exhausted.[38]

Yet even before trust fund assets are exhausted, the Department of the Treasury faces a burden: it must come up with the funds necessary to transfer the cash necessary to pay the interest, when added to tax revenues, required to cover expenditures. Beginning in 2021 it must come up with the cash to redeem the U.S. securities credited to the trust fund accounts. Before 2013, in contrast, no actual transfers of cash were required, since tax revenues alone were sufficient to meet expenditures, rendering interest accruals as mere accounting adjustments.

In coming up with the cash, Congress will have only a few options: raise taxes, cut benefits, cut other federal programs and reallocate the resources, or borrow the money. The last option entails selling other federal securities to willing buyers in the marketplace. And since general obligation securities have the "full faith and credit" of the federal government behind them, they will be marketable, although large sales could drive up the interest costs—costs that future operating budgets will bear.

Still, even if Congress comes up with the money to pay back its debt to the trust funds, unless it changes the law the trustees estimate that OASDI tax revenues will be sufficient to cover only about three-fourths of program costs beginning in 2032.

The trustees based their projections on what they believe is the best estimate for the future. That estimate follows assumptions about each of the factors that affect the trust funds' tax revenues and expenditures. They include economic performance, wage growth, inflation, employment, birth rates, immigration, and mortality rates. For instance, if the economy performs better than assumed, and all other assumptions prove reasonably sound, the key dates discussed above will be moved back in time somewhat. Similarly, if mortality rates drop faster than expected, and all other assumptions square with reality, OASDI will have greater financial difficulty than the best estimate projects.

Options abound for fixing the problem. They include extending Social Security coverage to those currently exempted; increasing the retirement age; increasing payroll taxes; reducing benefits; allowing trust fund administrators to invest a portion of trust fund reserves in private capital markets (rendering that portion unavailable for use in paying for other government expenditures); and permitting participants to invest a portion of their Social Security tax in individual retirement accounts, from which they could make their own investment choices drawn from a set of defined options. The most radical option would do away with the present Social Security system altogether, replacing it with a system of forced saving, similar to those found in Singapore and Chile. With this option, individuals would have broad flexibility in directing savings into investment instruments, but their ability to tap those savings, short of retirement or for a defined emergency, would be greatly restricted. These last two options would fundamentally change the nature of the existing Social Security program. They would move it, in part or in whole, from a pay-as-you-go (PAYGO) system to one that is prefunded, in which individual and employer contributions grow in line with market yields to provide income in retirement.

Public opinion polls have traditionally shown that Americans overwhelmingly support Social Security. Demographics play a significant role here. With a highly favorable ratio of taxpaying covered workers to retirees, retirees enjoyed returns well in excess of contributions. For instance, a man with average lifetime earnings who retired at age 65 in 1980 received benefits nearly four times higher than he and his employer contributed during his working years. Women, with their greater longevity, did even better.[39] But young workers today can expect considerably less favorable returns when they retire, since there will be far fewer workers to support their benefits, likely necessitating tax increases or benefit cuts.

The options of raising taxes and reducing benefits most affect the needy. Since Social Security taxes are forms of proportional, not progressive, taxation, they weigh most heavily on low-income taxpayers. The fact that the law caps income subject to taxation magnifies the taxes' regressivity. Any increase in the tax rate would raise the relative financial burden put on low-income taxpayers. Across-the-board benefit cuts would disproportionately hurt those most dependent on Social Security for their retirement income. Thus it is not surprising that advocates for the needy look to benefit cuts targeted at high-income recipients as the answer. They

reason that Social Security benefits merely augment the income of high-income retirees, whereas low-income retirees rely on Social Security benefits just to make
ends meet.

These issues lead to a debate about the nature of the Social Security program.
Was it really meant to be a social welfare program under the guise of social *insurance?* Although there is no doubt that it redistributes income, policymakers may
have to grapple anew with the extent to which they make Social Security an instrument of even greater redistribution. That could be accomplished by such options as
removing the income limit on the payroll tax, or by phasing out benefits for participants having retirement incomes above a certain level, say $50,000 annually. These
indeed are tough options politically. They affect the economic interests of the best-
educated and most successful elderly—a political force with which to reckon.

Transition to some form of privatization would also have implications for the
low-income needy. As discussed earlier, retirees who earned low incomes during
their working years receive a higher rate of return on contributions than do high-income workers. Redistribution makes that possible. A pure system of privatization
would remove that dedistributional feature. To retain it, Congress would either
have to set aside a portion of Social Security tax revenue to augment the contributions made on behalf of low-income workers, or it would have to use general purpose tax revenues for that purpose.

THE SQUEEZE ON PUBLIC ASSISTANCE
FOR NEEDY FAMILIES

The fortunes of America's needy families improved in the 1990s. Employment gains
accompanying moderately strong economic growth reduced the percentage of poor
families, and welfare rolls fell sharply from their 1993 highs. America's needy families face an uncertain future nonetheless. One element of uncertainty surrounds the
economy. Although economic optimists exist who believe that the United States
has embarked on a "new economy," in which low unemployment and low inflation
can be sustained indefinitely, most economists hold that the business cycle is alive
and well, and that a downturn, complete with rising unemployment, is inevitable.
When it occurs, the working poor are likely to be affected first. As they lose jobs
that have kept them out of poverty, they will lose their eligibility for an Earned Income Tax Credit and increasingly turn to public assistance for financial help. But
will that help be there?

Welfare reform has limited the extent to which government will provide it. It
also constitutes the second element of uncertainty. Although federal block grants
and maintenance-of-effort requirements give the states adequate resources to meet
demand in a good economy, a deteriorating economy will test the adequacy of
TANF's fixed appropriations. No longer does public assistance for needy families
have a legal entitlement to whatever funds are necessary to aid all who meet eligibility requirements. Furthermore, work requirements and lifetime limits on eligibility constrict the extent to which the needy will or can avail themselves of support.

Some of the needy will opt out of the program due to its work requirements, as recent experience has shown. Others will not be able to find employment, despite their efforts, and will depend on public assistance, moving toward their five-year or lower limit on assistance. Of those who reach their limit on benefits, some will fall within the 20 percent exemption option exercised by the states. The others will have to turn to local governments and nonprofit social service agencies for help.

The impending Social Security crisis will also likely squeeze public assistance. Whenever the federal government needs to redeem the Treasury securities held by the trust funds, because Social Security tax revenues are insufficient to cover retiree benefits, the president and Congress will face the choice of raising taxes or using new debt to provide the necessary funding, assuming that no benefit changes are made. In that setting, Congress might be sorely tempted to lessen the impact by cutting the budgets of other vulnerable programs and reallocate their budget authority. TANF could be a prime candidate for cuts and reallocation, now that Congress has redefined welfare as a state (albeit, federally assisted) responsibility.

It all depends on how the public resolves its ambivalent feelings about welfare. As discussed earlier in this chapter, Americans are willing to provide financial support to poor families which are in need *despite* their breadwinners' best efforts to find jobs. Americans also believe strongly in the principle of just deserts, that effort is rewarded and that people get about what they deserve. They want to be assured that the needy are attempting to exercise personal responsibility and making the effort to provide for themselves and their children. Americans are willing to provide a helping hand in time of need, but they do not want that assistance to foster long-term dependence. Yet they do not want to see children go hungry and do without the basic necessities of life.

The 1996 welfare reform legislation embodies this ambivalence. It values personal responsibility while offering temporary assistance, and includes a number of provisions that guard against dependency. Time will tell, however, the extent to which its benefit limits and its work and behavioral requirements move people from welfare to work, or increase the ranks of those who fall through the cracks of capitalism, unemployed and unable to turn to government for help. Should the latter occur, the plight of the poor will likely become more visible in communities, and the media can be expected to depict that reality graphically. Americans' altruism will be tested. If, on the other hand, welfare reform meets its objectives, and its temporary assistance leads to economic independence for a growing number of former recipients, that success will reaffirm the very values of America's classical liberal inheritance.

NOTES

1. Louis Hartz, *The Classical Tradition in America* (New York: Harcourt, Brace, 1955).

2. *Public Perspective* 8, no. 6 (October/November 1997), 5.

3. Ibid., 4.

4. *Public Perspective* 8, nos. 6, 5.

5. *Public Perspective* 9, no. 2 (February/March 1998), 84.

6. Ibid.

7. Ibid., 34.

8. Ibid., 35.

9. This section incorporates and revises material written by the author and included in Dennis L. Dresang and James J. Gosling, *Politics and Policy in American States and Communities*, 2d ed. (Boston: Allyn & Bacon, 1999). It appears with the permission of the publisher.

10. Eugene Smolensky, et al., *Welfare Reform in California* (Berkeley, CA: Institute of Governmental Studies, 1992), 25.

11. Frances Fox Piven and Richard Cloward, "The Contemporary Relief Debate," in *The Mean Season: The Attack on the Welfare State*, ed. Fred Block, et al. (New York: Pantheon Books, 1987), 63.

12. *Poverty 1997* (Washington, DC: U.S. Bureau of the Census, U.S. Department of Commerce, September 1998), vii.

13. U.S. Census Bureau News Release, CB97-155 (April 8, 1997).

14. *Poverty 1997*; Committee on Ways and Means, U. S. House of Representatives, *1996 Green Book* (Washington, DC: 1996), Appendix H.

15. Ibid.

16. *Money Income in the United States: 1997* (Washington, DC: U.S. Bureau of the Census, U.S. Department of Commerce, September 1998), Tables B and 12.

17. Jeffrey L. Katz, "Long-Term Challenges Temper Cheers for Welfare Successes," *Congressional Quarterly Weekly Report* 55, no. 42 (October 25, 1997), 2605.

18. Council of Economic Advisers, *Explaining the Decline in Welfare Receipt, 1993–1996*, May 9, 1997.

19. Office of the Press Secretary, *Statement by the President*, August 22, 1996.

20. This and the following subsection incorporates and revises material written by the author and included in Dennis L. Dresang and James J. Gosling, *Politics and Policy in American States and Communities*, 2d ed. (Boston: Allyn & Bacon, 1999), 392–394. It appears with permission of the publisher.

21. Christopher R. Conte, "Will Workfare Work?", *Governing* 9, no. 7 (April 1996), 20.

22. Joint Economic Committee, U.S. Congress, *Handbook of Public Income Transfer Payments*, Paper 20, 1974; Henry Levin, "A Decade of Policy Developments in Improving Education and Training for Low Income Populations," in *A Decade of Federal Antipoverty Programs*, ed. Robert H. Haveman (New York: Academic Press, 1977), 123–189; Irene Laurie, "Work Requirements in Income-Conditional Transfer Programs," *Social Security Review* 52 (December 1978), 551–566.

23. Laurence Mead, *The New Politics of Poverty* (New York: Basic Books, 1992), 8.

24. Ibid., 15.

25. Charles Murray, *Losing Ground* (New York: Basic Books, 1984).

26. Mary Jo Bane, "Wefare As We Might Know It," *The American Prospect*, no. 30 (January-February 1997), 47–55.

27. Christopher Jencks, "The Hidden Paradox of Welfare Reform," *The American Prospect*, no. 32 (May-June 1997), 33–40.

28. Frances Fox Piven and Richard A. Cloward, "The Contemporary Relief Debate," in *The Mean Season: The Attack on the Welfare State*, 45–108.

29. *Testimony Delivered by Commissioner Kenneth Apfel Before the Senate Committee on Aging*, February 10, 1998.

30. Peter G. Peterson, "Will America Grow Up Before It Grows Old," *Atlantic Monthly*, 227, no. 5 (May 1996), 72.

31. *The Economist* 342, no. 7999 (January 11, 1997), 24.

32. *The Budget of the United States Government*, FY 1999, 230.

33. Joseph F. Quinn and Olivia S. Mitchell, "Social Security on the Table," *The American Prospect*, no. 26 (May-June 1996), 77.

34. *The Budget of the United States Government*, FY 1999, *Analytical Perspectives*, 331.

35. *The Budget of the United States Government*, FY 1993, 3-24, 3-27.

36. *1998 OASDI Trustees* Report (Washington, DC: Social Security Administration, 1998), *www.ssa.gov/OACT/TR/TR98*.

37. Six members, four of whom by virtue of their administrative position in government (the secretaries of the Treasury, Labor, and Health and Human Services, and the commissioner of Social Security), along with two public members.

38. *1998 OASDI Trustees Report*, www.ssa.govt/OACT/TR/TR98/trib.html#pgfld=45.

39. Quinn and Mitchell, "Social Security on the Table," 77.

CHAPTER 7

Contemporary Performance and Future Challenges Facing America's Political Economy

The results of the 1998 elections seemed to reflect the electorate's mixed feelings. Incumbents fared especially well. Only seven of the 401 House members seeking reelection proved unsuccessful in their quest, and only three of the thirty-four senators up for election lost. On face value, these results could be interpreted as a strong expression of voter approval for those in office. Yet the 1998 elections also represented the first time since 1934 that the president's political party gained seats in an off-year (nonpresidential) election. Instead of losing seats, as was expected, the Democrats gained five seats in the House and broke even in the Senate. Of the seven House incumbents who lost their reelection bids, six were Republicans. Two of the three incumbents defeated in the Senate also were Republicans.[1]

Pundits offer different explanations of the Democrats' ability to ward off the almost inevitable midyear loss of seats. Some attribute it to the public's negative reaction to what they view as Republican excesses in their pursuit of partisan advantage over President Clinton's sexual exploits with a young Whitehouse intern.[2] Others see voters as rejecting ideologically driven politics of the kind associated with House Republican leaders and reminiscent of the failed GOP Contract with America, in favor of a more moderate approach that focuses on the day-to-day problems facing working Americans.[3] Those espousing that interpretation point to the success of the Bush brothers in their 1998 Republican campaigns for governor. One observer, Larry J. Sabato, professor of government at the University of Virginia, attributes the victories of Texas Governor George W. Bush and Florida Governor-elect Jeb Bush to their successful strategies of inclusion, which incorporated a dedicated effort to woo the support of Hispanic and African American voters.[4] Still others look to the higher-than-projected Democratic voter turnout, particularly among minority voters, as the deciding factor in a number of tight races that fell into the Democrats' victory column.[5]

The unavoidable fact, however, is that the voters overwhelmingly returned incumbents to office. At the same time, they continued to express support for President Clinton's job performance, support which, parenthetically, remained unscathed even after the House impeached the president about ten weeks after the election.[6] Preelection polls done by the Gallup Organization and the *Los Angeles Times* showed that about two-thirds of those surveyed in both polls approved of the president's job performance.[7] Moreover, when asked by Gallup pollsters if they are satisfied or dissatisfied with the way things are going in the United States, nearly two-thirds reported their satisfaction.[8] And the condition of the economy appears to have influenced both reactions. A Gallup poll administered before the 1998 elections showed that three-quarters of those questioned felt that U.S. economic conditions were either good or excellent, the highest rating given the economy since that Gallup series began in January 1992.[9] Given these sentiments, it should not be at all surprising that voters overwhelmingly returned incumbents to office. Yet it is also true that Republicans did not do as well nationally as had been expected in this midterm election, an outcome for which House Speaker Newt Gingrich took a good share of the blame. Although GOP leaders recognize that a continuing strong economy will likely again aid incumbents in the 2000 election and work to keep Republicans in the congressional majority, they also realize that the coattail effect of a Republican presidential victory could enlarge their precarious margins, just as the election of a Democrat could pull along enough support to cost them control of one or both chambers of Congress. The question remains which party in the 2000 presidential election would benefit most from a continuing strong economy, and which would suffer the most from economic deterioration.

If voters hold incumbents accountable for any economic downturn, then the Republican members of Congress have the most to lose; however, a significant economic slide could well hurt the electoral prospects of any Democratic candidate closely associated with the incumbent presidential administration.

If the mood of the country at the turn of the century has indeed swung toward policy moderation and performance, as some observers suggest, then voters can be expected to be lured less by ideological stances, and more by their sense of how the candidates will work with others, including partisan opponents, to address the problems that voters consider important. A weak economy magnifies problem perception, just as a strong economy radiates a positive glow that spreads to other aspects of life. Given the uncertainty about what the condition of the economy will be in November 2000, the intervening period will likely see both parties assessing how they can improve their chances regardless of the state of the economy. For Republicans, that appears to lie with broadening their electoral base through a more inclusive and less ideologically stringent message—one that nevertheless builds on the popular tenets of fiscal conservatism and government restraint while still demonstrating that the GOP can take the lead in addressing the tangible problems that directly affect people's lives. For Democrats, it means continuing to mobilize their traditional supporters while being careful not to alienate Clinton's "New Democrats." Should Clinton's high job-approval rating decline, Democratic strategists will be faced with deciding how far they should push a policy agenda that appeals to their traditional constituencies and run the risk of alienating the more conservative Democrats who applauded Clinton's role in balancing the budget and reforming welfare. Stretching the limits too far could repel some New Democrats into a more moderate Republican camp.

A continuing budget surplus could give the Democratic nominee the fiscal room to pursue policy initiatives that would appeal to the Democrats' traditional voter base while otherwise steering a course of generally restrained government that has won widespread public support. For Republicans, a continuing budget surplus would take away from them the patently successful issue of deficit reduction, leaving them with staking out a position on what should be done with the deficit. The most attractive alternatives for Republicans include using the surplus to finance a tax cut or pay off some of the national debt. The latter option, although attractive to some, might be far too transparent to most. Another option, saving the surplus to be used later to postpone the day of reckoning for Social Security, probably provides little political capital in the present, particularly when people perceive the crisis to be over a decade away—a long time in politics.

Some selective spending issues might garner Republican support, such as spending on defense or physical infrastructure, although the ideological turf staked out by the party in the 1980s and 1990s leaves little room for major spending initiatives. Yet a shift to a more moderate stance that seeks to use government to empower individuals to help themselves compete more effectively in the market economy (borrowing a page from Clintonian rhetoric) could cover selective programmatic initiatives without departing significantly from the GOP's calls for fiscal discipline and government restraint. Nonetheless, the economic and policy successes of a good part of the 1990s have thinned out the would-be policy agenda at the end of the century.

Thinning Out the Policy Agenda

For most of the 1980s and 1990s, the deficit was at the center of America's policy agenda. Not only did it soak up both presidential and congressional attention; it also served as the focal point of political and economic commentary. Political commentators focused on the political implications of the deficit and on the partisan nature of budgetary politics. Economic commentators concerned themselves with the macroeconomic effects of the deficit. Politically, both the president and Congress seemed powerless to make a major dent in the deficit once they set it in motion through a fiscal policy of tax cuts and real-dollar defense-spending increases, or at least they appeared to lack the political will to do so. Consecutive large deficits piled up the debt, leading some economic observers to argue that America was weakening its economic foundation and mortgaging its future. The federal government was living beyond its means, financing the overspending by IOUs and placing a financial burden on future generations to service that debt. The federal government's string of annual budget deficits, accompanying a falling rate of personal saving, shrank national saving (the sum of private and government saving) as a percentage of the gross national product (GNP). As discussed in Chapter 3, national saving fell from nearly 21 percent of GNP in 1981 to just above 14 percent in 1993. From that low, it recovered to over 17 percent in 1997, the result of four years of continued deficit reduction. The Department of Commerce's end-of-the-year report for 1998 showed a modest continuation of that trend (an increase of one-third of 1 percentage point), driven by the transition from budget deficit to surplus realized during the 1998 fiscal year—even though the U.S. personal savings rate continued its freefall, turning negative in September for the first time since the 1930s.[10]

With a near $70 billion budget surplus reported for fiscal year (FY) 1998 and the Congressional Budget Office (CBO) projecting subsequent annual budget surpluses ranging from $120 billion to $266 billion between the 1999 and 2004 fiscal years,[11] it appears that, for the near term, deficit politics has been consigned to history. Those surpluses will also contribute to increased national saving. Yet that rosy scenario assumes no significant change in current policy or in the middle-range projections of moderately strong economic growth. Should Congress yield to the temptation to weaken its controls on discretionary and entitlement spending, or should the economy perform much worse than projected, deficit reduction could reappear as a challenge.

Since deficit reduction is off the national agenda, does that mean that debt is off the table as well? Although the answer is probably no, the urgency felt by some over debt reduction has clearly dissipated somewhat as debt held by the public began to fall from 1996 to 1998, and is projected to continue its fall. The CBO forecasts a sharp decline in debt held by the public between 1998 and 2004, both in current dollars and as a percentage of the gross domestic product (GDP). It projects publicly held debt to decline by $1.1 trillion over that period, falling from 44.3 percent to 23.7 percent of the GDP—about the level experienced in 1974. And if projected debt held by the Federal Reserve is excluded, the debt held outside the federal government drops from 38.8 percent to 16.4 percent of the GDP.[12] Moreover, the CBO projects that net interest payments on the debt will decline from $243 billion in 1998 to $164 billion in 2004, a savings of $258 billion over the six years.[13]

If policymakers take some comfort in finding the budget in surplus and publicly held debt and net interest falling, should they nonetheless worry about another deficit—the foreign-trade deficit? As noted in Chapter 4, the U.S. trade deficit for 1998 stood at $169 billion, reflecting a deficit in goods that outstripped a surplus in services.[14] Should a large and growing trade deficit be a cause for concern? What about when it occurs at the same time the economy looks healthy along other dimensions: when, for example, its GDP is growing at an acceptable rate, both inflation and unemployment are low by historical standards, and its national budget is balanced? Those conditions clearly describe the state of America's economy as it enters the last year of the twentieth century. The answer to both questions is no. The empirical evidence is clear: a country's trade balance does not drive its economic performance.[15] Instead, a strong domestic economy provides the income growth that enables its consumers and businesses to increase their spending, benefiting imports along with domestically produced goods. If, at the same time, a country's trading partners are experiencing much slower growth or have fallen into recession, that juxtaposition combines to further increase the former country's trade deficit, since its exports will attract less demand abroad. As economist Robert Eisner ironically reminds us, the United States can "cure" its trade deficit problem if it can create enough unemployment and hard times at home. A recessionary economy lowers demand, depressing consumption and thus reducing imports. It would be foolhardy to trade off economic prosperity for an improved foreign trade balance.[16]

This does not mean that U.S. policymakers should cease their efforts to bring about more open, fairer trade in this country's bilateral relationships, particularly those with Japan and China. Pressure from the president and Congress aimed at winning greater access to their markets has achieved some limited successes, and the effort is worth continuing. Both Japan and China, as well as many other trading partners, depend heavily on selling their goods in the United States. That need gives U.S. representatives considerable leverage in trade negotiations; however, both the United States and its trading partners realize that U.S. policymakers will resort to trade sanctions only as a desperate last resort, given the consequences to the U.S. economy.

Beyond the trade deficit itself, should Americans worry about the U.S. current account deficit, which rose to $233.4 billion in 1998,[17] a figure that also takes into account flows of income on foreign investments and unilateral transfers? The trade deficit, in practice, accounts for the lion's share of the current account deficit. Until as recently as 1995, the United States traditionally had a positive balance on investment income, meaning that income from U.S. investments abroad exceeded income from foreign investments in the United States. Its modest negative balances since then are no concern for worry. In fact, they can be viewed as reflecting foreign investors' confidence in the comparative strength of the U.S. economy. Investors shop around in today's global economy for what they deem to be the best value, and value takes into account both financial return on that investment and a sense of acceptable risk. It is no wonder that the United States looks attractive to many foreign investors. The size, diversity, and stability of the U.S. economy make it attractive to investors. It indeed has proved to be a relative safe-haven. Yet to the extent that investments in the United States become more attractive to foreign investors than do investments abroad appear to Americans, the value of the dollar stands to rise in international currency markets, all other considerations being equal. A rising dollar, in turn, contributes to a trade deficit—again, all other things being equal—as imports become cheaper and exports become more expensive. Is this reality a bad thing, or is it a product of prosperity that we do not want to sacrifice?

But what about the trade deficit's effect on jobs? Despite the reality that some workers will lose their jobs as a result of production growth on foreign soils, in the aggregate the trade deficit and the average rate of unemployment are pretty much unrelated over the long run.[18] Paul Krugman shows that new jobs created in sectors that are largely insulated from international competition, such as services, have far outpaced employment losses in import-competing sectors.[19]

Well, if the most important economic indicators are all favorable, or at least moving in the right direction, should Americans be complacent? Should they ask little of government policymakers, other than that their policymakers continue the policies that have appeared to work? That means continuing to manage the economy through proactive monetary policy, continuing on the course of surplus building, and continuing to promote economic efficiency through regulatory restraint and selective deregulation. Or are there problems that merit attention, whether they are pressing today or to be faced in the not too distant future?

PROBLEMS AND THE PROSPECTIVE POLICY AGENDA

The first two chapters discussed the importance of productivity growth to an economy's economic performance. Paul Krugman calls it "the single most important factor affecting our economic well-being."[20] Alice Rivlin sees increasing productivity growth as central to reviving the American dream, the theme of her best-selling book.[21] Yet both feel dismay that policies to improve productivity growth have not found their way onto America's public policy agenda to the extent needed. For Rivlin, a public commitment to increasing productivity must include greater investment in education and training—especially in literacy, mathematics and science, computer skills; and research and development—and improvements in public infrastructure.[22] Krugman is less inclined to offer prescriptions for increased productivity growth, arguing that we do not know why productivity stagnated in the first place. He reasons that if you cannot explain why a problem exists, you are not in a very good position to recommend how to solve it. At the same time, however, he acknowledges that prescriptions such as those offered by Rivlin would probably help improve productivity growth a bit; but because the linkage is tenuous, Krugman doubts that policymakers will make any significant commitment to these so-called productivity investments.[23]

Nevertheless, productivity in the nonfarm business sector rose by 1.8 percent a year between 1996 and 1998, about double the annual growth rate since 1973.[24] Does this three-year spurt represent a fundamental turnaround, or is it merely a temporary blip that defies explanation? Alan Greenspan believes that it might well represent the former. He suggests that rising productivity could be associated with new technological applications coming from recent advances in computers and their vastly expanded capabilities. In his view, the rise in productivity growth could represent a delayed benefit from the surge in capital investment in high-tech equipment that began in early 1993, as businesses learn how best to apply these new tools to enhance worker productivity.[25]

A recent paper by Jeremy Greenwood, professor of economics at the University of Rochester and a visiting Federal Reserve scholar, suggests that Greenspan may be right, although he notes that productivity stagnated during the 1970s and 1980s despite significant increases in information technology investment. Greenwood argues that things have changed, and American industry has found itself on a higher point of the learning curve. The United States is now disproportionately benefiting from the constructive feedback of working through the problems of earlier applications. If this is indeed happening, Greenwood suggests that the United States may be embarking on a period of sustained productivity growth—growth that will expand the GDP and the income derived from it.[26]

If both Greenspan and Greenwood are right, and higher productivity growth does contribute to rising real household income, Americans, overall, will see their living standards rise for the first time in almost thirty years. Real median household income has remained essentially flat since the early 1970s, declining in recession years and improving in recovery, but failing to gain ground over the period. Recent signs have been cautiously encouraging, as real median household income grew between 1993 and 1997. But that growth still left it about where it had been in 1989.[27]

Yet even if median household income continues to rise, history has shown that all Americans will not benefit equally. Economic analysts broadly agree that income inequality increased and the size of the middle class declined since the early 1970s, reversing a post–World War II period of declining inequality and expansion of the middle class.[28] High-income households did the best in this period of real income stagnation, especially the top 5 percent, while those in the middle actually lost some ground in relation to others. The lowest-income families stayed close to even when considering cash benefits only, although their lot improved modestly when taking the value of food stamps and medical assistance into consideration. (See the discussion in Chapter 1 for the details and documentation.)

What can we expect in the future? That is a difficult question because experts cannot even agree on what caused the growing income inequality experienced since the early 1970s. Some observers look to advances in information technology as not only spurring economic growth, but as widening the income gap as well. A survey of economists by the Federal Reserve Bank of New York found that they attributed income inequality more to technological change than to any other factor.[29] As more and more jobs have come to rely on computer-based applications, technological expertise has become more prized and better paid. As new technological applications assist workers to do their jobs more productively, those who have the skills and training to use them on the job stand to benefit. Those who do not can expect to find demand for their services in decline and far less well rewarded. Some will find themselves displaced by technology, having to make a job change, if they can find one. As long as the economy continues to perform well, and unemployment remains low, other jobs can be found but often at a lower wage for the less well educated and trained workers.[30]

Professor Greenwood, while recognizing the potential for growing income disparity in the short run, holds out the hope for broader benefit in the long run. He argues that as information technologies mature, the level of skill required to use them will decline. Although those who expand the frontier of technological innovation will continue to reap disproportionately high financial rewards, salary disparities will shrink among the appliers of technology, thus reducing income inequality.[31] Whether that derived reduction comes at the expense of flat or lower median income is to be seen, and it is significantly tied to the fortunes of productivity.

In addition to the potential productivity gains spawned by high-tech advancements in the private sector, does government have an important role to play in enhancing productivity? Alice Rivlin, Robert Reich, and David Aschauer, among others, argue that it does. Rivlin[32] and Reich[33] extend government's role to improving both human and physical infrastructure. Aschauer limits his case to physical infrastructure, referring to the state of public capital in the United States as "America's Third Deficit."[34] Writing during the 1990 recession, Aschauer advanced his case that reduced public capital investment spending since the late 1960s contributed significantly to the drop in productivity that followed. Critics responded one of two ways: that no dropoff in spending can be found to have occurred after making appropriate statistical adjustments; or that both public capital investment and productivity fell together, but that the drop in the former did not cause the drop in the latter.

One critic, John Tatom, an assistant vice president at the Federal Reserve Bank of St. Louis, branded Aschauer's conclusions the "mythical national infrastructural crisis."[35] Tatom acknowledges that the two variables do covary, but argues that no statistically supported case can be made that increased public capital investment raises private-sector productivity. He also contends that the data on public capital investment must be put in proper perspective. It should not be surprising, he notes, that governments' investment in physical infrastructure slowed after the 1960s, since the interstate highway system neared completion, as did the boom in school construction. Politically, Tatom views the myth of an infrastructure crisis as diverting the attention of policymakers from other more pressing challenges, such as reducing the budget deficit and lowering the national debt. However, with the budget in balance since his critique, and with the forecast of additional progress to be made on reducing the national debt and its interest requirements, the question turns to what other economic policy initiatives the federal government might take.

As the United States nears the beginning of a new millennium, both the president and Congress appear to have a limited appetite for disturbing what appears to be working reasonably well. Perhaps they are adhering to the old adage, "If it ain't broke, don't fix it," or perhaps they have been preoccupied with the congressional debate over impeachment. For whatever reason, it is clear that both the president and Congress have elected to let the present forces play themselves out. That sentiment can be seen in their willingness to defer to the Federal Reserve's management of the economy through the use of monetary policy; to pass on federal deregulation of the electric power industry, in favor of monitoring the effects of state deregulatory initiatives; as well as in enacting federal legislation in 1998 that imposes a three-year moratorium on state taxation of Internet commerce.

Although continued good economic times will tend to support this inclination, they will also provide the president and Congress with budget surpluses available to finance new programmatic initiatives. How the president and Congress respond to demands for new spending, or see their political fortunes tied to new initiatives, compared to the value they place on returning some of those surplus revenues back to taxpayers in the form of tax cuts or paying back a part of the national debt, will shape budgetary choices in the near future. Beyond the short term, the problem of Social Security shortfalls stands waiting in the wings. It will not go away if present law remains unchanged and current demographic projections prove to be close to the mark. The question is when will policymakers choose to address it.

A related question is how long will voters be satisfied with government riding the waves of economic prosperity, and when will they demand greater government activism. Survey results suggest that they may be willing to ride the wave for some time, being content with government restraint. If the American public believes that past government action has moved their country in the right direction—by turning the federal budget from deficit to surplus, reducing debt, increasing national saving, reforming welfare and reducing the rolls, and making significant strides in deregulation—they may well endorse holding the present course.

NOTES

1. *Congressional Quarterly Weekly Report* 56, no. 44 (November 7, 1998), 2980, 2984, 2990, 2994.
2. See, for example, *The Economist* 349, no. 8093 (November 7, 1998), 15–16, 23–24.
3. Karen Foerstel, "Voters' Plea for Moderation Unlikely To Be Heeded," *Congressional Quarterly Weekly Report* 56, no. 44 (November 7, 1998), 2980–2984.
4. Reported in Kirk Victor, "Year of the Insider," *National Journal* 30, no. 45 (February 7, 1998), 2608.
5. Richard E. Cohen, "The Head-Hunting Begins," *National Journal* 30, no. 45 (February 7, 1998), 2602–2605.
6. ABC NEWS Poll, abcnews.gocom/sections/us/PoliticalNation/langerpoll981221.html., December 21, 1998.
7. Ronald Brownstein, "Public's Support of President Found to Remain Strong," *Los Angeles Times*, September 14, 1998, www.latimes.com/HOME/NEWS/POLLS/story45.htm; The Gallup Organization, October 1, 1998, www.gallup/com/The_Poll/100198/subgroupviews.asp.
8. The Gallup Organization, October 7, 1998, www.gallup.com/Gallup_Poll_Data/mood/satus.htm.
9. The Gallup Organization, October 1, 1998, www.gallup.com/Gallup_Poll_Data/mood/ratecon.htm.
10. *Survey of Current Business, The Economist*, 349, no. 8094, (November 14, 1998), 80.
11. Congressional Budget Office, *The Economic and Budget Outlook: An Update*, July 1, 1999. Table 5.
12. Ibid., Table 10; *The Budget of the United States Government, FY 2000, Historical Tables*, Table 7.1.
13. *The Economic and Budget Outlook: An Update*, July 1, 1999, Table 10.
14. *Survey of Current Business*, April 1999, Table 1.
15. David M. Gould and Roy J. Ruffin, "Trade Deficits: Causes and Consequences," *Economic Review* (Fourth Quarter 1996).
16. Robert Eisner, *The Misunderstood Economy* (Boston: Harvard Business School Press, 1995), 82.
17. *Survey of Current Business*, April 1999, Table 1.
18. Paul Krugman, *The Age of Diminished Expectations* (Cambridge, MA: The MIT Press, 1994), 48.
19. Ibid., 45.
20. Ibid., 22.

21. Alice M. Rivlin, *Reviving the American Dream* (Washington, DC: The Brookings Institution, 1992).

22. Ibid., 68–70.

23. Krugman, *The Age of Diminished Expectations*, 22.

24. Bureau of Labor Statistics, *Uniform Business Productivity Index*, 1996–1998, July 6, 1999, http://146.142.4.24/cgi-bin/surveymost.

25. Alan Greenspan, *Testimony Before the Subcommittee on Domestic and International Monetary Policy of the House Committee on Banking and Financial Services*, July 22, 1997.

26. Jeremy Greenwood, *The Third Industrial Revolution* (Washington, DC: AEI Press, 1997).

27. *Money Income in the United States: 1997* (Washington DC: U.S. Bureau of the Census, U.S. Department of Commerce, September 1998), vi; *The Economist* 345, no. 8037 (October 4, 1997), 35.

28. Daniel H. Weinberg, "A Brief Look at Postwar U.S. Income Inequality," *Current Population Reports*, P60-191 (June 1996), 1–4.

29. Reported in Neil Munro, "For Richer and Poorer," *National Journal* 30, no. 29 (July 18, 1998), 1676.

30. Ibid., 1676–1680.

31. Greenwood, *The Third Industrial Revolution*, 23–24.

32. Rivlin, *Reviving the American Dream*.

33. Robert B. Reich, *The Work of Nations: Preparing Ourselves for 21st Century Capitalism* (New York: Alfred A. Knopf, 1991).

34. David Alan Aschauer, "Infrastructure: America's Third Deficit," *Challenge* (March-April 1991), 39–45.

35. John A. Tatom, "Paved With Good Intentions: The Mythical National Infrastructure Crisis," *Policy Analysis*, no. 196 (August 12, 1993).

Index